TOWARD THE MODERN ECONOMY

Toward the Modern Economy

Early Industry in Europe 1500–1800

Myron P. Gutmann

THE UNIVERSITY OF TEXAS AT AUSTIN

TEMPLE UNIVERSITY PRESS

Philadelphia

Temple University Press, Philadelphia 19122

First Edition
987654321
Copyright © 1988 by Alfred A. Knopf, Inc.

Library of Congress Catalog Card No. 87-051595
ISBN 87722-547-8

Manufactured in the United States of America

For Robert

FOREWORD

New knowledge and fresh understanding, the goals of all research, demand constant change in the way that research is conducted. At the same time, research in any field is the expression of a cultural tradition that largely shapes the questions asked, the methods used, and the results presented. This tension between new perceptions and established standards is the heartbeat of academic disciplines, and modern universities are organized to keep that tension high. Although no longer confident that this process guarantees the progress of civilization, we sustain it because in a more limited sense it works. Year by year we command more information and learn to organize and analyze it in ever more elaborate and sophisticated ways. Specialization is the serious price paid for such gains. New information can be acquired and its validity carefully tested within a narrow focus. It is more difficult to determine how bits of new knowledge should be integrated with what was known before.

The benefits of specialization and the problems it brings have been particularly significant for the discipline of history. Over the last generation, the study of history has expanded and changed as much as any discipline in the social sciences or humanities. It has done so in large part by borrowing heavily from them, while maintaining most of its traditional concerns. The interests, theories, and methods of sociology, demography, economics, anthropology, semiotics, and literary analysis, which are readily apparent in current historical writing, have also directly affected historical research.

Thus a score of specialties have been added to the familiar ones of period and place by which historical expertise is identified. In addition, the present continues, as it always has, to stimulate new perspectives on the past. Contemporary concerns—about social order, the family, welfare, racism, women's roles, and inequality; the experience of mass culture, political oppression, and demands for democracy; the fact that European power does not dominate the world as it once did; and increased knowledge of non-Western societies—have led historians to pose fresh questions about European history. The historical study of Europe is also now more international in the double sense that historians of many nations study the same problems and that they are less inclined to confine those topics within national boundaries.

So the discoveries and successes of one historical field quickly influence work in others. The emphasis in this generation upon social history has enabled us to learn more than ever before about all eras of European history and in particular about the attitudes and lives of ordinary people with little power. By definition, this type of social history explores detailed knowledge. Its larger significance requires that the disparate facts about daily life, local behavior, or the activities of unorganized groups be related to some general view of social relations and patterns of change. Theory is essential to analysis.

As historians mine old archives for new information, the meaning of which may only be revealed through complicated techniques of cultural or quantitative analysis, they do so because they have posed fresh questions. Minute research and (at least implicit) theory must be combined to create a history that integrates new knowledge of ordinary life with the larger fabric of historical interpretation. Discovering the significant patterns and establishing a coherent perspective that can encompass both new findings and what was known before remain the great challenges of historical study. The search for such a synthesis is the very essence of historical writing. That is not new, but in the past this quest was expressed primarily through a powerful rhetoric redolent of larger purpose and was organized in sweeping narratives that gave to chronological sequence the aura of cause and effect. Newer methods and more specialized knowledge have made those established devices more difficult and less satisfactory.

The modern synthesis is likely to move on several levels at once. It must define an important problem or set of problems, using evidence both to define them and to establish their significance. These problems must then be carefully placed in historical context. The modern synthesis, which must relate the latest findings to the relevant theories, is also expected to address the scholarly debates from which central questions derive. Thus coherence is less likely to result from narrative flow or rhetorical values than from a consistent interpretative argument. When well written, as of course it should be, the carefully elaborated historical synthesis can nevertheless join with the best of older historical writing in conveying the color and fascination of a way of life now passed and the intellectual challenge of seeking to understand a particular society.

The books in this series present that sort of modern synthesis.

The excitement of recent research, with its diverse topics and methods, makes this an excellent moment for such a publishing venture. And historical synthesis, which must operate on several levels at once, offers the advantage that it can speak to many kinds of serious readers—to freshmen discovering the patterns that make sense of the panorama of Western history, to advanced students interested in the meaning of historical context and important scholarly debates, to scholars ready to wrestle with a new perspective offered by a distinguished colleague, and to anyone who enjoys thinking about how to understand significant historical developments. The authors of these books have accepted the challenge of attempting in a single volume to accomplish so much. Active scholars building upon their own research, these authors set forth arguments that specialists will need to consider. Their assessment of recent findings and of the general scholarly literature will be especially helpful to graduate students and advanced undergraduates. Their perspectives on important aspects of European history should prove useful and stimulating to beginning students in introductory courses and to their teachers who wish to integrate current research into an established framework. In short, different readers can all appreciate the same well-written and intelligent book whether initially drawn to its broad picture of an important epoch, the scholarly debate of which it is part, or the new findings it presents—and that remains one of the glories of historical study even in an age of specialization.

No historical process more fundamentally transformed the world than industrialization, and recent efforts to understand it have benefited from a contemporary perspective. Although deeply rooted in European experience, industrialization has spread around the world; and that argues that scholars should search for the general conditions in which it flourishes. Machine manufacture no longer seems its essence but rather a phase of it, and England's early lead in that phase no longer seems the most striking issue to explain. Attention has turned instead to a long process of change, but historical processes are easier to describe in the abstract than to identify in specific times and places. Yet that is what historians insist on doing, while at the same time demonstrating the interconnectedness of economy, social structure, politics, and culture. Aided by recent research in economic theory and social history, they have come to focus especially on the European economy before the nineteenth century. Demographic change (as both cause and effect) and the evolving relations of urban and rural life must now be interwoven with previous findings about the role of politics and the state, of religion and social attitudes, of invention and investment, and of much else. To synthesize all that is a formidable challenge, and Myron Gutmann meets it by combining several approaches. He uses the latest scholarship and his own research to establish a periodization, three long cycles that carried Europe from the economy of the late middle ages to the nineteenth century. And he uses case studies (particularly from the Low Countries, an area especially fruitful for his task not just because it is often overlooked but because it experienced the major economic changes of the period) to show concretely how specific decisions in particular industries shaped the larger patterns. In this way long-term trends are connected with such immediate factors as available technology, the workforce, market opportunities, forms of competition, and regional circumstance. *Toward the Modern Economy* will enable beginning students to see in both broad and specific terms the transformation of Europe that led to the modern economy. At the same time and for identical reasons an original synthesis, this study will engage specialists. It exemplifies the high ambitions of current historical scholarship.

RAYMOND GREW
Ann Arbor, Michigan

PREFACE

This book began with the desire to solve a simple historical problem. It later evolved into a much broader subject. In 1979, when I started, historians had rediscovered cottage industry. Many were considering a model of behavior that linked industrial growth in the countryside to earlier marriage. In a region I had studied the problem seemed much more complicated, so I looked for other ways to make sense of it. I report some of my demographic and social research in this book, but the reader will see that the book is much more than that. It became impossible to think about the social and demographic side of early industrial growth without thinking about the economic elements in its organization, and it became impossible to tell the complete economic, social, and demographic story without broadening my focus beyond the eighteenth century in the southeastern Low Countries. This book covers a lot of time and a lot of ground, attempting to put a very large story in context.

In the process of covering time and space the argument of the book has broadened too, to encompass more than just the social and demographic sides of cottage industry growth. I discovered through my interest in the Low Countries that the antecedents of the Industrial Revolution look very different from the perspective of the European continent than they do from England, and I discovered that very few authors have written about those differences. The keys to those differences, I believe, were the more gradual changes from stage to stage that appeared to take place when one's perspective was Europe instead of England. Another was the inevitability of the mechanization. The argument of the book thus emphasizes the continuities as much as the discontinuities in the movement from phase to phase in the history of European industry. It emphasizes the integration of social structures with demographic evolution and economic change. Finally, returning to its intellectual roots, it shows the importance of cottage industry growth in the eighteenth century in the forging of a new population, a new society, and a new economy.

This book is addressed to several audiences. I hope it will give undergraduate students a new way of looking at the process of industrialization, one anchored firmly in the long continuities of European history. I think the interpretive framework offered will interest a much larger audience, however. I hope the way of looking at industry and its place in a longer and larger context will give my professional colleagues and a more general readership new and useful insights into the process of industrial development. I also hope my use of specialized case studies will help advanced students. The importance of case studies in explaining a long stream of history is one reason so much of this book is about the Low Countries, and specifically about an area now in eastern Belgium between Liège and the German city, Aachen. Only with that detailed perspective about local matters can some issues be explained clearly and succinctly.

Like every book, this one has spiritual benefactors without whose urging it could not have come about. Harvey Graff was the first to suggest to me that I might be capable of writing a book about this subject. Franklin Mendels inspired the thoughts that led to the structure of this book when he pressed me to contribute to the 1982 International Economic History Congress. He has served also as a point of reference and source of inspiration as I read and reread his work on protoindustrialization. His generosity and perseverance with his supporters and critics gave me the resolve to write about a big and difficult subject. René Leboutte has been an unflagging aid and colleague, listening when I wanted to talk about research and results, solving problems when we wrote together, and tirelessly tracking down research materials when I could not be in Belgium. Etienne Hélin has made it uncommonly attractive for a foreigner to work on Belgian history. At Alfred A. Knopf, David Follmer and Christopher Rogers, along with their series editor Raymond Grew, have encouraged me despite my delays. Ray Grew has done me the additional favor of reading and rereading the manuscript as it approached completion.

My colleagues in the study of Liégeois history have also given me help and motivation. Their work answers important questions and their suggestions have helped me come up with a better understanding of this topic. Etienne Hélin and Georges Hansotte are our common mentors and friends. René Leboutte, George Alter, Bruno Dumont, Paul Servais, and Silvana Patriarca have all helped me by sharing their knowledge and their research when I have needed them. To work on a problem in isolation would not have been nearly as satisfying as it has been working on it alongside these colleagues. Together we have worked in the archives and libraries of the region we study. I have been ably helped by the staff of George Hansotte at the Archives de l'Etat à Liège, and by the staff of the Municipal Archives in Verviers. There, Mme. Rutten and Mme. Douffet have been very helpful and cooperative. Closer to home, this research could not have been done without the assistance of others. Many of them have contributed to the collection and preparation of the material included here. Randy Wyrick, R. Julian Martin, James Boyden, Eric Rust, Paul Pedersen, Silvana Patriarca, and Amy Holmes all worked with me in analyzing documents. Amy Fairchild drew the maps. Thomas Linsley and Mark Milem wrote computer programs. Others helped by reading, listening, and encouraging. My Texas colleagues Janet Meisel and Standish Meacham have been good readers and sounding boards over the years it has taken me to complete this book. Jan de Vries, Paul Hohenberg, René Leboutte, Etienne Hélin, Silvana Patriarca, Brian Levack, James Boyden and Kenneth Cowan read the manuscript in draft and gave me valuable advice. The mistakes that remain are mine; without the help of these colleagues I would have persisted in still more.

A number of institutions have supported the research reported here. The National Institutes of Health, through grant number 5R23 HD 15385 from the National Institute of Child Health and Human Development, paid for demographic research done between June 1981 and May 1984. The American Council of Learned Societies gave me a fellowship for the academic year 1983–1984, as did the University Research Institute of the University of Texas at Austin. The University Research Institute has also provided other research support.

My family has given me the love and inspiration with which to write. During four years they have tolerated without complaint my good-natured but often futile attempts to balance home, travel, research, and writing. My son, Robert, was born the month I began work on this book, and he has grown and matured in wonderful ways along with it. It is his. My wife, Barbara, has been patient and encouraging at times, demanding at others. Her sense of when I need each is perfect. She has made a life at home and at work of knowing human beings and solving their problems. The study of history is the study of human nature in the past, and when she has helped solve problems in this book her deep understanding of human nature has made the formidable look easy.

MYRON P. GUTMANN
Houston, Texas

CONTENTS

ILLUSTRATIONS

MAPS

FIGURES

TABLES

ABBREVIATIONS

AEL	Archives de l'Etat à Liège, Belgium
AEL, FFP	Archives de l'Etat à Liège, Fonds Françaises, Prefecture
Annales ESC	*Annales: Economies, Sociétés, Civilisations*
AV	Archives de la Ville de Verviers, Belgium
AV, F.	Archives de la Ville de Verviers, Collection of Portfolios
AV, Man.	Archives de la Ville de Verviers, Manuscript Collection from the Public Library
AV, V.	Archives de la Ville de Verviers, Collection of Bound Registers
BIAL	*Bulletin de l'Institut Archéologique Liégeois*
BSVAH	*Bulletin de la Société Verviétoise d'Archéologie et d'Histoire*
Chronique SVAH	*Chronique de la Société Verviétoise d'Archéologie et d'Histoire*

TOWARD THE MODERN ECONOMY

CHAPTER 1

Introduction

Five hundred years ago the economy and the society of Europe were agricultural, not industrial. That changed during the long span of time from the beginning of the sixteenth to the beginning of the nineteenth century, and Europe became gradually industrial. More and more people bought fabric, paper, metal goods, and glass, instead of making these products themselves or using inadequate substitutes, and more and more people were occupied in the process of making those things. Europe was remade in the process of that change. What had been a few industrial cities before 1500 blossomed into many urban workshops and many rural cottages by 1800. The location of industrial production moved, and moved again, as consumers and the businessmen who served them sought to find the best combination of quality products and low prices. The Europe remade by the growth and change of industry found itself transformed after 1800. Machines replaced workshops. A new kind of society replaced the old. The momentum of rapid change has not stopped since.

The creation of industrial society has never failed to interest those who have lived through one of its many stages.[1] Today that interest continues. Many historians have emphasized the stark novelty of machines and factories. This book has other goals. It is an interpretive essay about how we should understand the process of industrialization. The chapters that follow narrate a long history of industrial change, from the end of the Middle Ages to the first decade of the nineteenth century. They focus on the history of the European continent. And they emphasize people, their organizations and their choices.

A LONG HISTORY AND ITS THREE TURNING POINTS

Between 1500 and 1800 patterns of industrial organization were transformed and the location of industry moved. The chapters that follow narrate a history of industry, from its condition in the thirteenth century to its condition in the nineteenth century. There are three main turning points, each with social and demographic, as well as economic, facets. We pick up the history of industry in the late Middle Ages. At that time some industries were wide-spread in Europe, but textile production, the important industry for international trade, was concentrated in certain areas, above all in the Low Countries, as well as in Italy and southern Germany. Later England also developed. Most of the medieval textile industry was located in cities and towns, and very often it was organized into regulated guilds. Monopolistic practices were common, designed to maintain the guild's control over production of some commodities within the town, and the city's control over their production within its region.

In the late fifteenth and early sixteenth centuries a "first crisis of urban industry" set the stage for the end of regulated, guild-organized production. This is the first turning point. The first change that took place was the loss of Flanders' dominance over the international textile trade. It was battered by wars and the rise of competition in Italy and England. The older urban industry in cities such as Bruges, Ghent, and Ypres could not compete. First they became weak relative to the English and Italians who had better access to English wool. Later they could no longer compete against other production centers in the Low Countries, such as that at Hondschoote, which made use of low-cost rural labor. By the sixteenth century two kinds of industrial centers prospered. Hondschoote was one of them, buoyed by the ability to produce the "new draperies," which were lighter-weight cloth, at relatively low costs. The other kind was spurred both by the prosperity of the age, which made many kinds of business profitable, and conversely by the military and religious disruption of the sixteenth century, which changed trade routes and sparked the migration of Protestants from militantly Catholic territories. Under these pressures cities such as Leiden, in the Low Countries, and Venice, in Italy, grew, despite the fact that their urban labor forces were not competitive.

In the seventeenth century a "second crisis of urban industry" brought with it the rise of large-scale cottage industry in towns and, especially, in the countryside. This is the second turning point. The overall economic stagnation of parts of Europe during the seventeenth century slowed the growth of demand for industrial goods and increased competition among industrial producers. Urban centers such as Venice and Leiden lost, for the last time, their industrial prominence. Very large-scale cottage industry developed—producing metal and other goods as well as textiles. In the eighteenth century this large-scale cottage industry matured, bringing with it new forms of production. Europe's businessmen perceived a need to concentrate and control manufacturing even before the mechanization of industry, which led them to build primitive factories for their workers. The next logical step was mechanization, first in the English cotton industry, then in wool in England and on the European continent. The turn to mechanization is the third turning point.

The first turning point is the subject of Chapter 2; the growth which followed and the seventeenth-century crisis of industry are the subjects of Chapters 3 and 4; the maturing of cottage industry and its society are the subjects of Chapters 5, 6, and 7. The last turning point, mechanization, is the subject of the Epilogue. This book has as its subject industry in Europe, but it focusses much of its attention on the region in the Low Countries between the Belgian city of Liège and the German city of Aachen.

The story told here narrates and explains the process of change in urban industry that led to the first factories. Why did the mostly urban forms of industrial organization prevalent in the late Middle Ages die out in favor of the mixed urban and rural forms that prevailed in the seventeenth and eighteenth centuries? Why did those forms give way to mechanized factories in the late eighteenth and nineteenth centuries? There are many answers to those questions. The long cycle of industrial development coincided with a long cycle of other economic changes, determined by weather and agriculture, disease and population. Industry responded to big changes in the demand for goods in an agricultural population subject to forces often outside its control. But industry was also shaped by the attitudes and behavior of businessmen and the changing nature of a society of producers and consumers.

The point of view presented here emphasizes the shape of society, population, and markets—and the attitudes and behavior of those involved—in the transformation of industry in early modern Europe. This is partly at the expense of technological innovation as an explanation for industrial change. Whereas great historians have shown the dramatic accomplishments of technological change, I want to shift the accent from technology and the late eighteenth century to a longer span of time and a complex of causes which included business attitudes and the structure of population and society. This different emphasis assumes that industry was already strong prior to mechanization, and that the conversion from cottage industry and traditional urban industries to mechanized industries was more gradual than some readers might think.

While we can identify a technological school of industrial history that emphasizes the building of machines in the last third of the eighteenth century, we should not attribute to them a disdain for the pre-factory era. Many works have emphasized the strength of industry before mechanization, including all the best histories of the industrial revolution. David Landes's *The Unbound Prometheus* is among the most sensitive to the early period. In it he identifies ". . . a crucial element in the rise of industrial capitalism: the spread of commercial manufacture from the towns to the countryside. It was this that enabled European industry to draw on an almost unlimited supply of cheap labour and to produce at a price that opened to it the markets of the world."[2] For Landes the evolution of industry prior to the late eighteenth century was essential for the later growth of industry. The technological changes nevertheless brought on the real transformation to nineteenth- and twentieth-century industrial forms. This argument can be disputed only with difficulty.

The Industrial Revolution school has a characteristic point of view. For them, the introduction of machines to spin cotton thread, the invention of Watt's steam engine, and the use of coal in the production of iron are central to the history of industry. They characteristically begin their analysis with the year 1750 or 1760, and obviously emphasize the history of England, where all three of the developments mentioned above happened.[3] The best representatives of this approach—Landes's *The Unbound Prometheus*, Phyllis Deane's *The First Industrial Revolution*, and Peter Mathias's *The First Industrial Nation*—are all sensitive to a broad range of changes in industry, trade, agriculture, and society and yet adhere to a basic premise that stresses the importance of technology.[4]

Despite the predominance of the Industrial Revolution school, new approaches that emphasize the period before the factories have flourished. Moreover, they reflect an older tradition. In *The Age of Manufactures, 1700–1820,* Maxine Berg's interest is industry and society in eighteenth-century England, and she emphasizes some of the same processes that are emphasized here.[5] She concerns herself with the period in which traditional manufacture, as opposed to mechanized industry, dominated the English economy and society. Looking back at the historiography of industrialization, she found an interest in traditional industry in a number of early twentieth-century authors, the best known being A. P. Usher, George Unwin, and Alfred Marshall.[6] Since they wrote, there have been other strong advocates of industrial development in the centuries before 1780. John Nef stands out among these. He argued in the 1940s that the real origins of the Industrial Revolution can be found in the widespread adoption of coal as an energy source in sixteenth-century England.[7]

Since Nef's time, and especially in the past two decades, a group of historians appeared who look at the emergence of industry in a new way. This we might call a "gradualist" school. Berg is an important member of this group. So are several quantitatively oriented economic historians who have published results in the past decade that diminish the role played by the new industrial segments in the British economy and make more gradual the process of eighteenth-century industrial growth.[8] Another key contributor is Franklin Mendels, who published in 1972 an article called "Proto-Industrialization: The First Phase of the Industrialization Process."[9] The concept of protoindustrialization introduced by Mendels has generated a great deal of debate, and it has spurred the work of a number of authors.[10] The word protoindustrialization promoted by Mendels has become a kind of shorthand for emphasis on industrial development before the factories, and for the linkage of social and demographic change to that development.

The protoindustrialization model of development has economic, social, and demographic components. Mendels's work has two important elements. The first is an emphasis on the last stage of cottage industry development (mostly in the eighteenth century) as a necessary prelude to the later mechanization of industry, so that he calls protoindustrialization "the first phase of the industrialization process."[11] The second important part of the protoindustrialization idea is the linkage of social and demographic behavior with short- and long-term economic fluctuations involved in the growth of industry. Mendels's protoindustrialization model provides a starting point that reemphasizes continuities and the integration of population, society, and economics, but it should not become a restrictive formulation.

The variety of perspectives that exist about industrial development before 1800 have caused a terminological mess. Many authors use the term "preindustrial" to describe the era that ended in the late eighteenth century; but we can be sure that industry predated 1800. This terminology arose in an age when the word "industry" meant only large scale industry, that which took place in big factories powered by steam engines.[12] Because the word has been so broadened in meaning, we should now distinguish between *early industry* and *mechanized industry*—the latter specifying the stage of industrial development in which machines became widespread, and the former specifying the era of large-scale (but not mechanized) industry that preceded it. These are the terms used in this book. This is not to say that no other terms are used here. *Cottage industry* signifies the organization of manufacture wherein a merchant employs workers at their homes on his materials. *Protoindustrialization* is used in ways suggested by Mendels or other advocates of that theory.

INDUSTRIAL HISTORY AND THE LONG CYCLES OF EARLY MODERN EUROPE

This book is about the contexts in which industrialization took place. The most important of these contexts is the long cycle of economic and demographic growth and decline that animated Europe before the nineteenth century. There is much debate about this cycle, but no one will disagree that its points of punctuation came in almost every century: economic growth preceded a crash in the fourteenth century, resumed in the sixteenth century, stagnated in the seventeenth century, and returned dramatically in the eighteenth century.[13] The changes were most dramatic in the middle ages, and there has been a brisk debate about their causes.[14] The economy and population of Europe grew dramatically beginning in the ninth or tenth century, fed by a spectacular improvement in agriculture and trade. Environmental and economic reversals—most visibly the Black Death of the mid-fourteenth century, but also resources that were unable to accommodate a growing population—then led to a fourteenth-century depression. This long reversal erupted into growth in the late fifteenth century, a period that lasted in much of Europe until the first quarter of the seventeenth century. By 1650, with few exceptions, economic and demographic growth disappeared, turning to decline in a few places and stagnation in most others. Only after 1730 did growth resume everywhere.

Although Europe's economy was primarily agricultural, these economic and demographic ups and downs shaped the development of industry. A prosperous countryside housed a population that consumed industrial goods. When the overall economy was healthy, the industrial economy did well. Conversely, when the overall economy did badly, the market for industrial goods declined and sales were more difficult to obtain. Most economic historians would agree, however, that the early industrial economy was driven as much by supply as by demand.[15] Supply was increased by technical innovation (which was not widespread before 1750), by adding workers, and by creating new ways to organize production. The general welfare of the rural economy affected these changes, by changing the supplies of energy available (there is some reason to think that the large population of the seventeenth century led to energy shortages, especially of charcoal) and by changing the supply of manpower available.[16] When the rural population was underemployed, the number of would-be cottage industry workers grew.

Between the fifteenth and the nineteenth centuries, religion and politics contributed to the forces driving economic change. One side of this is the growth of state power—most visibly in France and Spain, but everywhere else too. State power rose at the expense of competing powers within society, especially the cities and the aristocrats. The state's new ability to dominate economic life helped transform industrial organization at every level. Religious life changed alongside political life. The Reformation of the sixteenth century and the ensuing long struggle to stabilize religious life had momentous consequences for industry. Early in this century Max Weber argued that Protestantism engendered a new way of looking at economic life; more recently, W. W. Rostow and others have attributed the industrial growth of England to its tolerance of religious nonconformity.[17] Such ideas are stimulating, but they will not play a role in this book, which deals with an economic Europe in which Catholics as well as Protestants became economic leaders. Nonetheless, religion was a powerful force, especially as it interacted with state power and politics. The ability of religion and politics to affect industry was clearly evident in the Low Countries, which gained in the sixteenth and seventeenth centuries from the Dutch acceptance of skilled religious immigrants, and lost in the seventeenth and eighteenth centuries as mercantilism and state power elsewhere closed the markets of large, well-organized states like France.[18]

The end of regulation generally led to more productive and lower-cost industry, but we should not assume that there was a steady movement away from it. Regulation was ended most readily at the level of the independent city or the very small state, yet the growth of power by large states in good measure compensated for the loss of power by individual cities and small states. Whereas the towns of Italy, the Low Countries, and Germany lost the power to control industry and saw their prosperity shift elsewhere, the rise of state power in France sometimes damaged productivity there. Regulation and the revocation of the Edict of Nantes in 1685, which drove out the Huguenots (French Protestants), crippled the French papermaking industry in the late seventeenth century.[19] Papermaking was not the only industry affected by the rules imposed by growing state power and wartime trade restrictions. War, as well as other state and local policies, constrained industry by opening or closing markets and by making investment attractive or impossible.

Paul Hohenberg and Lynn Hollen Lees have taken the importance of rural industry and developed a model of the relative significance of urban and rural production in Europe at different times in the past thousand years.[20] They suggest that the location and organization of industrial production were related to very long cycles of prices and prosperity. In boom times, and in the downward part of the cycle that followed, industry was concentrated in cities. In times of economic depression, and during the period of growth that came after, industrial production in the countryside did better. Hohenberg and Lees offer a good general verification of this very general principle; its quantitative proof will be difficult. Nevertheless, the reader of this book will see that their model describes fairly well the repeated shift from urban to rural industry which is part of the story told here. Urban industry was strong, for example, during and shortly after the sixteenth-century boom. Once the European economy reached bottom in the mid-seventeenth century, rural industry grew. The analysis that follows emphasizes long cycles, but shorter cycles were important too.[21] At some stages in these decades-long cycles innovation and investment were much more likely to occur than at others. We need to be on the lookout not only for the points of change and innovation brought on by very long cycles but also for the moment within a long cycle when shorter cyclical conditions brought about change.

When we get to the introduction of machines in the Verviers industry in the early nineteenth century, a topic that is addressed in the epilogue, we will see the role of shorter cycles at work. About England, Rostow writes,

> On the whole, the impression one receives is that the Industrial Revolution, regarded as a process of plant expansion and the installation of new industrial methods and techniques, lurched forward in a highly discontinuous way, with a high concentration of decisions to expand, or to improve technique, occurring in the later stages of the major cycles.[22]

We can place the introduction of machines in Verviers at the same kind of juncture, near the end of a major upward cycle. Nor should we forget, as Herman van der Wee has recently reminded us, that individual products have their own life cycles.[23] When a product's life cycle reaches maturity, it is likely that a new product will take its place and often likely that the new product will be produced elsewhere because of the resistance of old producers to change.

INTEGRATING DEMOGRAPHIC AND SOCIAL CHANGE WITH ECONOMIC CHANGE

Society and its evolution played an integral role in industrial development, because it shaped the behavior of those who made industrial goods and those who bought them. Likewise population movements were important. The chapters that follow bring together the discussion of economy, society, and population, because it is almost impossible to explain changes in one without the others. We cannot explain why the independent masters and monopolistic regulatory system that dominated much of late medieval and early modern industry yielded to the competition of unregulated cottage industry beginning in the sixteenth century, without understanding the structure of urban and rural industrial communities and how their populations performed as industrial workers.

In Chapter 4, we will follow the transformation of the German town of Nördlingen from an economy dominated by independent masters to one dominated by a rapacious merchant manufacturer employing many former masters, only by understanding social relations before and during the change. And repeatedly the importance is emphasized of linked social, economic, and demographic changes that freed peasants from agricultural work to be employed part- or full-time in industry. Such a separation took place in the region around Verviers, Belgium, which is a subject of so much of this book. When farming changed—beginning in the sixteenth century—from arable crops to dairying, farms became smaller and the population was less fully employed. An industrial population grew, and the growth of this population provided a labor force for expanding textile and metalwork production.

The behavior of rural industrial populations plays a crucial role here. Their attitudes about the land may be the key question. Many historians have believed for some time that the land shaped the fundamental attitudes of those Europeans who inhabited the countryside before 1800. Access to farmland was vitally important, so all sorts of behavior was conditioned upon it. This was especially so for marriage and the formation of families: only land and the income it brought could ensure support of a family, so young couples waited to acquire land before marrying. In northwestern Europe this produced a high age at marriage. The recent strength of the protoindustrialization theory called this supposition into question and created a new one. Land may not have been so important for cottage industry workers, because they could earn from industrial work an income sufficient for a family.

Marriage ages declined, and the community that was based on common assumptions about the land deteriorated.

This book challenges both the old and the new orthodoxy. Even in northwestern Europe, attitudes about land and its importance varied tremendously. If young men and women waited for land in some regions, they must have waited for other reasons elsewhere. And if the rise of cottage industry brought down marriage ages under some circumstances, it did not always do so.[24] We cannot yet understand fully how this process worked, mostly because there has been relatively little research into the detailed interplay of land, work, social relationships, and demographic behavior. The second half of this book offers some suggestions. The integration of rural society and population with economic change is vital. More important, there was tremendous variation from place to place, within a general pattern that saw emerge a rural labor force with new attitudes toward the land.

Between 1500 and 1800 the industrial organization of Europe changed. In 1500 most industry was still urban, and the work was done by skilled artisans working in small shops and operating hand-powered tools. Its performance was limited by rules imposed by municipal governments and corporate guilds. By 1800 much had changed. Although most goods were still produced by artisans in small workshops, some work had been taken over by machines and a great deal of work was done by less skilled workers in large shops or in the homes of cottage industry workers. In 1500 Europe was on its way toward the large-scale industrial forms we associate with the nineteenth century. By 1800 it was much closer, already partially mechanized and ripe for that change.

The chapters that follow narrate the end of regulated urban industry and its replacement by large-scale cottage industry, by primitive factories, and then by machines. Beyond the simple description of the change in industrial processes, the story calls forth a picture of economic, social, demographic, and even political change in Europe between 1500 and 1800. These changes involved the creation of a new kind of social life in which industrial work was carried on. It is not so much a global picture of change in Europe, however, as it is a picture of change in individual communities. These communities developed their own forms of industrial expertise, which they built, exploited, and eventually lost. Their stories give life to what follows.

NOTES

1. For a good discussion of the history of the Industrial Revolution, see David Cannadine, "The Past and the Present in the Industrial Revolution 1880–1980," *Past & Present* 103 (1984): 131–172.

2. The best example continues to be David Landes, *The Unbound Prometheus: Technological Change and Industrial Development in Western Europe from 1750 to the Present* (Cambridge: Cambridge University Press, 1972). It is strong on technology and the importance of its development, yet sensitive to the preceding period.

3. A classic example is T. S. Ashton, *The Industrial Revolution* (New York: Oxford University Press, 1964; originally published 1947).

4. Landes, *The Unbound Prometheus;* Phyllis Deane, *The First Industrial Revolution* (Cambridge: Cambridge University Press, 1967); Peter Mathias, *The First Industrial Nation: An Economic History of Britain 1700–1914* (New York: Scribner, 1969).

5. Maxine Berg, *The Age of Manufactures, 1700–1820* (London: Fontana, 1985). See also N. F. R. Crafts, *British Economic Growth During the Industrial Revolution* (Oxford: Clarendon Press, 1985).

6. A. P. Usher, *An Introduction to the Industrial History of England* (Boston: Houghton Mifflin, 1920); G. Unwin, *The Guilds and Companies of London* (London: Methuen, 1908); and A. Marshall, *Industry and Trade* (London: Macmillan, 1919).

7. John U. Nef, *The Conquest of the Material World* (Chicago: University of Chicago Press, 1964); and Nef, *Industry and Government in France and England* (Ithaca: Cornell University Press, 1957).

8. Crafts, *British Economic Growth;* and C. Knick Harley, "British Industrialization Before 1841: Evidence of Slower Growth During the Industrial Revolution," *Journal of Economic History* 42 (1982): 267–289. For another perspective, see Jan de Vries, "The Decline and Rise of the Dutch Economy, 1675–1900," in *Technique, Spirit, and Form in the Making of the Modern Economies: Essays in Honor of William N. Parker, Research in Economic History,* supplement 3 (1984): 149–189.

9. Franklin Mendels, "Proto-industrialization: The First Phase of the Industrialization Process," *Journal of Economic History* 32 (1972): 241–261.

10. At the 1982 International Congress of Economic History in Budapest there was a major discussion of protoindustrialization. See Franklin Mendels, "Proto-industrialization: Theory and Reality," in *Eighth International Economic History Congress, Budapest, 1982: "A" Themes* (Budapest: Akademiai Kiado, 1982), pp. 69–107.

11. Mendels, "Proto-industrialization: The First Phase."
12. Fernand Braudel, *The Wheels of Commerce*, vol. 2 of *Civilization and Capitalism: 15th–18th Century* (New York: Harper & Row, 1982; originally published Paris, 1979), pp. 297–298.
13. This statement of cycles has been most clearly expressed for France. For the Middle Ages, see Georges Duby, *L'économie rurale et la vie des campagnes dans l'occident médiéval*, 2 vols. (Paris: Aubier, 1962). For the modern period, see Denis Richet, "Economic Growth and Its Setbacks in France from the Fifteenth to the Eighteenth Century," in *Social Historians in Contemporary France: Essays from Annales*, ed. Marc Ferro (New York: Harper, 1972), pp. 180–211. It is stated somewhat more forcefully in Emmanuel Le Roy Ladurie, *The Peasants of Languedoc* (Urbana: University of Illinois Press, 1974; originally published Paris, 1966), pp. 289–312.
14. The recent debate has pitted "Marxists" against "neo-Malthusians" and has been relatively sterile. Robert Brenner began the discussion with an article in *Past & Present*. Most of the contributions have been collected in a book: T. H. Aston and C. H. E. Philpin, eds., *The Brenner Debate: Agrarian Class Structure and Economic Development in Pre-Industrial Europe* (Cambridge: Cambridge University Press, 1985). For a sensible approach, see the introduction to the English edition of Guy Bois, *The Crisis of Feudalism: Economy and Society in Eastern Normandy c.1300–1550* (Cambridge: Cambridge University Press, 1984; originally published Paris, 1976).
15. Joel Mokyr, "Demand vs. Supply in the Industrial Revolution," *Journal of Economic History* 37 (1977): 981–1008 (reprinted in *The Economics of the Industrial Revolution*, ed. Joel Mokyr [Totowa, N.J.: Rowman & Allenheld, 1988], pp. 97–118); and Donald McCloskey, "The Industrial Revolution 1780–1860: A Survey," in *The Economics of the Industrial Revolution*, ed. Mokyr, pp. 53–74.
16. Brinley Thomas, "Was There an Energy Crisis in Great Britain in the 17th Century?" *Explorations in Economic History* 23 (1986): 124–152.
17. Max Weber, *The Protestant Ethic and the Spirit of Capitalism*, trans. Talcott Parsons (New York: Scribner, 1958); W. W. Rostow, *The Stages of Economic Growth: A Non-Communist Manifesto* (Cambridge: Cambridge University Press, 1969).
18. This is the argument of Herman van der Wee, "De industriële ontwikkeling in de Nederlanden tijdens de 17de–18de eeuw. Enkele kritische bemerkingen naar aanleiding van het debat over de proto-industrie en poging tot aanvulling van het synthese-model," *Academiae Analecta* 46 (1984): 59–77.
19. Germain Martin, *La grande industrie sous le règne de Louis XIV (plus particulièrement de 1660 à 1715)* (Paris: A. Rousseau, 1898); and Warren C. Scoville, *The Persecution of the Huguenots and French Economic Development 1680–1720* (Berkeley: University of California Press, 1960), pp. 230–237.
20. Paul M. Hohenberg and Lynn Hollen Lees, *The Making of Urban Europe* (Cambridge, Mass.: Harvard University Press, 1985), pp.

113–120. Hohenberg originally put forward this idea in his contribution to the 1982 Budapest Congress (see note 10 above), "Toward a Model of the European Economic System in Proto-industrial Perspective, 1300–1800," in *La protoindustrialisation: Théorie et réalité. Rapports,* ed. Pierre Deyon and Franklin Mendels (Lille: University of Lille, 1982).

21. For example, W. W. Rostow, *British Economy of the Nineteenth Century* (Oxford: Oxford University Press, 1948); and A. D. Gayer, W. W. Rostow, and A. J. Schwartz, *Growth and Fluctuations of the British Economy, 1790–1850: An Historical, Statistical and Theoretical Study of Britain's Economic Development,* 2 vols. (Oxford: Clarendon Press, 1953).

22. Rostow, *British Economy,* p. 54.

23. Van der Wee, "De industriële ontwikkeling in de Nederlanden tijdens de 17de–18de eeuw," p. 65.

24. Myron P. Gutmann and René Leboutte, "Rethinking Protoindustrialization and the Family," *Journal of Interdisciplinary History* 14 (1984): 607–621.

CHAPTER 2

The First Crisis of Urban Industry

Large-scale industry has had a long history in Europe. At least one industry—the production of woolen textiles—was already old at the end of the Middle Ages. High-quality English wool had been traded since the time of Charlemagne. Most of the European cloth traded in the world's markets around 1300 was manufactured in Flanders, the French- and Dutch-speaking region near the North Sea in what is now western Belgium and northwestern France. Flemish cloth was already well known in Roman times, had been traded in Carolingian times, and dominated the world's trade in the twelfth and thirteenth centuries. The end of that dominance and the reasons for it are the subject of this chapter.

Put simply, the industry of Flanders (and of other textile-producing regions such as England and Italy) in the late Middle Ages was an urban industry. Virtually all the steps in the production of cloth took place in towns, and were regulated and controlled by town governments and the members of urban craft guilds. By the end of the Middle Ages that had begun to change. In short, although urban industry was not dead by the end of the Middle Ages—it never died—it was undermined by new forms of industrial organization, often located in the countryside. This evolution is extremely important, even though it was not completed until the building of the first factories. The end of the urban industries and their replacement by largely rural forms of industrial organization constitutes a key element in the argument to be put forward in this book.

Almost all the large-scale industries in the pre-factory era reached their maturity in a monopolistic environment. They may have controlled sources of raw materials, or labor, or markets for finished products, and they may have exerted this monopoly through economic or governmental means. Very often they controlled the production of a given article that others could not yet

15

produce. These places had a monopoly that depended on technological advantages. Sometimes the monopolistic power of mature industries befell them as a lucky consequence of their political or military good fortune, or the political or military bad fortune of their competitors. What is important here is that these mature industrial centers were protected by monopoly against competition; this protection permitted them to prosper and extend their dominance.

The power of the urban industrial centers was vulnerable so long as it was based on monopolistic advantages. The kinds of monopolies controlled by the Flemish towns, for example, were eventually broken. In the late Middle Ages monopoly-based industrial dominance began to be replaced by economically based industrial dominance. The new forms of industry that replaced those practiced in the Flemish towns prospered because they had a product for which there was great demand, and which they could sell at an advantageous price. While not complete by the sixteenth century, this process was under way; and the pattern was repeated in the sixteenth and seventeenth centuries, until what evolved was the kind of modern economy ripe for factories.

The crisis of Flemish urban industry was first noted at the beginning of this century by the great Belgian historian Henri Pirenne.[1] He described the decline of the old urban textile centers and the growth of new, rural textile producers in their place. According to Pirenne, the entrepreneurs who dominated the new rural industry were the first modern capitalists. If Pirenne is correct, his story is the perfect starting place for an examination of the growth of modern industry in Europe. It includes all the elements: the end of the dominance of the guilds; their replacement by unregulated workers in the countryside; the inability of the old organizations to adapt quickly and effectively; the transformation of business leadership from a group of noncompetitive masters to a group of large-scale capitalists; and the movement toward industrial production for export of large quantities of relatively inexpensive goods in place of small quantities of expensive goods.

This chapter, then, reports an expanded version of Pirenne's argument. First, we need to put that argument in context, by showing what other industries besides the Flemish textile industry existed in the late thirteenth century, and by showing what markets existed and how goods got to market. Second, we need to understand fully the organization of industry in the period of Flemish dominance. Then we can go back to the decline of Flemish industry and understand what replaced it: first the English and later a new form of Flemish industry, producing a new kind of fabric and located in the countryside.

THE INDUSTRIAL GEOGRAPHY OF THE LATE MIDDLE AGES

The Flemish textile industry reached its peak at the end of the thirteenth century. Its centers were the great towns: Arras, St. Omer, Douai, Lille, Tournai, Ypres, Ghent, and Bruges (see Map 2.3).[2] Its competitors were located in England, Italy, Catalonia, and the Hanseatic towns on the Baltic. Textile production was not the only industry in Europe in the late Middle Ages. Others were leather and metal and finished products made from them. Shipbuilding, papermaking, and glassmaking were also important. Some authors also include construction in the list of industrial processes; but construction was a process fundamentally different from the others and will not be discussed in what follows. Mining, like construction, is an ambiguous category. Overall, metals were most important after textiles and possibly leather: tin, lead, copper, and bronze, as well as silver and gold made their way into international trade. Other small metal goods, especially those made of iron, were traded (despite their weight and the widespread presence of iron ore in Europe); in general, they were produced in less densely settled parts of the Continent and consumed in more densely settled areas, where demand exceeded supply. Moreover, the Venetians sold metal goods to the most sophisticated consumers in the Middle East.[3]

Maps 2.1 and 2.2 show the distribution of industrial production (textiles in the one, mining and metalwork in the other) in the thirteenth century. Metalwork was spread fairly evenly through the parts of Europe where raw materials were found, especially Germany and eastern Europe. The contrast with textiles is striking, because in the thirteenth century textile production was mostly concentrated in Flanders and northern Italy. There are three reasons why more textiles were produced in Flanders than anywhere else. First, consumers believed that the Flemish produced the best quality textiles. Second, the Flemish

Map 2.1.   Textile Production in Europe in the Thirteenth Century

had a near monopoly on access to English wool, which was the best raw material. Finally, the Flemish had access to the largest markets—through the major trade routes to the Baltic and through the fairs of Champagne to the Mediterranean.

The geography of industrial production is only one side of late medieval industrial geography; the other sides are the market for industrial products and the trade routes that got them there. Identifying industrial markets is not easy, but it is necessary. Without knowing who was buying European industrial goods, and where they lived, we cannot understand the transformations in European industry that took place between the end of the Middle Ages and the time of factory construction around 1800. By the end of the Middle Ages, virtually every European used manufactured goods of one sort or another. In saying this, of course, a broader definition of "manufactured" is being used than was implied earlier. In this sense, a wooden or metal-edged plow, even if built at home or bought from a local craftsman, was

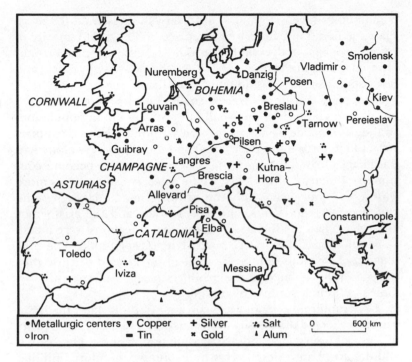

Map 2.2. Metal Production in Europe in the Thirteenth Century

manufactured. So was woolen cloth made at home or by a neighbor. The point here is that virtually everyone used things that were processed, prepared, or made.

To understand who used *industrial* products—in the narrower sense of those produced by specialists for trade in the larger sphere—we need to consider the general structure of late medieval European society. In 1250 at least 90 percent of all Europeans still lived in the countryside. It is important that we recognize nonetheless that these people were hardly primitive, and that even the poorest among them had access to some money (by 1250 a number were already paying rents and taxes in cash) and to traded goods. Still, most of the rural population had little need for industrial products at the end of the Middle Ages. They might buy iron (smelted elsewhere but fabricated by a local blacksmith) in the form of tools or a cooking pot, and they might purchase some fancier cloth to dress up for holidays. But these kinds of commodities (even clothing) could serve a household for more than a generation before being replaced. The great majority of rural Europeans at the end of the Middle Ages were not consumers of manufactured goods. They were too poor to buy much, and few had a taste for "fashionable" products.

The main consumers were a small minority among the rural population and part of the small but growing urban population. In the countryside, some of the clergy (though the vast majority were too poor to make purchases) and the aristocracy alone had the financial resources and the tastes required to become consumers of industrial products. In the cities, consuming was more widespread; but again, only the growing middle class of some craft masters, merchants, and bureaucrats, and the aristocracy and clergy, had the financial wherewithal. Weapons were a case apart, of course. They were costly but indispensable. The production of weapons led to technical advances; and because they were always profitable to the producer, their makers never had difficulty finding sources of capital.

Geographically, industrial consumption in late medieval Europe reflected the density of population, especially the density of clerical, bourgeois, and aristocratic populations. The church and the aristocracy were everywhere, and we therefore find that industrial goods had markets everywhere, although the wealth of these groups varied from place to place. The bourgeoisie constituted the best market because their numbers increased more rapidly than the population as a whole. Consumption was spread throughout Europe, with nodes of market densities where increasing activity in industry, trade, and government spawned urban growth. The greatest concentrations occurred in northern France and the Low Countries, northern Italy, and southeastern England, with smaller centers in the Rhineland, around the Baltic, and along the Mediterranean.

The major trade routes connected the large markets with the major producing areas, and connected the major commercial entrepôts with consuming centers outside Europe. Before 1300, European trade was divided into two spheres (a northern trade and a southern trade), which met in the middle to exchange goods. The northern trade was dominated by Germans, who exchanged the products of the Baltic (grain, tar, pitch, timber, and furs) for those of the Atlantic regions (fish and fine woolen textiles) and for whatever Mediterranean products they could acquire. The southern trade was dominated by Arabs and Jews, and by Italians (at first Venetians, but later Genoese and others). This trade exchanged European gold, silver, and cloth for the Mediterranean's wine and the East's spices and silks.

The meeting grounds for the northern and southern traders were periodic fairs, which were attended by itinerant merchants who traded with one another.[4] In the twelfth and thirteenth centuries, the most important fairs were those in the Champagne region of northeastern France, which constituted a cycle of six fairs (in four towns—Lagny on the Marne, Bar, Provins, and Troyes) each lasting six weeks.[5] In the fourteenth and fifteenth centuries, the Low Countries towns—Bruges and later Antwerp—eclipsed the Champagne fairs by encouraging permanent resident traders. At the fairs a Genoese or Venetian merchant might purchase Flemish textiles and sell silks or spices originally obtained in the Middle East. A merchant from Bruges or Antwerp might do the obverse, arriving with textiles and leaving with spices, silks, or cash (or bills of exchange payable later).

European textiles played a crucial role in cementing the trade of the late Middle Ages. Within Europe a number of grades of cloth were exchanged to supply everything from the everyday needs of bourgeoisie, clergy, and aristocracy to the holiday needs of every class from the peasantry up. For this market a large variety of mostly woolen (but also, sometimes, linen) cloth was produced, not merely the luxury cloths made in Flanders, England, and Italy but also less expensive textiles for the everyday needs of the middle class and the holiday needs of peasants.[6] Cloth varied by the kind of wool used and by the kind of finish it received. Fine, uniform wool was more desirable than coarse, varied wool. Smooth finishes were more desirable than rough ones. Brightly colored cloth, in reds, greens, and purples—dyed "in the piece" after weaving rather than "in the yarn" beforehand—were sought after. Rich people wore bright colors made from the best yarn and finely finished; poor people wore dull browns and greens, roughly finished. Outside Europe fine textiles became the European commodity easiest to sell. Russian, Arab, and even Chinese traders gladly exchanged their commodities for European goods. European textiles sold well outside Europe, building a market of their own and allowing European traders to impose conditions (such as increased production of silks) on their non-European counterparts.[7]

THE ORGANIZATION OF A LATE MEDIEVAL INDUSTRY: WOOLEN TEXTILES

Medieval industry was organized in a characteristic way, both technically and socially: it consisted of the relationships between the various persons involved from the sale of the basic raw materials through the sale of the finished product to a trader who took it to its final destination. We will concentrate here on woolen textiles, because they were the dominant industrial products of the time and offer us a pattern. They dominated because there were no real substitutes. Cotton, silk, and linen were known, but they were not available in sufficient quantity and variety of quality to meet large-scale needs. Wool is the key to the industrial economy of the Middle Ages. A rather large number of steps marked the production of woolen cloth in late medieval Europe, and the number of steps and its division into tasks undertaken by specialized workers is one of the most notable characteristics of this industry. As early as the late Middle Ages (if not earlier), the number of steps look very much like the kind of division of labor later described by Adam Smith, and specialization was capable of producing significant economies.

In the Middle Ages two primary kinds of cloth were made from wool and sold in international markets. These two varieties are usually called *woolens* and *worsteds* in English.[8] A woolen is made from short-staple wool and has a characteristic soft-textured appearance in which the nap of the fabric is raised so that one cannot see the weave (much as in a woolen blanket or very heavy woolen garment, such as an overcoat). A worsted fabric is made from long-staple wool and has a harder, smoother finish than a woolen. A brief description follows of the most important steps in manufacturing woolen cloth.

Sorting and Cleaning the Wool

The raw materials for wool cloth were complete fleeces, each of which had been clipped in one continuous piece off the animal.[9]

A fleece clipped from the sheep, rolled, and then sacked was not ready for weaving. It was dirty and greasy, not uniform, and contained burrs, seeds, twigs, and dirt, which needed to be removed. The first steps were therefore to clean the fleece and divide and sort it into different categories of quality. The dense fleece was opened up by a fleece-breaker, who spread it out and pulled out large pieces of debris. Then it was pulled apart and the wool sorted into three or four grades.

The sorted wool was ready for cleaning. First, any objects remaining in the wool needed to be removed. This was done, in medieval Flanders, by placing the wool on a rope net suspended from a wooden frame, and beating it with sticks. Next the wool was washed, in alternating hot- and cold-water baths, in clean and soapy water. If the wool was to be dyed before spinning and weaving, it was done after cleaning. Dyeing at this stage produced dull colors; for bright or light colors the cloth had to be dyed after finishing. Finally, the wool was oiled before it entered the true manufacturing operations. This was done by adding butter or oil. This lubrication made the wool workable, by reducing friction and breakage.

Carding or Combing

The next major step in the production of wool cloth was to take the still disorganized mass of wool that emerged from the cleaning and sorting operations and organize the fibers. Long-staple wool was *combed* for use in worsteds; short-staple wool was *carded* for use in woolens. In combing, the goal is to convert a mass of tangled, curling wool into a smooth tress in which all the curls, knots, and tangles have been removed and the wool fibers lie parallel and smooth. A comparison could be made with combing the hair of a person whose hair has grown for a year—unwashed, uncombed, and unbrushed. The comber uses two combs, holding the mass of wool in one and using the second, which has been heated to make the work easier, to comb through the wool. The result is a lightly gathered but linear bunch of straight wool fibers that can then be pulled out and spun for worsted cloth.

Short-fiber wool is carded because the fibers are too short to line up parallel and still hold together as useful yarn. The object of carding is, first, to remove tangles and knots and, second, to mix the short fibers in such a way that they constitute a cohesive bunch of wool that can then be pulled and twisted into yarn. A card is a rectangular block of wood with a handle; one side is covered with leather through which are placed parallel rows of wire teeth. The carder starts out with a bunch of wool placed on one card. With the second card he or she works the wool, still on the first card, in a circular motion. This removes knots and tangles, and mixes the wool so that the fibers hold together. Here the result is a ball of wool that can be pulled out and twisted as it is spun.

Spinning

The combed-out or carded bunches of wool must be converted first into continuous lengths of yarn. This process is called spinning, and it involves twisting the raw wool while pulling it into a thin, continuous thread. The twist is crucial because it makes the thread strong.

Spinning was the most labor-intensive part of the process. A single piece of finished cloth was a large undertaking, both in the Middle Ages and in early modern times. A broadcloth was more than 1¼ meters wide, and was 22–32 meters long. There are many estimates of how much manpower was required to produce such a cloth, and they often differ. The important point here is that it took several spinners to produce enough spun yarn for a single loom. One credible seventeenth-century English source says that it took two fleece-breakers to split up and six spinners to spin enough wool for a single coarse cloth of 28 meters length after fulling (see page 25). Carding probably required six girls, and the process of carding and spinning must have lasted two to three weeks. The weaving occupied two men and one boy and took another three weeks. A fine or superfine cloth might call for half again as many spinners as this (to spin the wool more tightly), and several more days.[10]

The traditional tool for spinning was the spindle and weight, used from at least Roman times. The spinning wheel began to be adopted in the late thirteenth century, at least for producing the weft, the yarn that is used for the side-to-side threads in woven cloth. Hand-spun yarn was considered stronger than wheel-spun yarn and therefore more appropriate for the warp, or lengthwise threads.

Weaving

Weaving produces cloth by interlacing yarn or thread at right angles so that an individual thread crosses over and under the threads at right angles to it. The broadloom is strung with the threads of the *warp*, which run from front to back, before weaving is begun. They are wrapped around a spindle at the front of the loom, and tied to another spindle at its rear. Then the weaver passes a bobbin holding the thread of the *weft* from side to side, going over some threads of the warp, and under others. After each thread of weft is added, the weaver compresses the finished cloth across its width to make it tight. Finished cloth moves away from the weaver and is wrapped on the spindle to which the threads of the warp had been tied. As that happens more warp threads are unwound from a spindle on the front of the loom, near the weaver. An over one and under one weaving technique produces a simple weave. More complex weaving patterns are possible, the most important for us being a twill weave, in which the thread passes over two and under two. The common fabric called serge is woolen or worsted cloth with a twill weave. A normal broadloom required three persons to operate it, often two adult men and one child. The weaver performed other tasks besides simply weaving. Very often he wound the warp and put the weft on the bobbins, in addition to the two to three yards of weaving he accomplished in a given day.

Fulling

Just-woven cloth was cleaned, softened, and finished before being sent to market. The cleaning and softening process is called *fulling,* and it works by mixing the cloth with chemicals that remove grease, and then pounding it. Fulling shrank and cleaned the cloth thoroughly, softened the fabric, and closed up any gaps left in the weave. Not all types of cloth were fulled. In some places worsteds were not fulled, but there was no simple rule; in Flanders, virtually all cloth was fulled. The chemicals used for fulling were various kinds of detergents and soaps: lye, stale human urine, ashes, and especially fuller's earth—all products that dissolved or absorbed fats.

In primitive fulling the cloth was folded, placed in a trough with water and chemicals; the fuller stood in the trough and stamped on the cloth with his feet. Periodically the cloth was removed, refolded, and returned to the trough, to make sure it had been evenly fulled. By the thirteenth century a water-driven fulling mill was gradually adopted in England and Italy; but in Flanders foot-fulling was considered preferable until the end of the Middle Ages.[11] A mechanical fulling mill used a water wheel to raise heavy wooden triphammers. When released, they fell on the cloth in the fulling trough.

Finishing

The cloth, once fulled, was dried and stretched by placing it on a wooden frame, or tenter. Then it was ready for finishing. The procedures to which the cloth was usually subjected were bleaching, dyeing, raising the nap (teaseling), shearing, and pressing. Of these, bleaching, dyeing, and pressing hardly need description.

The nap is raised by pulling out all the fiber ends from the cloth so that they are raised above the surface; it imparts a soft finish to the cloth, and helps hide the weave. This raising of the nap is done by brushing the cloth with the burr of the teasel plant, which is rubbed across the surface of the cloth. The craftsman who did this work was called a *teaseler.* The surface was then clipped smooth by a shearman, so that all the fiber ends exposed were the same length. Often this process was repeated, using smoother teasels at each stage, so that the resultant cloth was made softer and softer. The processes described here required an ever-increasing level of skill. The weaver had to be more skilled than the spinner, but the fullers, teaselers, shearmen, and dyers all required still more skill.

THE SOCIAL AND COMMERCIAL ORGANIZATION OF LATE MEDIEVAL INDUSTRY

Most of us have a picture in our minds of the organization of late medieval industry into guilds of masters, assisted by journeymen and apprentices. The master is a self-sufficient small-scale industrialist who owns both his tools (his fixed capital investment) and the raw materials (working capital) with which he and his assistants work. He controls all the stages of the manufacturing process from the moment at which he purchases his raw materials until he sells the finished product to its ultimate consumer. In this kind of industrial society, the guild or the city government strictly regulates the processes of providing raw materials to masters and of selling finished products. In the normal situation, masters must have ready access to raw materials at the prevailing price; no one may hoard them. At the other end of the manufacturing process, only masters in a given craft may sell finished goods at retail.[12]

We may think about a simple craft, that of baking. The master baker owns his ovens and produces bread with the help of his family and some journeymen and apprentices. The guild and the city government ensure that he can buy grain in the city's markets at a reasonable price and that no grain merchant can hoard grain with the intention of driving up the price. No one but a master baker may sell bread in the town, although the authorities usually impose a reciprocal requirement on the baker that he sell his bread at a regulated price.

Whether this society actually existed or not, it is an explicit vision of a harmonious industrial community. All masters are essentially equal: they have the same resources in terms of equipment and assistants, they buy raw materials for the same price, and they sell their product in a regulated market. No one profits at the expense of the others. In return for this protection, they contribute to the community as a whole by selling their goods at a "just price."[13] The commercial and industrial process is localized and integrated, and profits are limited.

In the late Middle Ages this kind of industrial society was already intermixed with a more complex variety. The idealized society had never existed because the masters and the guilds rarely had sufficient power to enforce their rules.[14] Moreover, they could not control raw material prices, and they could not control the way their customers spent their money. Means arose to deal with the problems of getting the special raw materials and specialized products demanded by consumers. This more complex society came into being to serve the long-distance trade in raw materials and manufactured goods. The existence of the long-distance trade meant that industrial society was no longer local in its focus. The masters of a single town could no longer be protected by not being allowed to compete among themselves; they had to worry about competition from outside. And as the amount of production increased, they had to find ways to rationalize and streamline the manufacturing process.

Nowhere is this alternative industrial society evident earlier than in the textile industry of the Flemish towns. The structure of industry, commerce, and society has already been alluded to in describing the tasks required to produce wool cloth. In the developed Flemish textile industry, from the twelfth century on, each of the tasks described was performed by a specialist. There were breakers, beaters, washers, oilers, carders and combers, spinners, weavers, fullers, tenterers, teaselers, shearmen, dyers, and pressers. While some of these workers owned their own tools and worked in their own homes or shops, none of them owned the raw materials. Rather, the raw materials were owned, and the work directed, by a businessman called a *draper*. Some of the workers, especially those employed in cleaning and preparing the wool, were his employees and worked in his shop. These unskilled workers were paid very low wages. Spinners and fullers, although relatively unskilled, had their own equipment; but they were provided raw materials by the draper, who then paid them a piecework wage. Even the relatively skilled weavers and shearmen were in fact the employees of the draper and subject to the regulation of the industrial "police," who guaranteed the quality of the product and were the agents of the drapers.

These workers often had their own guild organizations, and they had more freedom than the wool preparation workers because they could take in work from more than one draper; nevertheless, they still were not industrial craft masters in the sense that our baker was. The only economically independent individual was the draper; he was a member of the merchants' guild, a controller of working capital, and protected to a limited extent from competition from other drapers by his guild or by the city administration. Moreover, he could buy raw wool and sell finished cloth, something a weaver, spinner, fuller, or shearman could not. Finally, he was not limited to the retail trade, and special provisions existed for him to market cloth for the long-distance trade: he was required to lease a stall in the communal sales hall and to negotiate his wholesale transactions there. He could usually make retail transactions from his shop, but he dealt with international merchants only in the sales hall.[15]

This industrial and social structure was therefore clearly divided into an ordered hierarchy. At the very top were the drapers and the other merchants (sellers of raw wool, of dyestuffs, and of finished cloth) involved in the textile trade. Below them were the skilled craftsmen, who had their own organizations, owned their own tools, employed their own assistants, and felt they had a considerable amount of freedom and status in the community. Below them were the simple day laborers who washed or beat the wool; they were little more than the kind of proletarian factory workers who became so common in the nineteenth century.

Nowhere else was industry so large and developed as it was in Flanders in the thirteenth century, so nowhere else was social organization so fully developed. In England the system was remarkably similar to that in Flanders, but on a much smaller scale; growth of industry to surpass the Flemish did not occur until the late fourteenth century.[16] In Italy, although trade had developed to a considerable extent by the thirteenth century, industry was not so well established. For one thing, in the early thirteenth century the Flemish still controlled access to the best English wool. The manufacturing enterprises of Italy produced poor cloth. The area in which the Italians excelled, however, was in finishing cloth manufactured in Flanders. Their merchants bought unfinished or partially finished cloth at the Champagne fairs, and transported it to Italy for dyeing, teaseling, and shearing. The great centers were located at Genoa and Lucca, and especially at Florence.[17] They produced textiles with exquisite soft finishes and dramatic colors—especially reds—for sale in the eastern Mediterranean and Asia. They did this by employing the most expert craftsmen, who used the best Eastern dyestuffs, and performed the crucial processes of teaseling and shearing over and over until the cloth was perfectly smooth and soft.

At this stage in the development of the Italian industry, it exhibited a truncated version of the organization we saw for the northern industrial cities and towns. The finishing process was dominated in a town such as Florence not by drapers, who were members of the merchants' guild, but by members of the finishers' guild, the Arte de Calimala. They performed the same industrial function as the drapers, by organizing work and putting it out to specialists who did each task, but the members of the Calimala had no mercantile function. In thirteenth-century Flanders there was no bar to drapers entering into the trade that brought wool in or sent cloth out, and the greatest merchant industrialists of the time did just that. In Italy the finishers very rarely imported unfinished cloth and never retained its ownership until it was sold in the Middle East. Rather, they bought the cloth from importers and sold it to exporters. The manufacturing and commercial operations remained almost completely separated.

In the late thirteenth and early fourteenth centuries high-quality cloth production joined finishing as a major Italian industry. There are two reasons for this development. First, as the Italians became more confident in their role as the preeminent European merchants, they entered the English wool trade. Once they were involved in the trade for raw English wool, it was just as easy for them to send it to Italy as to Flanders. For the first time, Italian manufacturers could obtain access to the best raw materials. The second reason for the growth of the Italian industry had more to do with Flanders than with Italy. During the second half of the thirteenth century the Flemish industry was constantly interrupted, because war between Flanders and France led to embargoes and other disturbances in the trade between England and Flanders, and between Flanders and the Champagne fairs. Moreover, as trade conditions became uncertain, labor unrest erupted in Flanders. The workers became increasingly restive under the yoke of merchant domination of towns and industry. The quarrels between workers and manufacturers ended around 1300 in a workers' victory, but the victory came only after long battles that sapped the Flemish industry's strength. Although Flanders was hardly eliminated at this time, an increasing amount of industrial work was shifted from Flanders to Italy.

The social and commercial organization of the Italian textile industry resembled the Flemish organization, preserving only the distinction observed earlier for the finishers: the Italian drapers were members of their own craft guild, not the merchants', and only very rarely became involved in trade, either to acquire raw materials or to sell finished cloth. What did distinguish Italian from Flemish industrial society as the fourteenth century progressed was the growing power of the drapers over the people who worked for them. The Italian industry became more and more concentrated. The power of the drapers meant that among the crafts only the finishers retained any independence. The workers—even those who worked at home—became obligated to a single draper, and very often they ceased to own their tools. Most of the industry's workers became industrial proletarians.

THE RISE OF THE ENGLISH TEXTILE INDUSTRY

The story told thus far is about the miracle of medieval urban life. The growth of population and trade that began in tenth-century Europe sparked the development of a sophisticated urban society capable of remarkable economic activities. Once this society emerged, it became the base on which the whole edifice of modern civilization was built.[18] That it was clearly in place by the twelfth century, almost immediately after the end of the decline of urban life that characterized the Middle Ages, is a sign of the intellectual power of medieval Europeans and of the close lines that connect them to us.

Yet despite the achievement we see in the rise of the Flemish and Italian textile towns, we should not assume that the development from then to now was straight and linear, or that medieval urban society worked so well that it continued in only modified form to modern times. Rather, strains soon arose in the towns of Flanders and Italy, and their industrial preeminence, so marked in the twelfth, thirteenth, and fourteenth centuries, waned. Why this happened is extremely important, not only for understanding the state of industry in Europe at the beginning of the sixteenth century, but because it presents us with a model of the way in which industry and industrial society evolved during subsequent centuries. This is Pirenne's "industrial crisis." It is our first crisis of urban industry; through it we will see the pattern with which we can understand later industrial developments.[19]

Several forces provoked the first crisis of urban industry. One problem the Flemish faced was that they gradually lost access to English wool at competitive prices in the fourteenth and fifteenth centuries. The first step was the end of Flemish domination in the trade in raw English wool. Through the middle of the thirteenth century Flemish merchants dominated this trade, buying large quantities of fleeces directly from the monasteries that produced them.[20] Between 1264 and 1275, however, domestic political difficulties in England and their transformation into war between England and Flanders led to a series of trade closures and seizures of foreign property by both sides. By the time the Flemish merchants returned to England, growers had become sensitive to the political risks involved in dealing with parties considered the king's enemies, and the Flemish lost their preeminent role in trade. Their place was taken by Englishmen and Italians, who obviously felt no obligation to provide wool to the Flemish so long as there were other customers.

Not long after the Flemish lost their dominant role in the wool trade, they lost their key place in the trade that took finished products out of Flanders. In the twelfth and early thirteenth centuries, Flemish merchants took their cloths to Champagne to trade at the fairs. In the second half of the thirteenth century the same set of conflicts that brought the English and Flemish to blows raised tensions with France. Champagne became part of the French domain in 1285, and the French king repeatedly cut trade between Flanders and Champagne after 1297. Moreover, the French kings wished to bring Flanders into France, whereas the Flemish strove to preserve their independence. By 1312 the French-speaking districts of Flanders, including the textile towns of Lille and Douai, had been ceded to France (as Arras, the former center of the textile industry, had been ceded in the late twelfth century). Cession to France brought, or at least confirmed, economic stagnation. During the thirteenth century Ypres, Bruges, and Ghent became the most important Flemish textile towns, and cloths no longer were taken by Flemings to Champagne. Instead, they departed directly from the harbor of Bruges for points abroad, in the care of Italians.

The Flemish suffered still further from the competition of their neighbors in the duchy of Brabant. While Flanders was deeply involved in international conflicts in the late thirteenth and early fourteenth centuries, Brabant steered a relatively neutral course, keeping its ports open to English wool.[21] And the duke stood behind the merchant patriciate in Brussels, Antwerp, Louvain, and the other towns, so that urban workers were unable to disrupt industrial activity. The stability of ongoing trade and the relative absence of social unrest gave the merchants and craftsmen of the Brabant towns the opportunity to perfect their techniques and open markets into the world. By the early fourteenth century they had overtaken the Flemish as manufacturers of high-quality cloth in the Low Countries. Both Flanders and Brabant were weakened after the middle of the fourteenth century, as access to English wool was further restricted by heavy export duties placed on it. That wool exports should be taxed was natural in late medieval England, considering that the wool trade was the largest part of the nation's cash economy, and that it provided a foreign trade surplus that could be converted to bullion, with which the king could pay his troops in France.[22] The export trade in wool had long been taxed, but in 1336 Edward III raised the tax on wool from 6s. 8d. a sack to 40s. a sack.[23] While this tax was not yet permanent, and was felt more by producers (who were forced by the merchants to absorb the tax in the form of lower prices paid to growers) than by Flemish purchasers, the rate of taxation approached one-third. At the same time, the export tax on cloth was a nominal 2 percent.

By 1364 the tax was permanent. Virtually all English wool was forced to pass through the near monopoly Staple in Calais, which was controlled by English merchants who had the exclusive right to export English wool to Flanders. These policies may have had the effect of pricing the Flemish out of the market. In any case, they were forced either to change their goods or prices, or to look elsewhere for wool. The duty on raw wool exports meant that Flemish drapers paid one-third more for their wool than their English competitors. The English moved quickly to fill the gap by increasing production and raising quality. The Flemish found themselves unable to meet the prices offered by the English. The English began by taking over their own domestic market, so that few cloths made outside England were sold in England itself. Ultimately the English were able to conquer not only foreign markets elsewhere in Europe and the Middle East but the Belgian market itself, selling English cloths—via Antwerp—in Brabant, Flanders, and elsewhere. Prohibitions against the import of English cloth, such as the one enacted in 1434, did little good against products selling at a price advantage.[24]

The relative failure of the Flemish industry in contrast to the

Brabantine and especially the English was up to this point largely a consequence of external affairs. The Flemish industry had prospered because of its monopoly of English wool. It later lost market share (to use a twentieth-century business term) because it could not get enough raw material and because the supplies it received cost too much: the monopoly had ended. The same circumstances later eroded the strength of Brabantine industry. This situation arose because of the fiscal policies of the English government. Although those policies were not exclusively protectionist in their intent, they became extremely effective protective measures. An infant industry grew to maturity in the context of that protection. This point is important because it shows that the urban Flemish industry did not fail at first because it was urban but because it was Flemish. The Low Countries towns, facing difficulties, either failed completely to devise a solution that would return them to prosperity or responded only very slowly.[25]

Nonetheless, there was a truly urban industrial crisis at the end of the Middle Ages, one that was not just Flemish but English also. This situation, too, involved the failure of the industrial towns to respond to a change in the economic environment—in this case the first emergence of large-scale rural textile production. Its two elements taken together, the crisis of urban industry of the late Middle Ages show us key patterns we need to search for in later industrial history. The failures in industrial leadership reflect the failure to adapt quickly to a changing industrial environment.

There are two versions of the rise of large-scale English industry in the late Middle Ages. One version, which has been put forward by E. M. Carus-Wilson, tells us that growth coincided with the rise of rural textile industry. This in turn may have had as its starting point the invention of mechanized fulling and its widespread adoption in England in the thirteenth and fourteenth centuries.[26] The first mention of a fulling mill in England is in 1185. They were increasingly common thereafter. Being dependent on water power, these mills were primarily placed away from the traditional textile towns, in the countryside and along swiftly running streams.[27] Labor costs were lower for producers in these new locations because the fulling mill was as much as twenty to fifty times as efficient as foot-fulling, which was very labor-intensive.[28] At first, rural fulling mills were used to finish cloth that had been made in town; but before long the presence of fullers in the countryside attracted other textile crafts there. Because work in the countryside was not subject to nearly as much regulation as in the guild-dominated towns, rural industry grew still further as it took advantage of lower costs.

As one might expect, the older textile towns objected vigorously to the adoption of mechanized fulling, in England and in Flanders. In 1298 the London fullers demanded the abolition of mechanical fulling, because its product was inferior to foot-fulling and because it put fullers out of work. The citizens of York objected to all rural textile work in 1304, stating that their charter gave them an exclusive right to produce cloth in their neighborhood. In Flanders and later in Brabant, mechanical fulling was perceived as producing lower quality cloth than did foot-fulling. As a result, mechanized fulling did not develop in those regions. Only in Italy was mechanical fulling combined with continued urban dominance.

The other version of the growth of the English industry—most recently put forward by A. R. Bridbury—repudiates the economic argument based on prices and diminishes the importance placed on the fulling mill.[29] For Bridbury, the major explanation of the growth of English textile production was the improved quality of the cloth. This in turn was the consequence of both the introduction of foreign workers into England and the gradual maturing brought about by growing domestic markets. It is difficult to decide between these two explanations, so the most logical course is to accept something from each. There were economic grounds for the rise of the English industry: there was a move to rural filling that put more workers in the countryside; and there was a dramatic improvement in the quality of English cloth that made it more competitive both at home and abroad.

Improved quality, protection from competition because of low raw material prices, and the advantages of relatively free access to mill-fulling and unregulated rural industry gave an enormous boost to the English cloth industry. Carus-Wilson and Olive Coleman published figures showing the evolution of English exports of raw wool and cloth from 1280 to 1547 (see Figure 2.1).[30] Wool exports reached a plateau in the fourteenth century and from about 1350 moved steadily downward. They

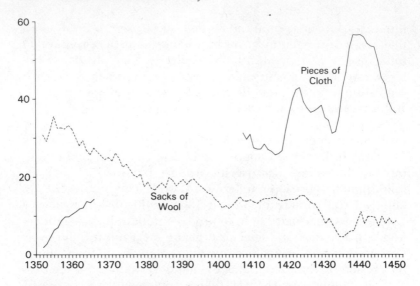

**Figure 2.1.   English Wool and Cloth Exports, 1350–1450
(in thousands; five-year moving means)**
SOURCE: E. M. Carus-Wilson and O. Coleman, *England's Export Trade,
1275–1547* (Oxford: Clarendon Press, 1963).

reached half their former level by the end of the fourteenth
century and one-fourth by the mid-fifteenth century. Thereafter
English wool exports amounted to a trivial 5,000 or fewer sacks
of wool per year. Their quantity fell by 90 percent from peak
levels.

Cloth exports grew as wool exports declined. From a low level
(rarely more than 10,000 cloths per year) in the mid-fourteenth
century, England exported 40,000 cloths a year at the end of the
fourteenth century, roughly 80,000 at the end of the fifteenth
century, and about 120,000 by the middle of the sixteenth century. English industry converted the island from a producer of
raw materials that were worked by others, to a producer and
exporter of finished goods. Wool previously sent to Flanders was
made into cloth in England. The cloth made in England was
almost exclusively broadcloth (as opposed to worsted, which sel-
dom exceeded 1 percent of the export market), manufactured in
the traditional way described earlier.

If manufacturing techniques were stable, a novel social and
commercial organization evolved in the English woolen industry

in the fifteenth and sixteenth centuries. First, the great industry moved out of the old towns and into the countryside and small towns, in new sections of England. Half the country's cloth production came from the west of England, "especially in the southern Cotswolds, in the Stroud valley and along the Bradford Avon and its tributaries, where [there] were abundant supplies of fine quality wools, water power and fuller's earth."[31] Other major new centers were in Yorkshire, East Anglia, Norfolk, and the West Riding. Their production was traded out of Bristol and London, not by the masters of the old Staple (which sold wool) but by the merchant adventurers, whose name derived from their courage in trading a new product—cloth—in distant markets.

The novelty and freedom of the fifteenth-century English woolen industry went beyond its location. Its development reflected a new way of doing industrial business. Part of its freshness came from the role played by the numerous Flemish and German migrants who were attracted to England as English industry grew and Continental industry declined. But another part of that freshness was a consequence of the absence of regulation that prevailed in the countryside. Except for minimal standards, any sort of cloth could be produced, and whatever would sell *was* produced. A great deal of experimentation took place. And no longer did the old drapers dominate the industry. In their place arose a group called *clothiers,* who were not involved in trade but merely in organizational matters. Here lies the first large-scale spread of the putting-out trade, where an entrepreneur obtains wool and then delivers it—first to the carder, then to the rural spinner, weaver, fuller, dyer, and so on. The clothier sold the finished product to a draper, who was involved only in the long-distance trade. Another striking change from older systems was the possibility for almost anyone to become a clothier. Under the old urban system, a draper could not combine his tasks with another craft. He had to give up any manual work (weaving, dyeing, or fulling, for example) before being accepted into the drapers' guild or merchants' guild, and only members of those guilds could buy and sell cloth. In the countryside no such guilds and regulations evolved. A weaver, a dyer, a merchant, or even a lord might work as a clothier, and all of them did, on different scales. The consequence was a much more dynamic industrial environment.

THE RISE OF THE FLEMISH "NEW DRAPERIES"

The remains of Flemish urban industry faced a world of bleak prospects in the early fifteenth century. The amount of English wool exported fell during most of the century until it averaged only 8,000 sacks per year, enough to make roughly 35,000 cloths—and not nearly enough to support the number of Flemish workers who had been supported in the fourteenth century. The rest of the English wool produced was being exported in the form of cloths sold at prices below those possible for the Flemish, whose markets as well as their raw materials were thus cut off.

Flemish industry could not respond to these new conditions by waging direct battle against the English. Other responses were necessary. Ordinarily, industries respond to losing their raw materials or markets by searching for new products that permit the industry to discover new markets. Where the local industry is textile production, the common path is to shift the quality of what is produced upward or downward until a new niche in the market is found. Therefore, for a region producing low-quality goods, a shift in external conditions might cause them—if there are workers present with enough skill—to move to medium- or high-priced textiles. For an industry producing for the middle market, a movement upward or downward is possible; for a high-priced industrial region, all that is possible is a shift to lower quality and lower prices.

In the late Middle Ages, the number of options theoretically available to the industrialist were more limited than they are today. To move up in the scale of quality was much easier than to move down, because late medieval business thought still held that to earn a larger profit on each of a smaller number of transactions was preferable to earning an equivalent or greater total profit by means of smaller earnings on each of a larger number of transactions. Thus the majority of Flemish business people, when subjected to the pressure put on them by the English, attempted to produce still higher quality fabrics that they could sell for more (this is *economic efficiency*), rather than searching for ways to produce the old quality cloth for less per piece (this is *technical efficiency*).[32]

The obvious way for the Flemish industry to compete with the English would be to imitate it: adopt mill-fulling, employ unregulated workers in the countryside, and shift to lower-cost (preferably domestic) wool. Indeed, rural production attempted to blossom in the fifteenth century. Yet in almost every case the towns moved rapidly—usually through the courts but sometimes by armed expeditions into the countryside to smash looms—to quash any such efforts. A period of "urban imperialism" ensued. So long as the towns remained powerful and kept up some level of economic activity, these measures were successful. They persisted, and the towns maintained their domination of the economic lifeblood of the textile industry, until the very end of the fifteenth century.

There were, however, efforts to introduce new products or expand the production of old products that were outside the mainstream of the old heavy broadcloths. Such efforts grew in the fifteenth century, and although still limited at that time they were to suggest the kind of salvation that lay ahead for Flemish industry. The products which emerged at that time are the so-called *new draperies*—lighter cloths which became fashionable and widely marketed in the sixteenth century.[33] These cloths did not require the highest-quality English wool; they were usually made of other varieties—Scottish and lower-quality English wool in England, and European wools on the Continent.[34] Some of them were mixed cloths, which used linen and wool, or goat hair and wool, to give a different feel and appearance.

The most successful of the new draperies produced in Flanders were *says.* [35] Says are lightweight worsted textiles that characteristically are given a twill weave. Most Flemish says were made of wool raised in the Low Countries, France, Germany, or Spain.[36] The warp of a say is very strong, made up of a doubled or tripled twisted worsted thread coated with starch to make it smooth and easy to weave. The say was only very lightly fulled. The production of says in Flanders grew beginning in the late fourteenth century, especially in a region extending from Tourcoing to Poperinghe, centered in the villages of Langhemarck and Neuve-Eglise. During the fifteenth century the production of these new cloths spread through Flanders just as it spread in England, in Holland, in France, and elsewhere. The vogue of the new draperies permitted regions overtaken by the English dominance of the market for the old broadcloths to persist in the fifteenth century.

In the late fifteenth century the development of the say industry in Flanders was heavily influenced by domestic politics in the Low Countries, as it had been previously and as it would be again in the sixteenth century.[37] Throughout most of the late Middle Ages the territories that now make up Belgium, the Netherlands, and Luxembourg were divided into a number of essentially independent principalities. After 1375 the French dukes of Burgundy gradually acquired these principalities (see Map 2.3), beginning with Flanders (1384) and continuing with Namur (1421), Hainaut, Holland, and Zealand (all in 1428), Brabant and some of Limburg (1430), and Luxembourg (1451).

This is the environment in which Duke Charles the Fearless (1467–1477) put all the Low Countries principalities under considerable pressure to obey his wishes—pressure that the older Flemish textile towns resisted and to which Antwerp, which was then growing in importance, acquiesced. In the period of instability that followed Charles's death in 1477, Antwerp supported his successor, Maximilian, whereas the Flemish towns opposed him. In return for Antwerp's political support Maximilian permitted free entry of English textiles. This led to the complete demise of the old broadcloth industry, because Antwerp had close ties with England and served as the port of entry to the Low Countries for English finished textiles.[38] The opposition of the old textile towns to the free entry of English textiles came to nothing, especially after the victory of Maximilian.

By 1500, Bruges, Ypres, and Ghent were almost dead as large-scale industrial centers. Forced by English competition to lower prices, the industrialists of the Flemish towns made piecemeal economies in the quality of the cloth they produced. Over time, these economies meant that their cloth, although still attractive, was unable to compete in price or in quality. One by one the markets for fine Flemish cloth dried up. The response of the Flemish towns was not to emulate the English but once again to seek protection. The guild merchants of Ghent as late as 1539 requested the prohibition of all industry within a radius of three leagues (about 12 kilometers) of the city. Ypres complained at about the same time that the cause of the city's decline was the failure to enforce the prohibition against rural industry. They made no move to lift regulation in an effort to find a way out of the crisis; instead, they constantly reaffirmed the old regulations. Courtrai in 1496 restated a regulation limiting master weavers to

Map 2.3. **The Burgundian State in the Low Countries Before 1550**

a single loom (more looms would have permitted a weaver to staff them with journeymen or apprentices and lower his labor costs). In Bruges in 1536 the shearmen opposed the presence of foreign workers brought in to introduce a new kind of cloth in the town.[39]

Only the towns that produced the new draperies were dynamic in the sixteenth century. From about 1500, as the broadcloth industry died, the say and serge industry of West Flanders boomed, led by the little Flemish town of Hondschoote. Around 1500, Hondschoote exported some 15,000 cloths annually. By the late 1520s the number had doubled. It reached 50,000 around 1550 and nearly 100,000 by 1570. These production levels probably made Hondschoote the largest single producer of cloth in mid-sixteenth-century Europe.[40]

The organization of this industry differed from that associated with the traditional Flemish medieval broadcloth. Hondschoote did have an old textile industry organized in a craft guild, so its industry cannot be said to have grown completely outside a regulatory environment. Nevertheless, demand for Hondschoote says grew so rapidly in the early sixteenth century that its drapers had little choice but to find labor wherever they could. The town itself was small—really just a market center in an agricultural region—so the obvious choice of the industrialists was to search for workers in the countryside outside the town. That they did, and it seems every farm contributed to textile production in the early sixteenth century. As the industry matured and neared its peak around 1570, more and more of the workers lived in the growing town, and the rural character of the industry disappeared, although not the cottage industry organization.

The relatively flexible organization of the industry extended to the roles taken by workers and to commercial relations as well. Workers often performed both industrial and nonindustrial functions, combining weaving with trade in dyestuffs or sale of cloth; or combining spinning with sale of food to other workers, and so on. In this, the West Flanders industry resembled the English. Equally dramatic was that this meant the absence of the traditional sales hall, which regulated the sale by drapers to long-distance merchants. Rather, the Hondschoote equivalents of the English clothiers sold their cloths directly to the new breed of long-distance merchants at Antwerp, without regulation of prices or sizes, or competition within the town. Pirenne reports, "From [Antwerp] the merchants received orders for hundreds, even thousands of pieces. In 1555, a certain Jacob Colaert purchased nearly all the serges produced at Bergues."[41]

The preeminence of the Hondschoote say industry was not very long-lived. Born as an indirect consequence of changing political fortunes in the Burgundian Netherlands, it died because of the next round of transformations. In the early sixteenth century the Spanish king, emperor, and Burgundian duke, Charles V, continued to add to his power. In 1521 he gained Cambrai and in 1543 Tournai. Moreover, he added the lands north of the Rhine: Friesland in 1523–1524; Utrecht and Overijssel in 1528; Groningen, the Ommelanden and Drenthe in 1536, and finally Gelderland in 1543. By the time he stepped down in favor of his son, Philip, in 1555, the Netherlands was virtually a single state consisting of seventeen provinces that shared a common sovereign. Only the principality of Liège remained outside its orbit.

The centralizing and monarchical interests of Charles and Philip ran up against two powerful forces. One of these was the continuing sense of individuality and independence felt by the old provinces, their chief towns, and their aristocracies. The other was the gradual spread of Protestantism. The story of the Dutch Revolt is well known and need not be repeated in detail here.[42] Opposition to Philip grew after 1560. By 1568 that opposition had turned to civil war. For eighty years thereafter the situation awaited a resolution, as armies and diplomats in turn sought stability. The final settlement created two states: the United Provinces in the north, Protestant, republican, and centered in Holland; Spanish Netherlands in the south, monarchical, Catholic and centered in Brabant and Flanders. In the process the economy of the West Flanders industries and of Antwerp were disrupted, as wartime conditions limited trade and Protestants emigrated. Furthermore, Antwerp's ships navigated the Scheldt River to reach the Atlantic. The 1648 treaties closed the Scheldt to navigation from the Spanish Netherlands, essentially closing off Antwerp's role as an entrepôt. These political changes transformed the economic situation of the growing industries of the Low Countries.

Were the creation of the flexible industries of England in the fifteenth century and of West Flanders in the sixteenth century the first real signs of modern capitalism? A number of the great historians who wrote during the first half of the twentieth century thought so. Much of what we know about the Hondschoote new drapery industry was the result of research spurred by the famous Belgian historian Henri Pirenne. Pirenne argued forcefully that the new conditions of production and sale—in which regulation was limited, and in which middlemen were absent and competition was permitted—was entirely novel. Moreover, the idea that one could profit from producing a vast quantity of less expensive goods, from which one derived a smaller profit per piece, struck him as the key to the origins of modern capitalism and the Industrial Revolution. The rule of the great urban industries, which depended on economic efficiency (getting the most profit from the smallest investment of fixed capital), was over. The great factories, which produced technical efficiency (getting the most profit from the smallest total investment), were just around the corner.

What we will see in the next two chapters is that while England and West Flanders had taken a first step on the way to modern capitalism, much was left to be done. A great deal of the English production continued to be the very highest quality cloth, about which it is difficult to claim a truly novel approach (although it is true the social organization of the west of England textile industry was novel). And the Hondschoote industry did not lose the quality of a hectic boom town until its industry was virtually destroyed by the revolution against the Spanish successors to the Burgundian dukes, which began in the 1560s. As reported earlier, production in Hondschoote peaked about 1570 at nearly 100,000 pieces of cloth per year. A dozen years later, in 1582, it had sunk back down to virtually nothing. Although Hondschoote would partly recover in the seventeenth century, it would never again stand as a great center of industrial production. That role passed elsewhere, and the rise and fall of some of those new centers is the subject of the next two chapters.

NOTES

1. Henri Pirenne, "Une crise industrielle au XVIe siècle. La draperie urbaine et la 'nouvelle draperie' en Flandre," in *Histoire économique de l'occident médiéval* (Bruges: Desclée, De Brouwer, 1951), pp. 621–643. This article originally appeared in *Académie Royale de Belgique, Classe des Lettres. Bulletins* (1905).

2. On the overall history of the woolen textile industry in the Middle Ages, see E. M. Carus-Wilson, "The Woolen Industry," in *The Cambridge Economic History of Europe*, ed. M. Postan and E. E. Rich, 7 vols. (Cambridge: Cambridge University Press, 1942–1978), 2:355–428. The list of towns cited here is found on p. 372.

3. On metalwork, see Rolf Sprandel, "La production du fer au moyen âge," *Annales ESC* 24 (1969): 305–321; Sprandel, *Das Eisengewerbe im Mittelalter* (Stuttgart: Anton Hiersemann, 1968); John U. Nef, "Mining and Metallurgy in Medieval Christendom," in *The Cambridge Economic History of Europe*, 2:433–441; and Philippe Braunstein, "Innovations in Mining and Metal Production in Europe in the Late Middle Ages," *Journal of European Economic History* 12 (1983): 573–591.

4. Pirenne, *Economic and Social History of Medieval Europe* (New York: Harcourt Brace, 1937), pp. 144–147. The following essays from *The Cambridge Economic History* are also useful: M. Postan, "The Trade of Medieval Europe: the North," vol. 2, pp. 119–250; R. S. Lopez, "The Trade of Medieval Europe: the South," vol. 2, pp. 250–354; R. de Roover, "The Organization of Trade," vol. 3, pp. 42–118; and O. Verlinden, "Markets and Fairs," vol. 3, pp. 119–156.

5. Pirenne, *Economic and Social History of Medieval Europe*, pp. 96–102. Henri Laurent, *Un grand commerce d'exportation: La draperie des Pays Bas en France et dans les pays méditerranés, 12e–14e siècle* (Paris: E. Droz, 1935), passim; and R. M. Bautier, "Les foires de Champagne," in *Recueils de la Société Jean Bodin*, vol. 5: *La Foire* (Brussels: Librairie Encyclopedique, 1953), pp. 97–147.

6. The best description of cloth types can be found in G. de Poerck, *La draperie médiévale en Flandre et en Artois*, 3 vols. (Bruges: De Tempel, 1951). See also Emile Coornaert, "Draperies rurales, draperies urbaines: L'évolution de l'industrie flamande au moyen âge et au XVIe siècle," *Revue Belge de Philologie et d'Histoire*, 28 (1950): 59–96; and D. C. Coleman, "An Innovation and Its Diffusion: The New Draperies," *Economic History Review*, 2nd ser., 22 (1969): 419.

7. Lopez, "The Trade of Medieval Europe: The South," pp. 308–309.

8. On the differences between woolens and worsteds, see Herbert Heaton, *The Yorkshire Woolen and Worsted Industries*, 2nd ed. (Oxford: Oxford University Press, 1965), pp. 259–263; Ephraim Lipson, *A Short History of Wool and Its Manufacture* (Cambridge, Mass.: Harvard University Press, 1953); and Coleman, "An Innovation and Its Diffusion," pp. 419–420.

9. On kinds of wool and their classification, as well as on all questions of the technology of medieval wool production, see de Poerck, *La draperie médiévale;* Walter Endrei, *L'evolution des techniques du filage et du tissage* (Paris: Mouton, 1968); and the appropriate sections of N. W. Posthumus, *De geschiedenis van de Leidsche lakenindustrie*, 3 vols., vol. 1: *De Middeleeuwen* (The Hague: M. Nijhoff, 1908). For a briefer description of medieval textile technology, see R. Patterson, "Spinning and Weaving," in *A History of Technology*, ed. Charles Singer et al., 8 vols. (Oxford: Clarendon Press, 1954–1984), 2:190–210.

Other descriptions can be found in Heaton, *The Yorkshire Woolen and Worsted Industries*, pp. 322–359; and in Julia de Lacy Mann, *The Cloth Industry in the West of England from 1640 to 1880* (Oxford: Clarendon Press, 1971), pp. 255–307; but these works are not specifically devoted to medieval production methods.

10. De Lacy Mann, *The Cloth Industry*, pp. 316–319.

11. R. van Uytven, "The Fulling Mill: Dynamic of the Revolution of Industrial Attitudes," *Acta Historiae Neerlandica* 5 (1971): 1–14; and E. M. Carus-Wilson, "An Industrial Revolution of the Thirteenth Century," in *Medieval Merchant Venturers: Collected Studies* (London: Methuen, 1967), pp. 183–210.

12. S. L. Thrupp, "The Gilds," in *The Cambridge Economic History of Europe* 3:230–280. For a traditional view, see L. F. Salzman, *English Industries of the Middle Ages* (Oxford: Oxford University Press, 1923), pp. 305–351; and Ephraim Lipson, *The Economic History of England*, 3 vols., 12th ed. (London: A.&C. Black, 1959), 1:308–439.

13. R. de Roover, "The Concept of the Just Price: Theory and Economic Policy," *Journal of Economic History* 18 (1958): 418–434.

14. A. R. Bridbury, *Medieval English Clothmaking: An Economic Survey* (London: Heinemann Educational Books, 1982).

15. Georges Espinas, *La draperie dans la Flandre française au moyen-âge* (Paris: Picard, 1923), 2:407–514.

16. E. M. Carus-Wilson, "The English Cloth Industry in the Twelfth and Thirteenth Centuries," in *Medieval Merchant Venturers*, pp. 211–238.

17. Carus-Wilson, "The Woolen Industry," pp. 388–389.

18. See the discussions by Carlo M. Cipolla and Jacques le Goff in Carlo Cipolla, ed., *The Fontana Economic History of Europe*, 6 vols. (London: Fontana, 1972–1974), 1:1–22, 71–106; and Paul M. Hohenberg and Lynn Hollen Lees, *The Making of Urban Europe, 1000–1950* (Cambridge, Mass.: Harvard University Press, 1985).

19. Pirenne, "Crise industrielle."

20. E. Power, *The Wool Trade in English Medieval History* (Oxford: Clarendon Press, 1941); and T. H. Lloyd, *The English Wool Trade in the Middle Ages* (Cambridge: Cambridge University Press, 1977).

21. Carus-Wilson, "The Woolen Industry," pp. 405–408; Pirenne, "Crise industrielle," pp. 625–628; and Henri Laurent, *Un grand commerce d'exportation*, pp. 115–206.

22. John H. A. Munro, *Wool, Cloth and Gold. The Struggle for Bullion in Anglo-Burgundian Trade, 1340–1478* (Brussels: Editions de l'Université de Bruxelles, 1972).

23. Power, *Medieval English Wool Trade*; Lloyd, *English Wool Trade in the Middle Ages*; Munro, *Wool, Cloth and Gold*, pp. 33–41; and F. R. Barnes, "The Taxation of Wool, 1327–1348," in *Finance and Trade Under Edward III*, ed. George Unwin (London: Longmans Green, 1918).

24. Pirenne, "Crise industrielle," p. 625.

25. See the discussion of urban decline and adaptation in Myron P.

Gutmann, "The Dynamics of Urban Decline in the Late Middle Ages and Early Modern Times: Economic Response and Social Effects," in *Ninth International Economic History Congress, Bern, 1986: Debates and Controversies* (Zurich: Verlag der Fachvereine, 1986), pp. 25–56.

26. Carus-Wilson, "The Woolen Industry," pp. 408–413; Carus-Wilson, "An Industrial Revolution"; and van Uytven, "The Fulling Mill."

27. This is the point made by Carus-Wilson in "An Industrial Revolution." There have been differences of opinion. The most strongly stated is Bridbury, *Medieval English Clothmaking*. See also Edward Miller, "The Fortunes of the English Textile Industry in the Thirteenth Century," *Economic History Review* 18 (1965): 64–82; and A. Rupert Hall and N. C. Russell, "What About the Fulling Mill?" *History of Technology* 6 (1981): 113–119.

28. Maurice Aymard, "Production, commerce et consommation des draps de laine du XIIe au XVIIe siècle," *Revue Historique* 499 (1971): 5, citing Walter Endrei, "Changements dans la productivité de l'industrie lainière au moyen âge," in *Produzione commercio e consumo dei panni di lana (nei secoli XII–XVIII)*, ed. Marco Spallanzani (Florence: Leo S. Olschki, 1976), pp. 630–631.

29. Bridbury, *Medieval English Clothmaking*.

30. E. M. Carus-Wilson and O. Coleman, *England's Export Trade, 1275–1547* (Oxford: Clarendon Press, 1963), pp. 122–123, 138–139.

31. Carus-Wilson, "The Woolen Industry," p. 417.

32. Herman van der Wee, "Structural Changes and Specialization in the Industry of the Southern Netherlands, 1100–1600," *Economic History Review*, 2nd ser., 28 (1975): 203–221.

33. Coleman, "An Innovation and Its Diffusion."

34. A. Verhulst, "La laine indigène dans les anciens Pays-Bas entre le XIIe et le XVIIe siècle," *Revue Historique* 504 (1972): 281–322.

35. On these developments, see Emile Coornaert, *Un centre industriel d'autrefois: La draperie-sayetterie d'Hondschoote (XIVe–XVIIIe siècles)* (Paris: Presses Universitaires de France, 1930).

36. Pirenne, "Crise industrielle"; Verhulst, "Laine indigène"; and Coornaert, *Un centre industriel.*

37. Henri Pirenne, *Histoire de Belgique*, 7 vols., 3rd ed. (Brussels: Lamertin, 1923–1927), vols. 3–4.

38. Pirenne, "Crise industrielle," pp. 626–627.

39. Ibid., p. 630.

40. Coornaert, *Un centre industriel*, pp. 28–29.

41. Pirenne, "Crise industrielle," p. 637.

42. In addition to Pirenne, *Histoire de Belgique*, see Pieter Geyl, *The Revolt of the Netherlands* (New York: Barnes and Noble, 1958); and Geoffrey Parker, *The Dutch Revolt* (Ithaca: Cornell University Press, 1977). The most recent work is in Dutch, the *Algemene Geschiedenis der Nederlanden*, ed. D. P. Block et al., 15 vols. (Harlem: Fibula Van Dishoeck, 1980), vol. 5.

CHAPTER 3

The Emergence of a New Industrial Territory: The Liège-Aachen Region, 1500–1650

By the middle of the sixteenth century the fate of the grand industrial regions of the Middle Ages was apparent; their preeminence in the marketplaces of the world had evaporated. No longer could the products of Flanders, southern Germany, and northern Italy dominate the fairs. Only slowly did their competitors emerge, but by 1650 their identity was clear: England, the Netherlands, and the Walloon region between the Meuse and Rhine rivers were among the places that began to dominate Europe's industrial markets. To a remarkable extent, the places that grew in importance in the sixteenth and seventeenth centuries continued to play an important role in European industry at the time of the Industrial Revolution. In this chapter we will consider the emergence of these places, especially the territory between the Meuse and Rhine rivers, centered at Liège, Verviers, and Aachen. These are the birthplaces of the Industrial Revolution on the European continent.

Much of the story told in this chapter is that of the city and the principality of Liège. The city of Liège lies in the eastern part of Belgium, not far from the German and Dutch borders. Today Belgium includes a province of Liège, with the city of the same name as its capital. In the past, however, the city and territory of Liège was not always ruled by the same government as the rest of the territory that is now Belgium; rather, it was an independent principality, part of the Holy Roman Empire but ruled by its own nonhereditary prince, who achieved that position by being elected bishop of Liège. The old principality of Liège was larger than the current province and cut a broad north-south path, mostly along the Meuse River, separating the duchies of Limburg and Luxembourg from the rest of the Spanish Netherlands.

At the end of the Middle Ages the principality of Liège and the regions that surrounded it were not well known as industrial centers.[1] The city had cultural and religious functions, and several towns in the vicinity had small but growing groups of producers. Most notable among these were the cloth industry at St. Truiden and Hasselt in the Dutch-speaking regions to the northwest, and in the copper-working shops at the Mosan towns of Huy and Dinant. By the late seventeenth century all that had changed, and whereas the small centers of production at places such as Hasselt and Huy had stagnated, the principality as a whole had become one of the great industrial centers of Europe. Three broad industrial grouping led this growth: the extraction and sale of coal and alum; the production of metal goods, most notably nails and weapons; and the production of woolen cloth. The industrial centers that evolved included the city of Liège, but most of the others were new. Production took place in the countryside, and the most notable center of production outside Liège itself was in the area east of the city, at the northern edge of the Ardennes forest, centered in the village of Verviers (which became a town in 1651).

Some of the reasons for the growth of industry around Liège are the same as those we saw earlier for the growth of England and Hondschoote—inexpensive supplies of good raw materials and manpower—but others are different. Liège also prospered because of its good communications and transportation facilities, because of the principality's neutrality in a bellicose age, and because of the misfortunes of its competitors. Whatever the causes, the results were stunning; by the end of the seventeenth century Liège and its hinterland were dominant forces in several industries, sending a stream of workers and entrepreneurs elsewhere in Europe to start subsidiaries and copy processes. The power of Liège in European industry and the convergence of several industries in one region make it an ideal testing ground for the development of industry and the population that grew up to support industry. This chapter introduces that history; later chapters will show how the industry worked in the golden age after 1650 and how the citizens of the newly developing society lived.

THE CONTEXT OF INDUSTRIAL GROWTH IN THE SIXTEENTH AND EARLY SEVENTEENTH CENTURIES

Everywhere in Europe economic growth marked the period from the late fifteenth to the early seventeenth century. This "long sixteenth century" had all the appearances of a boom, in which expansion seemed inevitable and possibly endless. Along with agriculture and trade, industry grew; and the growth of the Liège industry took place in this milieu. Despite the fact that we know there was tremendous growth, the nature and causes of sixteenth-century growth can be difficult to specify. To say the least, the century was characterized by dramatic demographic expansion. Starting from a very low base brought on by the catastrophes of the fourteenth century, the population of Europe grew by at least 50 percent in the sixteenth century; the populations of some regions may have doubled. But a larger population hardly explains all the change. Successful population growth over a long period implies agricultural change, because a large population must consistently be fed to continue growing. Provisioning a larger population implies increasing trade and transportation, because supplies must come from a greater distance. Trade grew in the sixteenth century not only because food had to be brought over long distances to the growing cities of Europe but because of the opening up of ocean exploration of Asia, Africa, and America, and the trade that accompanied it. Finally, the growth of population, trade, and wealth coincided with, and may have caused, a growth in governmental power and wealth. All these forces acted together to sustain the expansion of the sixteenth century.

This book is not the place for a complete survey of sixteenth-century growth. What is needed instead is a rapid examination of the special conditions of the sixteenth century to see how they interacted with the development of industry. Population is the starting point. During the second half of the Middle Ages, between the tenth and the early fourteenth centuries, the population of Europe grew. After 1300, and especially after 1340, that growth was reversed by a number of forces, the most important being epidemics of bubonic plague. A population that in 1340 may have been as large as 60 million for Europe excluding Russia and the Balkans dropped in a century by one-fourth, to about 45 million. After 1450 the population expanded again, reaching about 55 million in 1500, 70 million in 1550, and nearly 80 million in 1600, before stabilizing and perhaps falling back during the seventeenth century (see Figure 3.1).[2] In 1700 the population of Europe as a whole was only slightly larger than it had been in 1600, although there was some growth in northern and western Europe. After 1700 the population started growing rapidly again, expanding from 81 million to 123 million in a century, another gain of over 50 percent. Eighteenth-century population growth is discussed in Chapter 5.

The dynamics of population change in the sixteenth and seventeenth centuries are not difficult to explain, despite a painful shortage of data. Populations grow when there is an excess of births over deaths, or of immigration over emigration. For our purposes, the role of migration is inconsequential, both because there was not yet a lot of migration into or out of Europe and because what there was represented only a tiny proportion of the continent's overall population. What population growth took

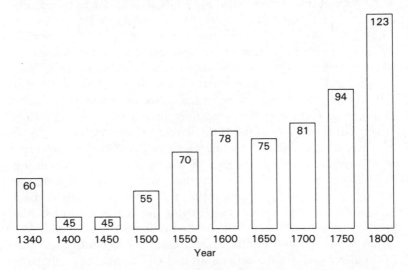

Figure 3.1.   The Population of Europe, 1340–1800 (in millions)
SOURCE: Based on J. C. Russell, "Population in Europe 500–1500," in The Fontana Economic History of Europe, ed. Carlo Cipolla, 6 vols. (London: Fontana, 1972–1974), 1: 36; and Jan de Vries, European Urbanization 1500–1800 (Cambridge, Mass.: Harvard University Press, 1984), pp. 36–37.

place after 1450 was the result of more births than deaths. Some of that excess came from a fall in mortality; the rest came from a temporary rise in fertility. The fall in mortality is easy to explain: mortality levels had probably been moderate during the late Middle Ages, but they increased dramatically in the fourteenth century. Mortality is described in terms of the average life expectancy of a person at birth, and we can speculate that the expectation of life fell from about 40 years in the thirteenth century (equivalent to a crude death rate of about 25 per 1,000) to about 25 years in the fourteenth and early fifteenth centuries (equivalent to a crude death rate of about 40 per 1,000). Needless to say these are averages; during the midst of an outbreak of plague the death rate might double or quadruple, and the life expectancy temporarily fall to 8 or 10 years.

After 1450 plague outbreaks became less frequent, and the overall death rate declined. Life expectancy gradually rose to between 30 and 35 years. The limited evidence we have suggests that the level of mortality was static during the first half of the sixteenth century and improved in the second half of the century. E. A. Wrigley and Roger Schofield chart an increase in the expectation of life at birth in England from about 34 in 1551 to about 41 in 1576—years they call "the golden period of low mortality."[3] The period of low mortality continued until the mid-seventeenth century in England, although there is some evidence that it ended earlier on the European continent. After the middle of the seventeenth century, if not earlier, life expectancy gradually diminished and mortality gradually increased, although they never deteriorated beyond early sixteenth-century levels.

This evidence about mortality tells us that fifteenth- and sixteenth-century population growth was accelerated by declining mortality, which may have occurred in two waves, one during the second half of the fifteenth century and one during the second half of the sixteenth century. During the entire period births probably exceeded deaths, but we do not know by how much. We do know that couples did not consciously try to control the size of their families. Rather, a woman had children at a steady pace of one birth every two and a half to three years, from the time she married until the time she or her husband died, or she reached menopause (usually at about age 40). Family size was determined by the age at which a woman married, because that established the number of years within which she would have children. In northern and western Europe, most young people married rather late, at least in comparison to the twentieth century and to other parts of the world.[4] In the sixteenth, seventeenth, and eighteenth centuries, the age of women at first marriage was rarely less than 23 years. Men were usually about three years older. In the mid-seventeenth century, women living in some European regions usually married when they were around 25 years old (see Table 5.11). Fifteen years lie between the ages of 25 and 40; at one child every three years, a couple would have five children if both lived that long. Had they married when the woman reached menarche (the time when she was first able to bear children), at about age 16, they would have had three more. Five children is already many (although at most three would have survived to adulthood, given prevailing mortality rates); eight would have severely strained the couple's ability to provide for them.

Marriage ages were high because social customs made it appropriate for young couples to wait before marrying. Why those social customs developed is very difficult to explain, but the explanation most often put forward is that it made possible a fairly stable social order in a peasant society where land ownership was critical to economic well-being. Lawrence Stone explains the logic behind a marriage age of 28 for peasant men and 25 for their wives in this simple way: The wife of a man who marries at about age 28 will bear his first son two to three years after marriage. At that time the man will be about 30, and his expectation of life is another 28 years. When the father's generation dies out, at age 58, their first sons will be age 28 and themselves ready to marry and begin the cycle anew. Each generation, in this simple scheme, replaces itself perfectly. Although the reality is not so simple, this gives us a good sense of why the European scheme worked so well.[5] It kept the population from growing far too rapidly.

In the fifteenth and sixteenth centuries, levels of mortality fell and fertility may have been stable. The result was a rapidly growing population, because the number of births was larger than the number of deaths. In the seventeenth century the situation reversed. The level of mortality increased after 1600 in the area around the Mediterranean, and later elsewhere in Europe, because of a new wave of epidemics, poor weather, and wartime disruption. Fertility at the same time declined, because marriage ages increased. A balance was achieved in some places and may even have tipped in favor of deaths. The seventeenth century was marked by a stable or declining population in much of Europe. Only the most prosperous regions—England, the Low Countries, and Scandinavia—grew, and those regions grew more slowly in the seventeenth century than earlier.

Population growth was accompanied by economic growth, although it is difficult to ascribe cause to one phenomenon and effect to the other. The European economy in the sixteenth century was primarily agricultural: almost 95 percent of the population lived in the countryside in 1500, and virtually all of that population worked full-time in agriculture.[6] The relatively small number of city dwellers worked in services, trade, government, church, and industry, with the largest numbers employed in services and trade. All sectors of the European economy grew in the sixteenth century, but agriculture grew the most of all, to provide an expanding population with food. Agriculture in the already developed parts of Europe became more intensive, but there was tremendous growth in north-central Europe (today's Germany), where grain was grown on large estates and shipped via the Baltic Sea to the cities of western Europe. A large-scale trade developed, which moved Baltic grain to Atlantic ports. The growth of agriculture and trade were interconnected, and they spurred the growth of both the rural and the urban population. The rural population produced more food, for itself and the cities. The urban population was fed by the new grain supplies and was occupied in the new trade that developed in food and other commodities. The population of cities with 10,000 or more inhabitants grew by nearly 75 percent in the sixteenth century (from about 3.5 million to nearly 6 million), increasing from 5.6 percent to 7.6 percent of the European population.[7]

The growth in trade was by no means limited to food, and it had wide-ranging effects. Europe's overseas trade blossomed in the late fifteenth and sixteenth centuries, bringing connections with Asia, Africa, and the Americas.[8] The expansion of trade with northern Europe made that region's inhabitants better customers for products from western Europe and overseas sources. New opportunities for trade thus reinforced the growth of agriculture and population, making Europe more prosperous. The centers of the new trade-based prosperity were at first the regions that had been strongest in the Middle Ages: Italy and the Low Countries. But the transformations in local importance described in the last chapter continued, so that the location of power in northwestern Europe continued to evolve and concentrate. The great Flemish cities stagnated, while the towns of Brabant and Holland grew. Antwerp was the great success story of the sixteenth century, capturing a central place in European trade. Its preeminence was destroyed in the Dutch Revolution, and Amsterdam took its place as the major Atlantic entrepôt. Simultaneously, London grew, so that by the mid-seventeenth century it was the second-largest city in Europe, outranked only by Paris. By 1700, London was the largest.

The final element in the equation of growth is the state. The economic and demographic growth of the late fifteenth and the sixteenth centuries sustained the rise of national states in Europe. Already in the late Middle Ages the monarchs of larger states, such as Spain and France (and possibly England) were increasing their powers. The growth of population and wealth after 1450 allowed them to accelerate that process. They attempted to monopolize military force, and to monopolize the benefits of trade and population for their domestic and international advantage. The classic example of this process of state growth on the back of trade was Spain, which used the power to tax a growing population and its share of silver imported from America to support its international political activities. Spain eventually lost its sources of income, and the state lost its eminence. France enjoyed a more lasting benefit. We see the consequences in the size of Paris, the largest city in Europe for most of the seventeenth century. Paris combined the role of governmental, trading, and industrial center for northern France. It symbolizes the interaction of the state, the economy, and population in early modern Europe.

The related rise of the state, of population, and of trade provide the context in which industrial growth took place in sixteenth- and seventeenth-century Europe. As population increased, demand for consumer goods like cloth increased. Increasing production of consumer goods and agricultural products led to a demand for tools. Perhaps most important, the growth of the state sparked a rise in warfare, an increase in the size of armies, and a demand for new weapons. Much of that growth was in northern Europe, because of the steadily increasing power of France and the wealth of the Low Countries. This is the environment in which Liégeois industry evolved in the sixteenth and seventeenth century.

THE RAW MATERIALS INDUSTRY

The basic industry around Liège in the sixteenth and early seventeenth centuries was the mining, processing, and sale of chemical raw materials—mostly coal, alum, and sulphur—and the production of refined chemicals such as gunpowder. The manufacture of these chemicals hardly demands great scientific knowledge or technical skill, but they were very widely used and therefore in great demand—coal and gunpowder for their obvious uses, alum and copperas for the dyeing of cloth, and sulphur for a variety of chemical processes (including the manufacture of gunpowder). Like so much of early modern industry, all were dependent on the presence of raw materials and the ability to find markets, rather than on superior technical skills or innovations.[9]

The raw materials trade had its origins, however modest, in the late Middle Ages. The oldest segments of this trade were the production of coal and iron, and they seem to have begun to be exportable commodities at least as early as the fourteenth century.[10] The other commodities grew in importance considerably later.[11] These industries grew to prominence in the sixteenth century because of the discovery of supplies in the Liège region, because of the availability of new markets (and the difficulties faced by old suppliers of those markets), and because of the emergence in Liège of a group of entrepreneurs capable of bringing the commodities to those markets. Moreover, they capitalized on a large hinterland rich in wood and iron, in the Eifel district to the east, and the Ardennes, Lower Luxembourg, and the Sambre-Meuse districts to the south and southeast.

The principal stimulus to the emergence of the chemicals industry was the existence of large coal deposits in and around the city of Liège. These coal deposits had been known for a very long time by the sixteenth century; some of the coal lay quite near the surface, and an active industry developed for extracting it. Large-scale production was somewhat more difficult, because it meant confronting the serious problem posed by the presence of water in the mines and the need to drain them. An increase in demand for coal in the sixteenth century led to a solution to this problem, through the creation of a series of tunnels and pumps for draining the mines. The production of alum, sulphur, and copperas called for no complex chemical processes, only the dissolving of the raw materials and the distillation of that liquid to extract the pure chemicals. The process requires only heat and was therefore well suited to the use of coal.

There were other demands for coal as well. One came from the growing metalwork industry, as we will see shortly. But the most important may have been the use of coal for domestic heating.[12] Like England, the United Provinces became very short of timber in the sixteenth century, due to a dense population and a thriving shipbuilding industry. Timber was too valuable to use for heat, and most alternatives, such as peat, were not available in sufficient quantity. The solution to this problem was the use of coal for domestic heat, and it was widely used for this purpose in Liège itself and in the Dutch cities. Liège, with convenient river access down the Meuse to the Dutch cities, became a major supplier to Amsterdam and Dordrecht by 1700.

The availability of coal for chemical processing sustained one leg of the requirements for a large-scale early industry in sixteenth- and seventeenth-century Liège—that of costs. Coal could be sold itself and it allowed Liégeois merchants to compete in terms of price in the chemicals industry. The second leg of the tripod was markets, which they found in a variety of locations. The most important single market was the United Provinces, which absorbed the majority of Liégeois exports. The political emergence of the United Provinces and the growth of the Dutch economy played a role equal to that of coal in the growth of the Liégeois raw material and chemicals trade. The final element needed for the growth of a home-based industry was the presence of home-grown entrepreneurs and capitalists who could exploit the availability of low-cost products and markets to make fortunes. These Liège had in sufficient numbers by the mid-sixteenth century to sustain the growth of its industry.

To identify these entrepreneurs we need to consider the organization of industry in the Liégeois region.[13] Most of the industries that grew to importance in Liège in the sixteenth and seventeenth centuries—chemicals and raw materials, iron and textiles—employed at least some capital-intensive equipment. Coal mining and metallurgy always demand capital investment—for mine construction, furnaces, and forges. The chemicals industries likewise needed financing—for equipment to distill and refine the chemicals. And the textile industry made use of water-driven fulling mills. In sixteenth-century Liège there were few capitalists rich enough, and sufficiently willing to expose themselves to risk, to own and operate one of these mills alone. Rather, the most common form—in iron work, in coal mining, in the production of alum or fulled cloth—was joint ownership by a number of individuals. Joint ownership made it possible to finance capital investment internally.

Two forms of ownership characterized the capitalism of Liège in the sixteenth century. In those industries, such as metalwork and textile production, where the investment was for the machinery used to produce a certain product, the partners in a fulling mill or furnace owned a time-share in it. For example, a partner in a furnace might have the right to use it one week in four to smelt his own iron. Or he might own the right to use it during three weeks or six weeks or three months of the year. During the rest of the time he would work to refine and forge that iron. A partner in a fulling mill might own the right to use it during certain hours each day or certain days each week. His partners would use it to full their cloth during the rest of the time.

In the coal mines, where the investment was not so much for the machinery (though that could be considerable) but the capital expense involved in obtaining mineral rights, opening the mine, paying miners, and keeping the mine in shape to operate, a rather different system operated. The partners in Liégeois coal mines were very often not miners but "white-collar" entrepreneurs who put up capital to get a suitable return in the form of coal to sell or to use. A manager ran the mine, collecting the funds for its operation from the owners (these partnerships rarely had much working capital in hand) and distributing its production to them, usually in kind, in proportion to their share in the enterprise. They then sold the production or used it themselves.

Both forms of ownership and operation just described had fairly long histories in the Liégeois region, because they evolved naturally from each kind of business. The system used in furnaces and fulling mills is a natural evolution from older corporate systems, where a group of masters combined to construct a piece of costly equipment that no one person could afford, and shared its use. That system would be hard to employ in the coal mines, so a different system evolved there. These business arrangements suggest the social status of industrial owners and workers in sixteenth-century Liégeois industry. In the processing industries, such as textiles and metallurgy, the early entrepreneurs were the direct descendants of craft masters, who used an investment in manufacturing equipment to process a relatively small quantity of materials they themselves owned. The size of the wage-labor force in these operations must have been small. In mining, on the other hand, the owners were not necessarily the operators and workers, and therefore came from a somewhat higher social stratum, made wealthy by trade, office, or land. Here the wage-labor force was larger.

In the second half of the sixteenth century, just as the new chemical industries began to emerge, the prevailing system of ownership in Liège underwent a transformation. More and more of the investors in industry were merchants whose wealth rested on selling goods, rather than craft masters who manufactured products themselves. Therefore, while the chemical processing shops might have lent themselves to the form of ownership that traditionally characterized furnace or fulling mill, in which a master made use of the distilling and refining equipment for a set amount of time each week or month to produce his own sulphur or alum, they were not organized that way. Rather, they were organized more like the traditional coal mines, in which the partners employed workers and simply received a share of the product, either in cash or in kind. The transformation slowly took place in the iron industry as well, and for similar reasons: the old form of organization did not permit any one partner to accept large orders and assure continuous production. The change was this: originally, partnership represented the right to work in a shop and use the equipment there; by the end of the sixteenth century, most industrial partnerships in Liège represented a share in the production of a shop that was staffed by salaried craftsmen.[14] This move from active to sleeping partners is an important part of the transformation of business in the sixteenth and seventeenth centuries, demonstrating how industrial concentration could occur.

The eventual outcome of this transformation, which took a very long time to complete, was the concentration of these industries in the hands of a smaller number of richer entrepreneurs. The first development was the investment by very rich merchant-industrialists in many operations. Between 1549 and 1582, one Arnuld des Champs owned shares in nineteen different coal mines.[15] By the end of the sixteenth century and beginning of the seventeenth, however, concentration took another form. Entrepreneurs owned mines or industrial operations outright or in partnerships of two, three, or four partners. The class of salaried workers increased dramatically. The transformation as a whole signals the conquest of Liégeois industry by a stratum of very wealthy industrialists.

The most famous of these wealthy entrepreneurs was a man named Jean Curtius, who assembled the largest fortune in the region during the last quarter of the century.[16] Curtius was the son of a minor court functionary in Liège who died before Curtius was 7 years old. Although he did not inherit a fortune, by the time he was 25 Curtius was munitioner to Don John of Austria, Philip II's governor of the Spanish Netherlands. Curtius continued in this profitable relationship until the Twelve-Years' Truce ended hostilities in 1609. By then his fortune was made. Enriched by the gunpowder trade, Curtius extended his fortune both by expanding that industry in Liège and by entering into others. To build up the production of gunpowder, he found workers and equipment as far away as Germany and France, and brought them to Liège, where inexpensive coal was available. He purchased land (the traditional outlet for the excess fortunes of rich merchants), became a partner in coal mines and in alum works, and finally in 1616 entered into a deal with the Spanish crown to establish a metalwork and armament industry in Spain itself, under his direction.

The end of Curtius's career is as instructive as its beginnings, because it prevents us from becoming too grandiose about the

Liégeois business environment. Curtius left Liège. So did Louis de Geer, another famous Liégeois industrialist, who moved his business to Amsterdam before establishing himself in Sweden. The economy of Liège did not always have access to very large markets. It was not itself an entrepôt, and it was not part of a large state. Many businessmen saw its limitations and looked for opportunities elsewhere.

THE METALWORK INDUSTRY

Like coal, iron was an old product in the eastern Low Countries, its ore found in some abundance. Around the city of Liège, the iron industry had medieval origins; until the sixteenth century, the primary activities were mining and smelting. In the sixteenth and seventeenth centuries that concentration—in terms of geography, product, and markets—changed.[17] The region experienced enormous growth during the first two-thirds of the sixteenth century, a period in which the smelting industry grew dramatically in the role of provisioning the Antwerp market. The 1560s changed all that, and the Liégeois iron industry, like the coal and chemicals industry, felt the consequences of the Dutch Revolution and the rise of the Dutch economy. The smelters of the Liège basin could not compete, but the processing portions of the industry could. New centers of smelting developed in the southeastern Low Countries. By the early seventeenth century an enormous market for certain Liégeois products—nails, armaments, and other hardware—emerged in the Netherlands because of a reputation for high quality and low prices.

Liégeois prices were low because of technical advances and the availability of coal and charcoal. By the end of the fourteenth century the water-powered blast furnace, which may have been invented in the region of Liège, was in use there. In the sixteenth and seventeenth centuries coal still could not be used for smelting iron because its impurities found their way into the iron. The same problem was not nearly so severe for the working of iron that had already been smelted. The iron needed to be heated repeatedly in order to refine it and then shape it into useful products. For the smelting stage the ample wood supplies that could be taken from the Ardennes provided charcoal. For working the iron, Liégeois workers used mineral coal, which was abundant locally and far less expensive than charcoal. Their products thus had an advantage in terms of price.

The costs of Liégeois iron goods were lower than those of competitors for another reason—a technical advance that became available in Liège by the late sixteenth century and that dramatically increased the efficiency of finishing operations. This was the adoption of water-powered rolling mills for the production of sheet goods and for the refining of steel for armaments.[18] Since the fourteenth century water power had been used in Liégeois forges to drive a heavy hammer (a *marteau*) and thus speed up the process of forging the iron bloom into usable wrought iron. In the fifteenth century the water mills were connected to bellows to provide sufficient draft to improve the smelting of iron. By the early seventeenth century a further refinement had been achieved: the marteau was supplemented by a rolling and slicing mill, which consisted of two sets of rollers—one smooth and the other "bladed"—through which the heated bar was passed, first to reduce its thickness to the desired level and then to slice it into usable widths for nails or more complex hardware items, such as eating utensils. This innovation, although not unique to Liège, was rare elsewhere, and its combination with Liégeois coal supplies and proximity to Dutch markets made it extremely significant.

A single rolling mill, called a *fenderie* in Liège, could produce some 200 tons of sliced iron rods a year;[19] by the mid-seventeenth century there were ten such mills in the Liège basin, and it is this innovation that entrepreneurs such as Curtius attempted to export. The output from the *fenderie* served as raw material for the enormous nailmaking industry that evolved in the Liège basin in the seventeenth and eighteenth centuries. The bars that were produced by the rolling mills were the property of the large-scale businessmen who controlled the mills. These merchant industrialists then provided the bars to an army of cottage workers, who converted them into nails in home forges. The organization of this industry was like any other cottage industry; the merchant provided raw materials to families, who worked at home to process it and received payment either in kind or in cash.[20] (The process is described in more detail in Chapter

7.) The nails were sold throughout Europe, but their primary market was in the Dutch Republic, where the shipbuilding industry consumed them in great quantities.[21]

THE WOOLEN TEXTILE INDUSTRY

The third industry of the Liège region was the production of woolen cloth. This too had its origins in the late Middle Ages. Although the city of Liège had a drapers' guild, the medieval centers of production were elsewhere.[22] The last outposts of the Flemish textile industry were the cities of St. Truiden and Hasselt in Liégeois territory.[23] Their economic ties were to Bruges and later Antwerp, however, rather than to Liège. Another center of activity in the textile industry was the imperial city of Aachen, some forty kilometers east of Liège.[24] These centers of textile industry in the late Middle Ages followed the technical lead of the Flemish industry and produced a heavy cloth using primarily English wool. Like their Flemish masters, they could not compete with English production, and in the early sixteenth century the Aachen and Hasselt wool trades began a long, slow decline.

Hasselt and Aachen were controlled by strong guild organizations that were not flexible enough to compete in the new economic environment of the sixteenth century. Their products were too costly compared with English cloth and increasingly out of fashion after the introduction of the new, lighter cloths, such as those from Hondschoote. Their response to competition was nearly always a mixture of staunch adherence to the old ways of the guild and modest acceptance of the new innovations. In Hasselt, the city purchased Spanish wool for its drapers, and the guild readily permitted the manufacture of new styles of cloth after 1550, as well as the purchase of those cloths elsewhere to meet local demand. But they prohibited other activities that might have made their industry more competitive, especially any attempts to reduce labor costs by allowing masters more looms and more apprentices and journeymen to operate them, or the use of workers in the countryside, outside the jurisdiction of the city and its guild. The city and guild leadership demonstrated their commitment to the old system by obligating each master to produce at least four cloths in the old Hasseltois style each year, whether there was a market for them or not.[25] Moreover, because many textile workers were Protestants, the problems were only exacerbated by the repression of Calvinism in Hasselt, Aachen, and Maastricht before 1632.

The decline of Aachen and Hasselt did not mean the end of an important textile industry in the Meuse-Rhine region, however. To take their places a number of new centers emerged, unburdened by the strictures of guild regulations and free of the high taxes and high costs associated with providing for an urban labor force. The greatest of these centers was Verviers, in 1500 a large village on the Vesdre River at the northern edge of the Ardennes forest. Verviers itself had a textile industry at the end of the Middle Ages, which seems to have grown up in the fifteenth century.[26] The soft water of the Vesdre, rising from the clay soils of the swampy land near the present-day border between Belgium and Germany, was suitable for all the processes involved in the manufacture of woolen cloth. At the beginning of the fifteenth century there were already four or five fulling mills in Verviers, symbols of a fairly active woolen cloth industry. Seven more were constructed between 1450 and 1500, and another four between 1500 and 1550.[27] The growth of the industry at this time signals the origins of the great prosperity that was to last in Verviers until the end of the nineteenth century.

The growth of the Verviers industry has been attributed to the availability of water and power, and that was certainly the case. Verviers sits in a long level stretch of the Vesdre basin about midway between Liège and Aachen. The Vesdre falls some 200 meters in the twenty-kilometer distance between its headwaters and Verviers, and this water power for mechanical fulling as well as the softness of the water itself made the Vesdre a prime location for the woolen industry in the fifteenth and sixteenth centuries. The level run of the river in Verviers itself meant that mills could easily be constructed, and it obviously permitted their concentration. There were commercial reasons for the growth of the industry too. It grew large when its small-scale entrepreneurs discovered they could find a ready market for their cloth at the Frankfurt fairs (probably in the early seventeenth century) and began to send there convoys of wagons filled with cloth.

Verviers was not the only center that grew up between Aachen and Liège in the sixteenth century. Verviers is in Liégeois territory; smaller concentrations of industrial activity emerged elsewhere on the Vesdre—below Verviers at Ensival (also in Liégeois territory) and above it at Limburg and Eupen in the duchy of Limburg (Spanish Netherlands). Moreover, as Aachen faced the stagnation of its industry and growing divisions between Catholics and Calvinists, there was a steady trickle of Protestant cloth merchants from Aachen—first into its suburb, Burtscheid, and later into Monschau, a picturesque Ardennes valley town on the Roer River in the Eifel district.[28] None of these industrial centers were as active as Verviers in the sixteenth, seventeenth, and eighteenth centuries, but all were noticeable producers and sellers of woolen cloth.

The organization of industrial activity in these small-town and village-centered areas was quite different from that found in the traditional medieval industrial centers. At the very core of the difference lay a new way of thinking about the industrial segment of the economy. The rationale behind the guild regulations of the medieval system was the need to preserve the well-being of all the members of the corporate group that made up the guild. Efforts to devise new products that might compete unfairly with the old products favored by the group, or efforts to reduce costs or monopolize raw materials or markets, were discouraged as detrimental to the best interests of the group, even though they might be to the advantage of individuals.

The new societies that grew up in the sixteenth and seventeenth centuries were far less fettered by the old constraints. New competition grew up, and to survive and prosper in this new competitive environment business people had to lower their costs; the shortage of labor-saving equipment meant that the greatest savings could be obtained by lowering labor costs. To put matters simply, the new industrial producers of the sixteenth and seventeenth centuries, such as those at Verviers, Eupen, and Monschau, prospered by virtue of low labor costs. That fact shaped the structure of their businesses.

These new industrial concentrations can be called towns only with great caution. Verviers, the largest of them, had only 300 houses in 1569 and a population of 1200 to 1500 persons.[29] Yet as we have seen, it already had fifteen fulling mills along its stretch of the Vesdre. These were in fact large villages, and the industrial activities that took place in them were necessarily quite limited. In the textile industry, the easiest way to think of the organization of business is to see certain operations taking place in the large villages such as Verviers, Eupen, Burtscheid, and Monschau: trading and warehousing, the cleaning operations at the beginning of the process, and the finishing operations—fulling, dyeing, and shearing—at its end. These processes demanded access to water, primitive machinery (fulling mills and shearing equipment), and relatively high levels of skill (dyeing). According to Herbert Kisch, it was these processes—rather than the simpler carding, spinning, and weaving—that first found their way out of the city to the countryside.[30] They moved from Aachen to the suburbs and villages in search of lower labor costs for these labor-intensive industries. In the Verviers segment of the industry the rationale for the establishment of operations may have been somewhat different, but the outcome was the same, the creation of a center of cloth processing and finishing in a small semiurban center. From that base the rest of the industry could grow.

The centers of the textile industry were in the large villages and small towns. There the drapers, who were the industrialists of the age, kept their warehouses, the equipment for cleaning raw wool, and the simpler tools for finishing the cloth.[31] In the sixteenth and seventeenth centuries most owned a share (on average one-tenth to one-twelfth) of a fulling mill, rather than a mill of their own. With preparation and finishing located in the larger villages, the other operations were more spread out. Carding and spinning the wool, and then weaving it into cloth, were sometimes done in the central villages; but these tasks were just as often performed in outlying villages, by a peasant population employed partly in agriculture, and partly in industry.

The drapers and the dyers were the key entrepreneurial figures in the sixteenth-century industry, and none of them in a large village such as Verviers was an especially large operator. Their ties to Aachen remained strong, in terms of both identity and raw materials. Most drapers purchased their wool from Aachen merchants, who had obtained it from farmers in nearby Jülich. Some wool came from Maastricht, and a small quantity from other places, but at this time the Vesdre textile industry had yet to turn to wool that came a long distance, either from Spain or from England.[32] Having obtained the raw wool, the Verviers draper had it cleaned in his own shop; he then either paid someone to card, spin, and weave it for him in his shop, using his equipment, or farmed it out to one or more individuals, either in Verviers or in outlying villages, to perform those procedures. When he had the woven cloth back in his hands, the draper had it fulled, brushed, and sheared, usually by his own employees (but in a very small business he might do these himself). Then he sent it out to a specialist dyer. Only after dyeing was the process finished and the cloth ready for sale.

If the raw materials trade and the metalwork industry found their largest markets in the United Provinces, the textile industry in the region between Liège and Aachen looked further for customers for its products. In the sixteenth century many cloths were sold to Aachen merchants for resale in farther markets. These cloths, like the ones sold directly by the drapers of Verviers, eventually found their way to one of the German markets—Frankfurt or Strasbourg in the west or Leipzig in the east.[33] We do not know where the cloths went from there; but we can guess that some stayed in Germany while others went farther east and south. The market in Poland, Russia, and Turkey for cloth from Verviers and neighboring villages cannot yet have been large, as it was to become in the late seventeenth and eighteenth centuries, simply because the total output of the villages between Liège and Aachen cannot yet have been very large.

THE CAUSES OF INDUSTRIAL GROWTH IN THE LIÈGE-AACHEN REGION

The industries that developed in the region between Liège and Aachen in the sixteenth and early seventeenth centuries occupy an intermediate place in the transition of European industry from a craft orientation and small-scale production to a factory orientation and large-scale production. That the industrial environment was changing is clear. We see this transformation in the organization of business activity. Increasingly, capital was concentrated in the hands of a relatively small number of rich investors drawn not from among the craft masters but from merchants and others with capital. These participants concentrated much more on the sales of industrial products than on their production. We see the transformation as well in the location of industrial activity, which moved increasingly to the countryside. This was natural for metallurgy, which had always been located near power sources, either water or heat; but it was not so natural for the textile industry, which was also moving toward rural production.

We must not ignore the conservative side of the development of these industries, however. Even by 1660, few of the industrial businesses operating between Liège and Aachen were very large. What large industrial producers existed—men operating on a scale similar to that of Curtius and his successors in the chemicals and nailmaking industries—operated out of Liège, not Verviers. They may have controlled large quantities of production, but the goods were manufactured in small workshops run (and often owned) by intermediaries. And while organization had changed, especially in metallurgy and in the chemicals industry, much remained traditional in the textile industry. There were no guilds in Verviers, but the key role played by the drapers there sustains the idea that old industrial forms persisted. The drapers had great flexibility in the absence of regulation, but they remained the masters of cloth production, still working at a modest level in the mid-seventeenth century.

We have seen that this intermediate industry grew up near Liège in part because of a number of happy accidents of geography and technology. Coal, water, alum, and sulphur were the resource bases for the growth of industry. Proximity to the Dutch Republic helped too, especially at a time when it was at war with potential competitors to Liège in the Spanish Netherlands. Finally, the development of the rolling and slicing mill made a major contribution. None of these accidents of geography and technology was sufficient, however, to create the seeds of large-scale industry, which were developing in the region in the sixteenth and seventeenth centuries. Other regions had coal, iron (Liégeois iron was not of the right quality for nailmaking), water, sulphur, alum. The rolling mill was known elsewhere as early as in the region of Liège.[34] There was nothing at all novel about the cloth-making industry that grew up in this period. Other, human, factors played a role. Some have already been touched on. The existence of large markets made industrial growth easier, and the presence of entrepreneurs in Liège, Aachen, and the smaller places such as Verviers to exploit those markets made a difference as well. Even that was not enough, however; and to understand fully the origins and growth of industry between Liège and Aachen, we need to consider the social and demographic milieu in which it grew.

It is very difficult to understand the human side of the evolution of early industry in Europe while speaking in general terms, so much of the rest of this chapter, as well as some later chapters, will focus on the people of individual towns and villages in the region between Liège and Aachen. The main subjects will be Verviers, the heart of the textile-producing region, Limburg, a smaller town nearby, and Thimister, Soiron, and Ensival—three villages whose residents worked in the early industries of the region. These communities are located on Map 3.1.

All these places—even Verviers—were essentially farming villages. The ecological region that lies north of the Vesdre River is called the Herve Country. It is characterized by hilly, undulating terrain that is cut by streams. As in the rest of the Low Countries, rainfall there is abundant, and the land always looks a rich, dark green. Compared with other regions in nearby parts of Europe, the Herve Country became densely settled only after the end of the Middle Ages. People had lived there earlier, but the region is not especially well suited for the kind of traditional farming that was practiced in the Middle Ages in eastern Belgium. Those people who did settle in the Herve Country sometimes lived in villages, grouped around a parish church; but some also lived away from the center of the village, in small hamlets and on isolated farms.

Around 1500 the inhabitants of the Herve Country farmed like most of the other farmers near Liège. They followed a three-year rotation of crops, dividing their farms into three fields and planting two each year. They planted each field in a cycle. The first year the farmer planted a winter-sowed grain (rye, spelt, or maslin). The second year he planted a spring-sowed grain (oats or barley). The third year he left it fallow. Thus each year the farmer had one field of winter grain, which was used for bread, one field of spring grain, which might be used either for beer or animal feed, and one field left fallow, recovering its strength for the more strenuous phases in the cycle. Every farmer in the Herve Country had livestock, but in 1500 livestock did not yet constitute a major part of the region's farming. Even at this early date some land was not appropriate for plowing and the planting of crops. Instead, farm-

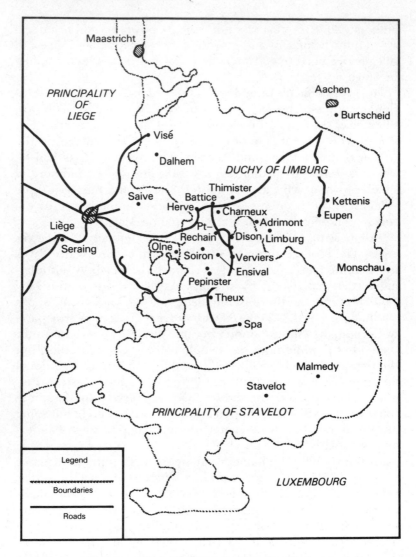

Map 3.1.   The Liège to Aachen Region in the Seventeenth Century

ers used it as permanent pasture—for cattle, sheep, or a plow-horse. These animals also fed on the stubble of the fields after harvest and whatever grew in the fallow fields.

Farming in the Herve Country changed dramatically but

slowly in the sixteenth, seventeenth, and eighteenth centuries, just as industry appeared. The traditional farms of the late Middle Ages, which had grown arable crops using a three-year crop rotation, gradually disappeared.[35] In their place a new kind of agriculture emerged, one that was almost totally dependent on dairy farming. The fields that had existed in 1500 were converted into pastures, to which the land of the Herve Country was much better suited. The pace of the change can be seen in Table 3.1. In the *ban* of Herve—an administrative unit consisting of Thimister, Battice, Charneux, and the town of Herve—the proportion of land devoted to pastures (about one-third) was the same in the early sixteenth century as it had been in the late fourteenth. But change began in the late sixteenth century and accelerated rapidly. Four-fifths of the land in the *ban* was pasture by 1611, 93 percent by 1682, and virtually all by 1705. Rather than produce grain that they consumed themselves, the farmers of the Herve Country began to produce butter and cheese for the urban markets of the Low Countries. The grain they consumed came from suppliers elsewhere in the Low Countries (and especially from the cereal-grain–growing regions west of Liège, the Hesbaye and the Condroz), and from the Baltic and other long-distance suppliers, via Amsterdam.[36]

The change to dairy farming made easier the development of early industry in the region around Verviers. The dairy farms were set up and operated rather differently from the traditional farms they replaced. First, they were smaller, because a farmer could support himself and his family on less land dairying than he could planting crops. He might earn a satisfactory living on

Table 3.1: The Evolution of Land Use in the Ban de Herve, 1500–1800

	% Cropland	% Pastures
1523–1543	67	33
1611	19	81
1682–1683	7	93
1705	1	99
1787	1	99

SOURCE: Joseph Ruwet, *L'agriculture et les classes rurales au pays de Herve sous l'ancien régime* (Liège: Faculté de Philosophie et Lettres, 1943), pp. 54–65.

one hectare, rather than two, and the gradual splitting of farms
meant that the region included more and more farms—and thus
more and more people—as time went on. Second, the work on
a dairy farm differed from that on a family-run traditional farm.
Raising a small number of grass-fed dairy cattle and using their
milk to produce cheese and butter is not a very labor-intensive
activity and would not occupy all the working time of a family.
Moreover, the labor required was very different. A farm producing grain needs strong (preferably young) men; a dairy farm can
get by under the care of women, children, and the elderly. The
change to smaller, less labor-intensive farms produced an increasing pool of underemployed people. These workers staffed
early industry. They were numerous and were partially supported by agriculture. Moreover, they were ripe candidates for
low-wage, part-time industrial jobs as nailmakers, coal miners,
and weavers and spinners of woolen yarn. Around 1500 the people of the region around Verviers had almost all been farmers,
and almost all of those farmers had still grown traditional grains.
By 1650 an increasing number of farmers—perhaps one-third—
operated farms that had been converted to dairying, and an
ever-increasing number of those farm families worked in the
growing industries of the region.

GOVERNMENT AND SOVEREIGNTY IN THE NEW INDUSTRIAL COMMUNITIES

In 1650 every community except Verviers was still a rural village
in substance, if not in governmental form. The farming communities all numbered fewer than 2,000 inhabitants in 1650 (Verviers had about 6,500 at that time), and the majority were
seigneurial villages in the contemporary legal terminology.[37]
They owed allegiance to a lord (a *seigneur*), who appointed the
village's judges and mayor, and who was responsible for repre-
senting it in dealings with the outside world. The only exception
was Limburg, which was an independent town. It was nominally
exempt from central government taxation; its two *burgermasters*
were elected by its citizens, while the seven judges (*échevins*) were
chosen by the sovereign's governor.[38] Towns had the additional
advantage of being entitled to build and maintain walls to defend

themselves. They thus attracted military garrisons, as Limburg did throughout the Middle Ages and until the end of the old regime. As a measure of its increasing economic importance, Verviers was transformed in 1651 from a village to a town, with the independence such status brought.[39]

The communities of the Verviers region did not, however, owe allegiance to the same national government. Verviers and Ensival were part of the principality of Liège. Limburg, Thimister, and Soiron were part of the Spanish Netherlands; they owed allegiance to the government in Brussels and, ultimately, to the Spanish government in Madrid. The differences between village and town meant little. Central governments, however, controlled foreign and military affairs, justice, and taxes; and it is in these areas that we should expect to see real differences between the lives of inhabitants of the villages in the different states. Of these potential differences, justice seemed to operate about the same everywhere and is not relevant to us. Taxes on property were not high and did not differ much between Liège and the Spanish Netherlands. On the other hand, import and export duties, designed to raise revenue and protect local markets, differed considerably from one place to another. Thus within the broad range of taxes, we need to be aware of the different strategies concerning customs duties, and their evolution, in the different states. Military and foreign affairs were the most important function of national governments. The region between the Meuse and Rhine rivers was often contested during the many wars of the sixteenth, seventeenth, and eighteenth centuries, because it lay at the intersection of principal routes both north-south and east-west, and therefore held a number of useful fortresses.[40] The long wars between Spain, France, and the Dutch Republic, which began after 1560 and lasted more than 150 years, made this territory important because it was close to the intersection of the three powers.

Varied sovereignty did not protect the inhabitants of the region from the hardships imposed by military occupation. Recruitment or the draft was not a major concern for the area's residents. The real burden was occupation by troops in passage or in preparation for a battle or siege. The nationality of a particular village offered little advantage or disadvantage during the period we are considering. Liège was nominally neutral, but the prince-bishop once or twice sacrificed any advantage by choosing sides in a conflict. In any event the principality did not have the forces required to protect that neutrality. It was readily occupied by the Spanish, French, German, English, Swedish, and Dutch armies that roamed the Low Countries, especially during the seventeenth century. The Spanish territories were treated more or less the same by all armies, including those of Spain and its allies. The armies occupied villages; lodged soldiers in peoples' homes, stables, and barns; and requisitioned manpower, food, and any other *materiel* they might need and be able to find. Differences imposed by war were slight, therefore, except that the Spanish and Dutch villages (of which there were some) did pay somewhat higher taxes during wartime to support their home government's military ambitions.

What mattered about sovereignty in the Liège-Aachen region was the fact that the region was militarily attractive. Every place suffered, producing a chain of consequences: military requisitions forced the village to go into debt; debt strained the fiscal resources of the community, forcing it to raise taxes; higher taxes put more demands on the citizens for cash, which then put them increasingly under the control of the richest citizens.

Where the differences between one sovereign and another were important was in the question of customs duties, because the common action of the age was to levy import and export fees (in Liège the normal fee was one-sixtieth of the value, levied both at entry and at exit) on all goods, even those in transit to an ultimate destination elsewhere or raw materials being processed before reexport as finished goods. The fact of varied sovereignty meant that in the case of textiles, wool from Spain might reach Verviers after a trip by ship to Amsterdam in the Dutch Republic, pass through Spanish territory on its way to Verviers, which was in Liégeois territory, and then be exported via Spanish territory to a final destination in Germany. In the worst possible scenario, the wool or cloth might be taxed at every border it crossed, both as it left one territory and as it entered the next.[41]

This situation affected the conduct of business. The industrialist's goal was to bring his raw materials and finished products through as few toll barriers as possible—that is, to attempt to cross as few borders as possible. To accomplish this, he had few options. Let us consider again the manufacturer of woolen cloth in Verviers. His basic raw material was Spanish wool. After the decline of Antwerp as an entrepôt in the late sixteenth century, Amsterdam became the logical place to purchase imported commodities, especially because the Dutch levied relatively light import and export taxes. Spanish wool could thus get into and out of the Dutch Republic virtually untaxed. But Verviers is in Liégeois territory, and the principal route (up the Meuse River) from Amsterdam to Liège crossed Spanish territory and toll stations, before entering Liège. The wool might be taxed by the Spanish, as well as by the Liégeois, on its way to Verviers.

By the eighteenth century, the manufacturers of Verviers had found a better solution. They imported their wool from Spain via the port of Ostend and then overland via the town of Louvain. Both Ostend and Louvain were in Spanish territory, so taxation was limited to the entry duty in Liège. To avoid that tariff the Verviers merchants found another solution. Verviers adjoins the village of Hodimont, which was so tiny in the seventeenth and eighteenth centuries that it was more a street than a suburb. Relations between the two communities were so close that residents of Hodimont went to church in the parish of Verviers. Hodimont was part of the duchy of Limburg and therefore Spanish territory. The Verviers manufacturers set up separate but essentially duplicate offices in Hodimont for the handling of Spanish wool. It was possible to avoid virtually all the customs duties that might be levied on the wool as it reached the manufacturer in Verviers-Hodimont. Once in Hodimont, border enforcement was so lax that the materials could be worked on wherever the manufacturer found it convenient.

POPULATION AND SOCIAL STRUCTURE IN THE NEW INDUSTRIAL COMMUNITIES

Most of the inhabitants of these early industrial communities were farmers, who grew crops and raised dairy cattle. In their spare time, they and their families worked in industry, primarily as nailmakers, miners, and spinners, while the rest of the industrial jobs—such as weaving, dyeing, and other processing of finished goods—were already filled by full-time workers, in the largest of the rural industrial communities, such as Verviers. We can get a rough idea of the occupations of the people who lived in Verviers in the middle of the seventeenth century, because a census was taken in 1649. The results are shown in Table 3.2. In the three-fourths of the city recorded in the part of the census that survives, virtually everyone worked in the woolen cloth industry or in service occupations that supported it. We cannot know how the residents of the rest of the city were employed. We can surmise, nevertheless, that the census records too few people in construction, crafts, services and hospitality. The best conclusion we can draw is that the village was not very agricultural in 1649, and that a large proportion of its inhabitants worked in the textile industry.

Verviers was the most industrial of the towns, even in 1650; so if we look at the amount of industrial work in the other towns, we should find fewer industrial workers. In terms of industrial employment there are three kinds of communities among our five places: Verviers was the most industrial, Limburg was in an intermediate position, and Ensival, Thimister, and Soiron had relatively little industrial employment, at least in the mid-seventeenth century. In Limburg the town fathers collected taxes every year from almost everyone who lived there. They not only taxed property, they also taxed every household head who worked. Therefore, their tax records include both the kind and the quantity of property held by each household, as well as identifying households that had no property. From these records we can estimate what proportion of the population was working in industrial jobs, because industrial workers were very likely not to own any land or to own very little. The earliest Limburg tax records that survive show taxes paid in 1670 (see Table 3.3). The records are divided between the village of Limburg itself and its industrial suburb, Dolhain.

Whereas there were few farmers in Verviers in 1649, between one-half and two-thirds of the population of Limburg was still farming in 1670. We know this by looking at the numbers of taxpayers who had land, or only a garden, or no land at all. In 1670, about 40 percent of all taxpayers in the two most important sections of Limburg—the part called Limburg proper and the

Table 3.2: The Occupational Structure of Verviers, 1649

BY ECONOMIC SECTOR		
	Number	Percentage
Textile industry	1,288	79.7
Food	70	4.3
Metalwork	17	1.1
Building	34	2.1
Leather	18	1.1
Clothing (nonindustrial textiles)	47	2.9
Rentiers and office holders	33	2.0
Professions	17	1.1
Hotels	7	0.4
Transportation	15	0.9
Miscellaneous	25	1.5
Sector not clear	45	2.8
	1,616	100.0
SOCIOECONOMIC CATEGORY		
Merchants	155	9.7
Artisans and industrial crafts	786	48.9
Day workers and industrial workers	611	38.0
Farmers	6	0.4
Rentiers and office holders	20	1.2
Professions	17	1.1
Miscellaneous	11	0.7
	1,616	100.0

SOURCE: Paul Bertholet, *La vie à Verviers au XVIIe siècle: Histoire Familiale (les de Sonkeux) et démographie historique* (Dison: G. Lelotte, 1978), p. 124.

part called Dolhain—paid tax on farmland. The remaining 60 percent had only a garden or no land at all. Those with only a garden or no land were employed by others, and we can assume that many of them worked as farm laborers while the rest worked in industrial jobs. Somewhere between one-half and two-thirds of the population, then, was probably involved in agriculture while the rest worked more or less permanently in industry. By the end of the eighteenth century, as we can see from the figures for 1780, the number of taxpayers with land declined by half, to about 18

Table 3.3: Taxpayer Characteristics in Limburg, 1670 and 1780

	1670				1780			
	Total Number Taxpay-ers	% No Land	% Garden Only	% With Land	Total Number Taxpay-ers	% No Land	% Garden Only	% With Land
Limburg	109	6.4	19.2	65.1	124	41.1	17.7	41.1
Dolhain	75	26.7	62.7	10.7	173	61.3	37.0	1.7
Total	184	20.1	37.0	42.9	297	52.9	29.0	18.2

SOURCE: AEL, Communes, Limburg, 299 (1780); and AEL, Thisquen, 139 (1670).

percent, and the overall proportion of agricultural workers probably declined to about one-third. By that time Limburg was very industrialized.

The two principal parts of Limburg were never divided equally in social and economic terms. The differences reflect the geographic setting of the town. Limburg proper sits on a knot of rock that rises above the Vesdre River (its original settlement took place because the rock made a perfect natural fortress). Its suburb, Dolhain, surrounds its base along the Vesdre. Most of the original settlers of Limburg lived on the hill, first farming the hillsides and then later spreading out into the surrounding region. Over time a social division emerged. The most prosperous members of the community lived in Limburg—on the hill—while their poorer neighbors lived in Dolhain—the valley. The valley was better suited to the cloth industry by its proximity to water, and most of the textile workers lived there. We see this very clearly in Table 3.3. Few residents of Dolhain ever farmed, even in 1670, and their role in the population declined during the eighteenth century. In Limburg, on the other hand, although the number of farmers declined in the eighteenth century, it always remained substantial. Never were fewer than 40 percent of taxpayers assessed on farmland.

If Verviers was fully industrial in the mid-seventeenth century and Limburg about one-third so, none of the other communities was heavily industrialized at that time. Almost all their people continued to work at farming jobs. While we have no documents for Soiron, Ensival, and Thimister that equal those for Limburg and Verviers, what documents we can consult—primarily lists of property tax payers—show populations made up largely of farmers and farm laborers. In Thimister in 1682 (the earliest document we can use), about 24 percent of all taxpayers had less than one-half *bonnier* (a *bonnier* is about .87 hectare), for most of them enough only for a garden. In neighboring Charneux, the proportion was 27 percent; and in Battice, 22 percent. These figures cannot be directly compared with those of Limburg, but they suggest that although the transformation to industry had begun, at least four out of five residents of these rural communities were still involved primarily in agriculture in 1682.[42] By the late eighteenth century, as we will see in Chapters 5 and 6, that was no longer the case.

Knowing roughly what part of the population worked in industry and what part in agriculture gives us a sense of how people lived in these communities.

The first part of the story told in this chapter is about the emergence of a powerful group of early industries in the region between Liège and Aachen. In the production of raw materials, in metalwork, and in the manufacture of woolen cloth, this region grew dramatically in the sixteenth and early seventeenth centuries, pointing toward future strength that would make this among the preeminent industrial regions on the European continent. The area was blessed with coal and alum, with abundant clean water, with a good location to profit from proximity to the Dutch Republic and German fairs, and with the simple good fortune to benefit from the competitive conditions of the sixteenth and especially the seventeenth century. By the mid-seventeenth century the territory east of the Meuse was already an industrial center, one that would grow still further in the late seventeenth and eighteenth centuries.

Natural resources and good fortune in the larger historical sphere contributed to the growth of this area, but the human contribution was more important. Without entrepreneurs, without technical innovation, and without competitive manpower, the area could never have grown as rapidly and as forcefully as it did. And it profited in all three ways, with men like Curtius and his peers, with innovations like the *fenderie,* and most important, with the development of a large and low-wage industrial work force, itself the result of the growth of Verviers and the transformation of the countryside of the Herve Country. The conversion from labor-intensive traditional farms to smaller, labor-extensive dairy farms, begun in the sixteenth century and well under way in the seventeenth, created a large and malleable labor force, partially supported by agriculture but available for industrial work. As we have seen, this labor force was socially stable and patient, marrying in their mid to late twenties. Older pressures to conform seem to have persisted. The labor force, more than any other factor, made the Verviers region ripe for its development as an industrial power and gave it competitive advantage over other industrial centers.

NOTES

1. There is no general economic history of the principality of Liège, but it is effectively described in studies of the economic history of Belgium. See the economic history chapters in Henri Pirenne, *Histoire de Belgique*, 7 vols., 3rd ed. (Brussels: Lamertin, 1923–1927), vols. 3–4; and the relevant parts of Laurent Dechesne, *Histoire économique et sociale de la Belgique depuis les origines jusqu'en 1914* (Liège: Wykmans, 1932).

2. The sources for these figures are given in Table 3.1. I have reduced de Vries's figure for 1500 to make the series more coherent.

3. E. A. Wrigley and R. S. Schofield, *The Population History of England, 1541–1871: A Reconstruction* (Cambridge, Mass.: Harvard University Press, 1981), p. 243.

4. John Hajnal, "European Marriage Patterns in Perspective," in *Population in History*, ed. D. V. Glass and D. E. C. Eversley (London: Edward Arnold, 1965), pp. 101–143.

5. Lawrence Stone, *The Family, Sex and Marriage in England, 1500–1800* (New York: Harper & Row, 1978), p. 51.

6. De Vries, *European Urbanization, 1500–1800* (Cambridge, Mass.: Harvard University Press, 1984), p. 39. De Vries defines urban areas as those having populations of 10,000 or more. This is rather high. Taking the minimum urban size as 5,000 or more would yield a somewhat higher figure as living in urban areas.

7. Ibid., pp. 30, 39.

8. See, for example, Ralph Davis, *The Rise of the Atlantic Economies* (Ithaca: Cornell University Press, 1973).

9. For the best simple description of the development of these industries and their importance and location, see the relevant chapters in Charles Singer et al., eds., *A History of Technology*, 8 vols. (Oxford: Clarendon Press, 1954–1984), especially those in volume 3, which covers the period c.1500–c.1750.

10. Georges Hansotte, "Pays de fer et de houille," in *La Wallonie: Le pays et les hommes. Histoire-économies-sociétés*, ed. Hervé Hasquin, 2 vols. (Brussels: La Renaissance du Livre, 1975), 1:269–294.

11. Jean Lejeune, *La formation du capitalisme moderne dans la principauté de Liège au XVIe siècle* (Liège: Faculté de Philosophie et Lettres, 1939).

12. For the similar and parallel English development, see John U. Nef, *The Rise of the British Coal Industry* (London: G. Routledge & Sons, 1932).

13. On the development of industrial organization in Liège in the sixteenth century, see Lejeune, *La formation du capitalisme moderne*, pp. 230–250.

14. This is the key argument made by Lejeune in ibid., p. 248.

15. Ibid., p. 261.

16. For the most accurate sketch of Curtius as an economic figure, see ibid., pp. 279–304.

17. Georges Hansotte is the historian of the Walloon iron industry. In general, see Hansotte, "Pays de fer et de houille." On the evolution described here, see Hansutte, "La métallurgie wallonne au XVIe et dans la première moitié du XVIIe siècle. Un état de la question," in *Schwerpunkte der Eisengewinnung und Eisenverarbeitung in Europa 1500–1650*, ed. Hermann Kellenbenz (Cologne: Böhlau Verlag, 1974), pp. 126–146.

18. On the technical evolution of the Liégeoise metallurgical industry, see Jean Yernaux, *La métallurgie liégeoise et son expansion au XVIIe siècle* (Liège: G. Thone, 1939), pp. 15–32.

19. Hansotte, "La métallurgie wallonne," p. 131.

20. Yernaux, *La métallurgie liégeoise*, Chapter 4: "L'organisation du travail," pp. 62–87; and H. Angenot, "Un marchand cloutier verviétois au XVIIe siècle," *BSVAH* 13 (1913):129–169.

21. Hansotte, "La métallurgie wallonne," pp. 136–137.

22. Dechesne, *Histoire économique et sociale de la Belgique;* Stanislas Bormans, *Le bon métier des drapiers de l'ancien cité de Liège* (Liège, 1866); and P. D. Spiegeler, "Le draperie de la cité de Liège: des origines à 1468," *Le Moyen Age* 85 (1979): 45–86.

23. A. Hansay, "Une crise industrielle dans la draperie hasseltoise au XVIe siècle," *Revue de l'Instruction Publique* 48 (1905): 261–271.

24. Josef Dahmen, *Die Aachener Tuchgewerbe bis zum Ende des 19. Jahrhunderts. Ein Beitrag zur Wirtschaftsgeschichte der Stadt Aachen*, 2nd ed. (Berlin: L. Weiss, 1930); H. Kley, *Studien zur Geschichte und Verfassung des Aachener Wollenaambachts wie überhaupt der Tuchindustrie der Reichstadt Aachen* (Bonn: H. Ludwig, 1916); and Herbert Kisch, "Growth Deterrents of a Medieval Heritage: The Aachen-Area Woolen Trades Before 1790," *Journal of Economic History* 24 (1964): 517–537.

25. Hansay, "Une crise industrielle dans la draperie hasseltoise."

26. E. Fairon, "L'origine de l'industrie drapière verviétoise," *Chronique SVAH* (1907): 77–84.

27. Ibid., pp. 82–84.

28. Kisch, "The Growth Deterrents of a Medieval Heritage," pp. 524–528.

29. AEL, Cour de Justice, Verviers, 173, folio 74, taille 1569; and I. Delatte, "Le commerce et l'industrie de Verviers au XVIe siècle," *BSVAH* 40 (1953): 7.

30. Kisch, "Growth Deterrents of a Medieval Heritage," pp. 523–524.

31. Delatte, "Le commerce et l'industrie de Verviers."

32. Ibid.

33. Ibid.

34. Georges Hansotte, *La clouterie liégeoise et la question ouvrière au XVIIIe siècle*, Anciens Pays et Assemblées d'Etats, No. 55 (Brussels: Editions de la Librairie Encyclopédique, 1972).

35. This process of change is described in Joseph Ruwet, *L'agriculture et*

les classes rurales au pays de Herve sous l'ancien régime (Liège: Faculté de Philosophie et Lettres, 1943), pp. 52–68.

36. On this kind of specialization in the early modern Low Countries, see Jan de Vries, *The Dutch Rural Economy in the Golden Age* (New Haven: Yale University Press, 1974).

37. For the structure of government, see Bruno Dumont, "Les communautés villageoises du Duché de Limbourg" (Ph.D. dissertation, University of Liège, 1987). There is a rich local history literature about these places. For a bibliography, see the individual listings in Hervé Hasquin, ed., *Communes de Belgique: Dictionnaire d'histoire et de géographie administrative*, 4 vols. (Brussels: La Renaissance du Livre, 1981).

38. J. Thisquen, "Histoire de la ville de Limbourg," *BSVAH* 9 (1907) and 10 (1908).

39. Jean Lejear, "Histoire de la ville de Verviers depuis son érection en ville jusqu'à la fin de l'ancien régime, 1651–1794," *BSVAH* 38 (1951).

40. On these wars and their impact, see Myron P. Gutmann, *War and Rural Life in the Early Modern Low Countries* (Princeton: Princeton University Press, 1980); and Geoffrey Parker, *The Army of Flanders and the Spanish Road, 1567–1659* (Cambridge: Cambridge University Press, 1972).

41. On the history of customs duties in the Liège-Aachen region, see Paul Harsin, "Etudes sur l'histoire économique de la Principauté de Liège, particulièrement au XVIIe siècle," *BIAL* 62 (1928): 60–161; Georges Hansotte, *La métallurgie et le commerce international du fer dans les Pays-Bas autrichiens et la Principauté de Liège pendant la second moitié du XVIIIe siècle* (Brussels: Academie Royale de Belgique, 1980); and Pierre Lebrun, *L'industrie de la laine à Verviers pendant le XVIIIe et le début du XIXe siècle* (Liège: Faculté de Philosophie et Lettres, 1948).

42. Ruwet, *L'agriculture et les classes rurales*, p. 247.

CHAPTER 4

The Second Crisis of Urban Industry and the Crisis of the Seventeenth Century

Despite the growth of rural industrial centers such as those between Liège and Aachen, the cities still dominated large-scale industrial production in the early seventeenth century. Although the figures do not exist with which to make statistical comparisons of production by region, or by city as opposed to countryside, the predominance of the cities is apparent in all the generally held views of the location of industry. Consider Jan de Vries's report on where industry was located at the end of the sixteenth century:

> Europe's industrial heartlands at the end of the sixteenth century could boast of considerable antiquity. Ever since the thirteenth and fourteenth centuries the cities of northern Italy and Flanders had been preeminent as producers of textiles and luxury furnishings. While metallurgical trades were, by their nature, widely scattered, Liège and Milan stood out as suppliers of armaments. Of course, many smaller centers had arisen to provide for regional needs, but a remarkable number of such centers could be found in the Rhenish, Swiss, and eastern French areas that connected Flanders with northern Italy. And within this area the location of industrial activity, although present in many rural districts, remained dominated by such cities as Venice, Milan, Augsburg, Liège, Amiens and Ghent.[1]

The emergence of new industrial territories provided competition to the older industrial cities, beginning in the late fifteenth century and with increasing force in the late sixteenth and early seventeenth centuries. In the face of this competition, many cities reoriented themselves toward new products, with some success. In the seventeenth century such reorientation became more and more difficult. Some of the older industrial cities de Vries mentions slid into near obscurity. This deterioration can be called the second crisis of urban industry, and it is the subject of this chapter. It is intimately associated with the long-term development of industry in Europe, as well as with another phenomenon often discussed by historians, a more general "crisis of the seventeenth century."

THE RISE AND FALL OF THE LEIDEN TEXTILE INDUSTRY

The Dutch town of Leiden is located in the southern part of the province of Holland, about two-thirds of the way down the north-south road that connects Amsterdam and the Dutch capital, the Hague. To understand the industrial crisis in seventeenth-century Leiden, we need to begin with that city's adaptation to the first crisis of urban industry, in the sixteenth century.

Leiden was a medium-sized textile-producing center in the middle of the sixteenth century.[2] Its population in 1574 and 1581 was between twelve and thirteen thousand. Its specialty was a high-quality heavy woolen cloth called *laken*. Competition gradually destroyed the market for this cloth during the mid-sixteenth century. As late as the early 1540s, Leiden produced 15,000 to 20,000 cloths per year; thereafter production fell, reaching a level below 1,000 per year in the 1570s. Leiden lakens were produced for export, and the export market for those cloths was restricted not only by oncoming war in the 1570s but by the growing competition of lighter fabrics of the kind made in Hondschoote.[3] During the years that Leiden's production fell from 20,000 cloths per year to virtually none, Hondschoote's production of says and other light cloths more than doubled, from 40,000 to 80,000 or more per year.[4]

In the 1580s the Leiden economy improved. The Dutch Revolution heated up, disrupting the Hondschoote industry; its work force began to emigrate.[5] Among many localities to which they moved, Leiden seems to have been first choice. By the end of the sixteenth century it emerged as the new textile center of northern Europe. Between 1583 and 1600 this town of 12,000 residents made homes for some 1,662 new burghers and their families, a 40 percent increase in population in less then twenty years. Hondschoote alone provided nearly one-eighth of those immigrants.[6] When the next census was taken, in 1622, the town's population had grown to 44,475, and by the early 1640s the best estimate by city authorities was a population in excess of 80,000.[7] From a city on the way to collapse in the 1540s, Leiden had become a demographic and economic center of considerable importance.

Production figures for the Leiden textile industry echo the growth of population (see Figure 4.1). By 1600 the total production of cloths of all kinds in Leiden was over 58,000 pieces. By 1620, it had reached nearly 100,000 pieces.[8] Very little of this was in the old lakens, a mere 1,539 cloths in 1620; rather, most was in the "new draperies." The city's looms produced about 50,000 says, about 22,000 fustians (a mixture of cotton and wool, with a worsted appearance), and 16,000 baizes (a light, felted woolen fabric like that used today to cover billiard tables).[9] Camlets—a mixture of wool and goat's hair—do not yet show up in the production figures. The city's artisans produced between 90,000 and 110,000 cloths a year from the 1620s through the early 1650s. Their output then rose to a new peak of 144,723 cloths in 1664. This signaled the end of Leiden's growth. By the late 1670s, production had fallen to 85,000 cloths, and it never again expanded.[10] This was so despite a new shift in production that saw says virtually disappear and the production of camlets and old-fashioned lakens increase. This decline continued in the eighteenth century, reaching a level of total production around 55,000 cloths in 1750 and around 30,000 in 1800.[11]

The rise and decline of Leiden is a story worth telling and worth explaining. Leiden became a great industrial center because it had a strong medieval base that attracted merchants and workers from the disrupted industry of the southern Netherlands. Without the base, and without the disruption that made these people available, it could not have grown as it did. Its decline is a different story. N. W. Posthumus, the historian of Leiden's woolen industry, suggested that Leiden declined because it could not compete effectively against the industries that were growing elsewhere. The strongest competition, he thought, came from the new manufacturing centers in the southeastern Low Countries, especially those in the Meuse-Rhine region.[12]

The organization of the Leiden textile industry tells part of the story. There were no guilds, and although the city regulated the industry, its administration was tolerant and flexible. Merchants were under little compulsion to have cloth produced ex-

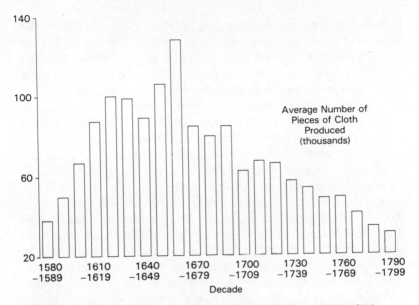

Figure 4.1.   Woolen Textile Production in Leiden, 1580–1799
SOURCE: N. W. Posthumus, *De Geschiedenis van de Leidsche Lakenindustrie*, 3 vols. (Leiden: M. Nijhoff, 1908–1939), 2:129; 3:930–931, 1098–1099.

clusively within the town walls, and they sent spinning and weaving to rural areas and smaller towns (some as far away as Prussia), where wages were low. The region between Liège and Aachen was among the localities in which the Leiden merchants had yarn spun and cloth woven before finishing it in their own city. After the middle of the seventeenth century a strong group of local merchants emerged in the principality of Liège and the duchy of Limburg. They displaced the Leidenaars in the main organization of the work, merely sending their nearly finished cloth to Leiden for the last touches and for sale on the international market. By the end of the seventeenth century even that dependence on Leiden disappeared. The merchants of Verviers were on their own.[13]

Patterns of migration to Leiden reflect the changing pattern of organization and concentration in the woolen industry of the Low Countries. In the late sixteenth and early seventeenth centuries, Leiden was a magnet for migrants from virtually every section of the Low Countries, northern France, and northwestern Germany. Among these were a significant number of new burghers from the principality of Liège and the regions that surrounded it. That migration peaked in 1638, when a decline in the migration of Liégeois to Leiden began. Moreover, some of those who arrived before 1638 later returned to their native city.[14]

The competition tipped in favor of Liège and Verviers after 1650. It cost far less to produce cloth in Verviers, where wages were only one-third those in Leiden.[15] For the differential in wages to be meaningful, however, the products had to be equal in quality. The Liégeois became competitive during the second third of the seventeenth century, and dominant during the last third of the century, because they changed the raw material in their cloth from local wool to the highest quality Spanish wool. The difference in cost combined with comparable quality gave the Verviétois a distinct price advantage, one they used to conquer first the markets of Germany and Switzerland, and later those of Italy and the Baltic.[16] The Dutch could not fail to notice the change, and they acted to exclude the Verviétois from the market for raw Spanish wool. Contrary to their usual commitment to free trade, they closed their border with Liège to the transfer of Spanish wool. This was ineffective, because the merchants of Verviers had ready access to Spanish wool through ports in the Spanish Netherlands and France.

The competition posed by the Liège-Verviers region was not exceptional. Leiden faced competition from a number of other areas, especially in England.[17] There were special fabrics that the Leiden artisans produced and that others could not effectively duplicate. This was notably so for the high-priced camlets. But in the area of low-priced cloths the Dutch were at a disadvantage, in terms of the cost of labor and materials, compared with both England and other Continental manufacturing regions. To meet that competition, the Leiden merchants were forced to lower their prices to a level at which their businesses were no longer profitable. When that happened, production in Leiden declined.

Leiden's woolen cloth industry became far less profitable during the seventeenth and eighteenth centuries. Figure 4.2 shows the changing ratio of cloth prices to wool prices between the 1620s and the 1780s. A high ratio of cloth to wool suggests profits were high, while a low ratio suggests profits were low. The ratio was high in the early seventeenth century, then declined after 1650. It was relatively level during the eighteenth century. The ratio is mostly sensitive to the price of cloth, because the

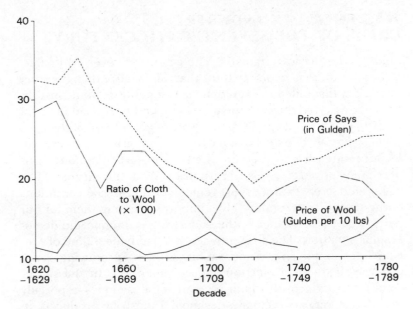

Figure 4.2.   The Ratio of Cloth to Wool Prices in Leiden, 1620–1789
SOURCE: N. W. Posthumus, *De Geschiedenis van de Leidsche Lakenindustrie,* 3 vols. (Leiden: M. Nijhoff, 1908–1939), 3:792–793, 853–856.

price of wool was more stable. Beginning in the middle of the seventeenth century, the prices received for woolen cloth declined, and they did not recover until the end of the eighteenth century. The price of wool rose again just as cloth prices improved. Because of their high labor costs and dependence on high cloth prices for profitability, the manufacturers of Leiden could not hope to compete with those who had access to a labor force willing to work for much lower wages.

Production in the Meuse-Rhine region was probably the inverse of Leiden's. There are few documents that quantify production, and none of them covers the whole region, especially in the seventeenth century. Pierre Lebrun believes that taxed production reached about 30,000 cloths in the 1730s.[18] This figure is surely an underestimate, because manufacturers tried to avoid paying taxes on the cloth they exported. He assumes that the entire region's production exceeded 100,000 pieces per year by 1750, a quantity roughly equal to the loss of production from Leiden in the eighty-five years following 1664.

WAS THERE AN INDUSTRIAL CRISIS OF THE SEVENTEENTH CENTURY?

Leiden's decline was dramatic. The city never reversed its fate. Moreover, there is reason to think that this is more than the story of one city that failed to overcome its competition. Some historians have asserted that Europe in general and European industry in particular were shaped by some sort of *general crisis of the seventeenth century*. [19] The debate over the general crisis of the seventeenth century has focused on whether the particular conditions of the time provoked unusual responses. What this means will be elaborated later. First we must remember the special conditions of the seventeenth century. Most important among them for our purposes was the change in the underlying economic and demographic situation. The sixteenth century had been a time of dramatic economic and demographic growth, producing large increases in both production and consumption. In the seventeenth century growth stabilized, and some regions—especially the Mediterranean—actually declined. Industrial producers in the seventeenth century witnessed changes outside the realm of the economy and population. In the political arena monarchical power grew, and in the international arena France and England asserted their power in ways they had not in the sixteenth century. Finally, religious conflict continued. States fought over religion until the middle of the seventeenth century, when the Westphalia peace ended the Thirty Years' War; but internal religious disagreements continued.[20] We see this in Louis XIV's revocation of the Edict of Nantes (1685) and the emigration of many Huguenots to Protestant countries.

Most participants in the crisis debate tell us that these underlying conditions produced dramatic changes in economic, political, international, religious, and intellectual life. A crisis is a "turning point," according to most dictionary definitions. To be a crisis, the seventeenth century had to be the "stage in a sequence of events at which the trend of all future events is determined."[21] The advocates of the idea of a "crisis" suggest that the outcomes were unexpected because so many of the contributing factors were unexpected and negative. This does not mean that the outcomes were regressive. Rather, a clear theme that runs through historians' discussion of the seventeenth-century crisis is that a positive or progressive outcome occurred because the inputs were so negative or regressive. This is the case in the famous essay by E. J. Hobsbawm, "The Overall Crisis of the European Economy of the Seventeenth Century."[22]

Hobsbawm's argument can be summarized in these terms: European economic history before the nineteenth century had three stages, roughly equivalent to the sixteenth, seventeenth, and eighteenth centuries. The first stage, during the sixteenth century, was one of growth; but according to Hobsbawm this growth was "contradictory" in that it failed to lead to industrialization. He illustrates this contradiction by pointing to the countryside, where growth impoverished potential rural customers for industrial goods. It did this by shrinking their holdings and forcing them to work for low wages and pay high prices for food. The seventeenth century constituted the second stage, when Hobsbawm sees the European economy thrust into a crisis by the contradictions of sixteenth-century growth. This stage was crucial, however, because the seventeenth century made use of its problems to find the organizational solutions that would permit later growth and change. The final stage, in the eighteenth century, combined the new prosperity with structural changes to allow the European economy to take advantage of its development and create modern mechanized industry.

The main organizational solution, Hobsbawm suggests, was concentration—which he sees in population, in urban power, in agriculture, and in industry. Concentration of capital and production was especially significant; and the growth of what Hobsbawm called "putting-out" industry, which provided for both the concentration of capital in a few hands and the concentration of production in certain regions, was vitally important. This concentration, arrived at through rural industry, eventually led to industrialization in the mechanized sense. This theory is attractive, because it connects the seventeenth century's difficulties with the eighteenth-century outcome. The only problem is that Hobsbawm gives few details about how processes worked, and this is crucial. He never says exactly how the newly concentrated rural industries led to eighteenth-century growth and factory industry. Nevertheless, Hobsbawm is fundamentally correct, and we will see below how his argument can be used to make sense of the history of early industry.

Hobsbawm's article provoked an initial flurry of criticism and disagreement. The main thrust of the critiques was the lack of uniformity in the seventeenth-century crisis.[23] The downturn did not occur everywhere at the same time, and certain regions— most notably the Dutch Republic and Sweden—did not experience any downturn at all. Nor was the response to economic and demographic retreat uniform. Some regions responded quickly and healthily, whereas others never recovered. There remained in Europe at the end of the seventeenth century a tremendous amount of variety, reflected in local patterns of development and responses to the century's generally gloomy material situation. These initial critiques have faded, as a consensus arose which agreed that the seventeenth century was a period of economic decline, one that saw the birth of new approaches to manufacturing and trade.[24]

In the wake of the debate about the economic crisis there followed another crisis debate about political developments. This debate, started by H. R. Trevor-Roper and continued by J. H. Elliott and others, emphasized the growth of state power and the reactions—often in the form of revolution—against that power.[25] The period from the mid-sixteenth to the early eighteenth century was certainly a turning point in the history of the state. This era saw the monopoly of power in the hands of the monarch confirmed, usually at the expense of older elites in the aristocracy or the cities. The largest and richest monarchies— eventually England, France, and the Spanish and Austrian Hapsburgs—used their new domestic power to assert themselves internationally. The result was a reshaped political world, making the seventeenth century a true turning point; the moment of crisis varied in different states, but it had a common form. The monarchs successfully turned back a challenge from older competitors for power.

The political and economic developments have more common threads than might be immediately apparent. The great and contradictory prosperity of the sixteenth century, which Hobsbawm said brought on the crisis of the seventeenth century and the concentration of the eighteenth century, also shaped the political world. This prosperity made it possible for the monarchies to monopolize power. Inflation sapped the power of the aristocracy. It also allowed the monarchs to increase levels of taxation to support more bureaucrats and soldiers. When deflation occurred in the seventeenth century, the reaction against taxes spurred the monarch's competitors to rebel; yet it also gave the monarchs the opportunity to prevail. A series of mid-seventeenth-century rebellions ended in royal victories. The economic growth of the sixteenth century and the economic reverses of the seventeenth century sustained the power of the monarchs. Conversely, the growth of royal power to sustain emerging industries shaped the outcome of the economic crisis.

There is much to learn from the idea of a crisis, despite the inability of historians to agree on many questions.[26] The seventeenth century was a turning point, provoked by its special conditions: economic and demographic stagnation, political and international change, the last burst of post-Reformation religious conflict. Long-term economic trends played a vital role in shaping social and economic life in the seventeenth century; deteriorating economic conditions underlie virtually every one of the general arguments. There was an economic depression in the seventeenth century;[27] and this stagnant or deteriorating economy cut into a world of unrealistic prosperity and optimism and led to new outcomes. Niceties of terminology do not preclude sustaining the point of view of those who perceive a crisis, and seeing the seventeenth century as one of creativity, in which a number of hardships were turned to advantage.

In the sphere of economic consequences, the idea of a crisis continues to make sense and helps us understand questions of historical interpretation. It suggests a turning point in European industrial history, one that had to arrive before the later developments, of which we know so much more, could follow. Urban industry encountered the final stage of a crisis in the seventeenth century. It was a crisis of profitability, and the creation of rural industry was both a cause and a consequence. The kinds of rural industry produced by the crisis made the later growth of factory industry particularly easy and nearly inevitable. The crisis of industrial profits existed not only on its own terms but by comparison with earlier times. The sixteenth century had been an era of easy profits and economic optimism, fueled by the demand of an ever-growing population and an age of inflation. Reality caught up with the economy in the seventeenth century. Industrial profits became considerably more difficult to generate. This was especially so for those producing in an urban environment.

Everywhere demand seemed to slacken, as the population

slowed its growth and prices for old-style industrial goods reached a peak and then eased off. Paul Hohenberg and Lynn Hollen Lees attribute the fall in demand for urban industrial goods to a number of processes related to Malthusian limits on rural population growth.[28] The growth of cities in the sixteenth century was largely sustained by "rents" drawn from the country-side. As the rural population approached a Malthusian maxi-mum, and demand for food was nearly as high as the productive limit of resources, conditions changed. Prices rose as the amount of surplus food diminished, and the amount of surplus rural income that could be transferred to the city declined as well. Demand for both rural and urban industrial goods declined, but the countryside was better prepared to absorb the shocks of overall decline.

In the face of slack demand and low prices for industrial goods, the costs of production remained high. On the other hand food prices in the great industrial areas did not peak until about 1650, and then only slowly receded. Where food prices were high, wages were high and difficult to reduce. On top of high wages, in many industrial areas in the seventeenth century pro-longed war brought on high taxes; the persistence of urban guild organizations led to high regulatory costs through inflexible quality standards and the maintenance of high prices and bureau-cratic personnel. All these cost pressures—wages, taxes, and regulatory costs—combined to squeeze the profits of many seventeenth-century industrialists. They found themselves hard-pressed to deal with those competitors who had found the means to produce similar goods at lower cost.

The means other entrepreneurs found to beat the profit squeeze was the placement of industrial activity in the country-side—where taxes were largely borne by the agricultural sector, where wages did not need to support a population employed in industrial work only part of the year (and might be one-half to one-third the level of urban wages), and where regulation did not exist. In this environment, those willing to break out of the older mold of industrial entrepreneurship could prosper—and did. The competition they offered to the older industrial centers was hardly new in the seventeenth century; similar patterns had emerged earlier. But the virtual completeness of this victory tells us a great deal about the scale of the profits crisis of the seventeenth century and about the entrepreneurial changes that accompanied it.

The long-term contribution of rural industries, which are the outgrowth of the industrial crisis of the seventeenth century, is crucial. They led the way to a new group of entrepreneurs who were oriented toward manufacturing large quantities at low prices, and therefore toward a kind of innovation that is vitally important for later industry. The movement of production to the countryside may well have motivated the owners to new styles of management. Workers were less skilled, and in any event bosses supervised their workers less closely. They had to break operations into simple and more standardized tasks, which prepared both workers and bosses for eventual mechanization.[29] Moreover, these were the entrepreneurs, fattened with the profits of early industrial production, who in the late eighteenth and nineteenth centuries financed the onset of factory industrialization. Finally, the creation of rural industries allowed the population to increase in such a way that there was, later, both a larger market and a larger work force to support industrial growth.

The foregoing discussion of the industrial crisis of the seventeenth century emphasized the transformation brought on by changing patterns of supply and demand. Other adjustments also took place. Political change made a major contribution by increasing monarchical and national power, and imposing mercantilist policies. Most of the declining industrial cities described in this chapter were independent city-states or were located in relatively small nation-states. Mercantilist policies gradually closed their markets in larger nations in the seventeenth century. They found it difficult to sell in France and England, for example. This put increasing pressure on them as they competed for markets outside the great powers. The Dutch Republic reacted to this situation by raising barriers to their competitors, as in the attempt to close off the access by Verviers merchants to Spanish wool. The Dutch did not have the power to emulate the larger states, nor did they have large domestic markets to protect. As noted earlier, Verviers merchants found sources for Spanish wool in the Spanish Netherlands and in France.[30] Finally, we need to remember that the impact of religious emigration did not end with the movement of Protestants from Hondschoote or other Flemish towns to Leiden. The emigration of the Huguenots from France after 1685 brought on a new readjustment in the placement of industry, as the urban industries in which they were concentrated (paper- and glassmaking among others) were dispersed to more congenial locales.[31]

SUPPLY, DEMAND, AND THE ORIGINS OF THE INDUSTRIAL CRISIS

The second crisis of urban industry arose out of changes that took place during the seventeenth century in the demand for and the supply of industrial goods. Most of the large export markets for woolen textiles of the type produced in Leiden existed not among the nascent consuming populations in developed western Europe (France, England, the Netherlands) but in less developed places in the colonial world or on the fringes of developed Europe. Eastern Europe, far northern Europe, southern Europe, even the Middle East, provided customers for the high quality fabrics produced by the western export centers. The distance between producer and consumer placed considerable pressures on manufacturers and the merchants who bought their products—at one of the German fairs, for example—for sale in still more distant places. In the seventeenth century, intelligence about factors influencing the size of demand—not to mention future tastes—was very difficult to obtain. Few producers or merchants could predict new competition; nor could they foresee a war or famine, which cut rural incomes and therefore potential expenditures on manufactured goods.

The uncertainty of demand and the inability to predict it left all levels of industrial society vulnerable. Manufacturers attempted to protect themselves against market variations, of course, but the production process often took too long for that to be fully possible. Even if one did not put wool into production until orders were received, the wool itself had to be ordered in advance and eventually paid for. Some cloth did need to be produced in advance, if only for samples, and most manufacturers and traders sent a supply of cloth along with their representatives to be kept in a warehouse in the market city. This followed the old practice of "venturing," in which merchandise was sent to a fair for sale even before orders were received. A disastrous year could leave everything unsold. If this happened, not only the manufacturers but the entire community suffered, because workers counted on a certain level of earnings from cloth production to get them through the year.

The demand—both long- and short-term—for exported industrial products such as woolen cloth was shaped by a number of factors.[32] Population, incomes, and tastes, as well as factors associated with production—such as price and the availability of the goods in question—all influenced demand. The size of the population and the level of incomes were most important, and had the Leiden manufacturer been able to predict their future in 1615, he could not have been sanguine. Southern and central Europe lost population during the seventeenth century, while northern and eastern Europe experienced only modest gains.[33] None of these consuming areas experienced much economic growth in the seventeenth century. Their economies had gained in the sixteenth century—the Mediterranean had profited from the direct and indirect spoils of empire, and central and eastern Europe had profited from the production of food for growing western populations—but these gains eroded in the seventeenth century. In other words, the populations of the consuming areas were not growing in a way that would foster continued industrial growth in the producing areas, and the incomes of their populations were not rising rapidly either. Income distributions were changing, especially in eastern Europe, in a way that concentrated more income in the hands of the elite. This may have been consolation to some producers of superluxury goods, but it was no consolation to those who catered mostly to farmers or the commercial and governmental middle class.

The fact is that our Leiden merchant looking out on the world in 1615 could not know about future demand. So he reacted to short-term changes in the marketplace: when orders slackened, he slowed or stopped production, cut prices, or looked for new products. But even by adjusting his production to perceived demand he could hardly control his economic world. Two forces were at work that put strong pressure on his business, and eventually would make it almost impossible to sustain: the emergence of new producers, and the renewed sensitivity of consumers to the price of the goods he sold. In the Middle Ages urban producers often had a virtual monopoly on the techniques for producing a category of industrial goods. Those technical monopolies slowly eroded, so that by the seventeenth century very few still existed, especially for low-priced goods. That is what allowed the Verviers industry to grow at the expense of the Dutch. The rigidities imposed on our Leiden merchant and his cousins in England, Italy, Germany, and elsewhere, and the economic pressures of competitors and price sensitivity, combined to force him to adapt or go under. The industrial problems of the seventeenth century were not limited to Leiden.

The weakness of some explanations of the economic crisis of the seventeenth century occurs because authors attempt to make the failures synchronous. In fact, the failures need not have been synchronous. What we must look for are similar sets of problems characteristic of the century that produced similar solutions. There is no reason why the industrial crisis in Leiden should have arisen simultaneously with that of Venice, and in fact, to have done so would have been impossible. The rise of Leiden, along with some other Low Countries producers of cloth, helped produce the crisis of the Venetian woolen cloth industry.

Venice

Venice, although often thought to have been primarily a commercial center or a manufacturer of specialized luxury goods—such as crystal, mirrors, or silk—was in fact a major producer of high-quality woolen cloth in, the sixteenth century. The city's production rose from under 2,000 cloths per year in 1516 to 26,500 in 1569 and a peak of 28,700 in 1602.[34] Most of the cloth was sold in the eastern Mediterranean. Just as rapidly as the Venetian cloth industry grew, it later declined. From the peak in 1602, annual production fell to 23,000 in 1620, 10,000 in 1665, and a mere 2,800 in 1701 (Figure 4.3).

The Venetian woolen cloth industry grew for reasons quite similar to those that somewhat later brought prosperity to Leiden. There had been an old, yet small, industry, which was part of a larger regional system consisting of the industrial towns of northern Italy. At a crucial moment, in this case the first half of the sixteenth century, Venice's competitors suffered from external problems—war in their territories, an unsettled Europe, and difficulties in reaching their markets. Venice found itself in a better position and profited from it by dramatically expanding

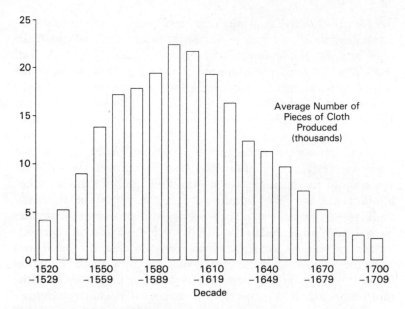

Figure 4.3.   Woolen Textile Production in Venice, 1520–1709
SOURCE: Domenico Sella, "The Rise and Fall of the Venetian Woolen Industry,"
in *Crisis and Change in the Venetian Economy,* ed. Brian Pullan (London:
Methuen, 1968), pp. 109–110.

its woolen production. When conditions in Italy generally improved, after 1569, Venice's expansion was complete; and while
it grew only slightly thereafter, it was able to hold onto its markets. The industry later declined because it could not compete in
those markets. It did not lose out to its Italian competitors, which
also lost ground after 1600 and especially after 1620. Domenico
Sella, who has written about Venice's woolen industry in this
period, attributes the decline to three causes: "one was the
deterioration of normal transport services between Venice and
the Turkish ports; another was the contraction in the demand for
cloth in the Levant; and a third was the entry of new competitors—England, Holland, and, in the later part of the century, the
Venetian mainland."[35]

All three causes ultimately took the form of pricing pressure
on Venetian exports. Venetian shippers had to use inefficient
Venetian ships to carry their merchandise, which raised their
costs; the decline in demand made buyers more choosy and
hence more careful about prices; and the new competitors
brought in similar products at lower prices. Venetian representa-

tives in the Middle East frequently reported this kind of example: "The English . . . 'offer cloth that looks better and costs less than ours, and the Turks more and more grow fond of it.' 'It is well known,' says another document, 'that Dutch woolens have displaced ours: being pleasant, light, and inexpensive, they have infected the mind of the Turks, so that . . . the latter no longer appreciate our draperies, which are heavy both to buy and to wear.' "[36]

Contemporaries blamed many factors for high Venetian prices in the face of competition. They recognized rigid regulations about production, which enforced quality standards not binding on Venice's competitors, high transportation costs, and high wages. Certainly all three were present; but when the regulations were finally eased in the 1670s, the industry did not recover. Moreover, Venice, far from clean fresh water and limited to a small territory, was not the ideal industrial town. In all likelihood the cost of labor and the availability of other investment opportunities are the most important pressures that kept prices high and then prevented them from decreasing. Most important, labor costs were high. Venice was a city of the very wealthy, partially isolated from the mainland. The cost of living must have been extremely high, and so was the floor under wages, even for industrial workers. Industrialists could therefore hardly reduce their costs (and consequently their prices) in industries that were dependent on human labor.[37] When their competitors offered similar merchandise at lower prices, the Venetians faced the unpleasant prospect of losing sales or reducing their prices and losing money on each sale.

The early Venetian industrialists escaped this no-win situation not by lowering prices and forcing their workers to accept less (which was probably impossible) but by turning their attention to other kinds of investments. Paul Klep has called the process by which declining urban industrial centers refocused their energies the "traditionalization of investments."[38] In the seventeenth century the Venetian trading economy, which had been hurt by the new sea routes from the East in the sixteenth century, was gradually restored to health and high profits. In the face of the potential for profits in trade and dwindling profits or losses in cloth production, there was little reason for the Venetian capitalist to linger in the latter. His investment, like that of all early industrialists, was limited. Faced with difficulty, he simply sold his merchandise as best he could and started afresh elsewhere or in a different business.

Leiden and Venice, taken together, tell us something about the ways the crisis evolved and the reasons it persisted. If we define an industry as the production of a certain product in a certain place, we can say that the textile industries of Venice and Leiden lost their competitive edge because of rigidities on the production side that could not keep up with changes in demand. Those rigidities need careful specification. Industrial centers were not unable to change products—both Leiden and Venice had done so quite effectively in the sixteenth century. Nor, in this case, can we blame an abrupt fall-off in demand, something that did happen from time to time in the seventeenth century. War, inflation, and devaluation caused an abrupt fall-off in German demand for English woolen textiles after 1615.[39] This was not so in Leiden and Venice, where price was a major rigidity. Industrialists in Leiden and Venice could not—or would not—lower their prices to compete with newer manufacturing regions that had access to lower-cost labor, the crucial expense that seemingly could not be reduced.

Nördlingen

The Swabian town of Nördlingen shows the second crisis of urban industry in a somewhat different way.[40] Its masters specialized in the production of *loden*, a coarse woolen cloth. Fully one out of six of its adult male citizens in the seventeenth century was a member of the wool-weaving craft. At the beginning of the seventeenth century, the industry was both regulated and free, the goal being to guarantee an equal income to all members of the craft. Regulations stated that all weavers should have equal access to wool, and that they be able to sell their finished cloth. No one could hoard wool, and merchants could not monopolize the supply entering from the countryside. The role open to merchants was a simple one: they could buy cloths from the weavers at the going price and sell them outside the city. The role of the merchants increased during the seventeenth century, just as the independence of the weavers waned.

The problem that faced the weavers and opened up new opportunities for the merchants was a result of the diminution of local markets. The town's population fell by half during the Thirty Years' War, and its control over its hinterland diminished. Thus not only was the number of potential customers less; the town's ability to enforce rules that prohibited the manufacture of cloth in the countryside (at lower cost) deteriorated. Rural cloth immediately captured the rural market, if not the export market. A substantial market for the kind of cloth produced in Nördlingen continued to exist in Switzerland, but only the merchants— not the weavers—had the capital and the time to carry cloth there and sell it. The weavers did not have the resources to invest in the long process of converting raw wool to a product for sale in a distant export market, so they came increasingly to depend on loans and advances from the merchants. And yet despite the increasing role played by the merchants, the weaving craft maintained much of its traditional organization until the end of the middle third of the seventeenth century.

The brutal transformation of the Nördlingen woolen industry began after 1650 and was the work of two merchants, Daniel Wörner and his son of the same name. By 1680 the Wörners were the leading exporters of loden cloth from Nördlingen, because they undersold their competition in the Swiss market. One example of this process occurred in 1697. The problem began when the Wörners stopped paying for cloth on receipt and instead paid only after they had sold it on the Swiss market, crediting to the weaver an amount determined unilaterally by the Wörners on the basis of the price they received. Besides delaying payment to the weavers, this procedure allowed the Wörners gradually to lower the prices they paid for cloth. When the weavers complained, the Wörners agreed anew to pay a fixed price on receipt if other merchants did so as well. The initial agreed-upon price was 14½ florins per piece of loden, but the Wörners were not to be defeated. Because of their large capital resources, they undersold their competitors on the Swiss market by offering "drastically reduced prices." This allowed them to drive their competitors out of the market completely and to offer the weavers whatever price the Wörners wanted. As Christopher Friedrichs, the historian who has written about the Wörners and Nördlingen, reports, "In the course of a few months the price had dropped first to 13 and then to 11½ fl."[41] Meanwhile, the Wörners controlled the supply of raw wool, which they sold at a price of 40 florins per hundredweight, enough to make three pieces of loden. The weavers were losing money.

The weavers, indebted to the Wörners because of earlier credit transactions, could not stop working even at a loss and were on their way to lives as salaried workers, no longer independent masters. The Wörner family's dominance increased during the early eighteenth century. Despite a 1698 city council ruling that forced them to pay a 4,000 florin penalty to the weavers, and the creation of a short-lived sales cooperative of masters, the family prevailed in their hesitant steps to create a capitalist-dominated industry in Nördlingen and its hinterland.

The story of Nördlingen and the Wörners is the story of a crisis of profits produced by the lowering of prices and the closing of markets to traditional producers. The Nördlingen weavers fell under the control of the Wörners because they had difficulty making a profit given the prevailing price for the commodity they produced. Second, the new organization created by the Wörners—a *Verlagssystem*, to use the appropriate German term—concentrated economic power in the hands of a very small group. Although the Wörners themselves faded from power in the mid-eighteenth century, it is precisely the masters of new forms of economic organization who accumulated the kinds of markets and capital that made the later transformation from *Verlagssystem* to factory possible and desirable. Nördlingen's experience reflects the basic nature of the industrial crisis and its importance in leading to modern industry.

Nördlingen's experience shows how competition operated to make small producers unprofitable and drive them out of independent business. Nördlingen was backward by the standards of industrial towns in the seventeenth century. The transformation to a system whereby merchants organized production from beginning to end took place earlier in the great cities. While Nördlingen and Verviers may have been somewhat similar in the seventeenth century, each supporting a substantial number of small producers, the "new" industrial towns such as Verviers operated without any regulations, giving merchants and would-be manufacturers much more freedom to maneuver. Nördlingen shows how new competitive environments eliminated profits in the seventeenth century, and how the rigidities of costs made adaptation by producers very difficult.

THE INDUSTRIAL CRISIS BEYOND TEXTILES

There was an industrial crisis in the seventeenth century, a turning point shaped by factors of supply and demand that led to new industrial leadership and new ways of producing textiles. That it occurred in textiles does not mean, however, that it occurred in other industries. There were a number of other industries in which we might look for a crisis. Construction vied with clothing in terms of overall importance and contribution to national product and incomes. But construction was by definition a local activity, one that responded to local supply and demand and specifically to the prosperity of individual communities. It cannot be compared with textiles. The metalwork industry is an alternative. Although not nearly as large as textiles, it was nonetheless important and growing. Metal goods were produced and exported in increasing quantities in the sixteenth and seventeenth centuries. If the locus of metal production began to change from urban to rural production we would be on the way to a broad generalization.

The Metals Industry

The metals industry was quite different from the textile industry in structure and location, as well as in markets. Virtually all textiles produced for large-scale trade eventually found their way to individual consumers for domestic use; the industry was distributed between town and country (with the majority of production still in cities at the beginning of the seventeenth century), but the sections of the industry that suffered the most during the seventeenth century were located in cities. The metals industry was very different. Primary metal production took place in the countryside, while finished goods were produced almost equally in town and country. Moreover, the market for the large-scale production of metal goods—tools, nails, and weapons—was destined for military use, for the construction of ships and houses, or for individual (but not necessarily domestic) use in farm or shop. The market for metal products reflected quite different forces than did the market for textiles. Mere population size and incomes had a proportionally smaller impact, while the volume of overseas trade and the level of military activity had a much larger impact. Fashion played no role at all. Because less metal work took place in cities, even a downturn in demand would not have had the concentrated impact of a decline in the demand for textiles.

There was not a crisis in the Liégeois metalwork industry in the seventeenth century. Its principal products were armaments and small hardware items, especially nails. The market grew during the century to supply the growing Dutch shipbuilding industry and to supply armies that grew larger as the century progressed. There was no crisis, no more than an occasional slump for a year or two. Only in the eighteenth century did the nailmaking industry suffer, as it became more rigid and vulnerable to competitors who used better iron to make harder nails.

In other metalworking regions, the experience was essentially the same as around Liège. The armament industry cities in Italy—Brescia, Milan, and others—did well in the seventeenth century. In part this was in response to consistent orders from the Spanish armies that passed through Lombardy on their way along the "Spanish Road" to the Low Countries.[42] The same can be said for the German and English cities that competed (albeit to a lesser extent) with the Liégeois and Italians. The agricultural uses of iron did not grow as much in Germany and Italy—where populations were fairly stable—as in England, the Low Countries, and Scandinavia. In the more dynamic economies of northern and western Europe, demand for metal goods rose so rapidly in the seventeenth century that there continued to be opportunities for all the producers, even with the introduction of new ones, such as Sweden.[43] Some of the large metalworking centers faced an energy crisis, a consequence not so much of slower growth in the seventeenth century as the aftereffect of more rapid growth in the sixteenth. Fuel became difficult to find in some parts of Europe because earlier demand for charcoal and wood had led to deforestation. That seems to have occurred in Italy and in Britain.[44] This gave further advantage to Scandinavian producers, who faced no such shortage, and to those in Liège, who had access to coal and knew how to use it for their needs. A characteristic set of factors influenced the metalwork industry, insulating it from the forces that reshaped textiles. The first influence on metalwork in the seventeenth century was its location and structure, always spread widely in Europe and often located outside cities and their regulatory environment. With this structure and location it is unlikely that the metalwork industry could have experienced the kind of urban crisis suffered by textiles. It was not big enough, not regulated enough, not urban enough. The second influence on the metals industry was its relationship to the state. Much of the strength of seventeenth-century metalwork came from the continuing stream of orders for weapons. These were possible despite the cyclical downturn in the economy because the great states continued to gain power and to need weapons for war and domestic peacekeeping. The metals industry grew and continued strong because the rise of state power made monarchs supreme and confirmed a new universe of international relations—with France, England, Austria, and Prussia at its center.

The Papermaking Industry

The papermaking industry shows a somewhat different pattern, it too shaped by the impact of state power. Papermaking was not an exclusively urban industry, because it demanded water and wind- or water-power.[45] The principal steps were the final preparation of the pulp, the manufacture of each sheet of paper by filling a mold evenly with wet pulp of the desired thickness, and the drying of the sheet by squeezing it in a press and then hanging it up. In the sixteenth and seventeenth centuries the French luxury papermakers had a very large market—perhaps a dominant one—throughout Europe.[46] Their position deteriorated in the 1680s, when high-quality paper production began to move to the Netherlands and England. The decline of the French paper industry had more to do with the state and the "state crisis" than with the cyclical crisis that transformed the textile industry. One cause of the decline of the French industry was the revocation of the Edict of Nantes and the emigration of Protestant workers. The importance of this factor should not be exaggerated, because there were not very many Protestants in the French regions in which papermaking was important.[47] It is nonetheless the case that there was emigration in the 1680s and that the Protestant emigrés to England and the Netherlands brought with them skills that bolstered already developing industries. The result was a large-scale development of rural papermaking in the two countries.[48]

The problem in French papermaking in the late seventeenth and early eighteenth centuries went beyond French religious policy to French foreign policy. This was an era in which France waged a series of aggressive wars—from 1689 to 1697 (the War of the Spanish Succession). The results were barriers—in the form of either high tariffs or wartime prohibitions against trade with the enemy—to the entry of French paper into its former markets. Exports of all French products, including paper, suffered. This situation gave foreign competitors an opportunity to develop their own home industries, at the expense of French producers.

A Crisis or Just a Turning Point?

The seventeenth century was a turning point in the history of European industry. Was it a crisis? That depends on the definition one chooses. Surely there was an urban industrial crisis in the textile industry. It was brought about by shrinking demand coupled with high costs and regulation in cities. A different transformation took place in other industries—those that were smaller, less urban, and less driven by consumer demand. The state experienced a dramatic turning point in the seventeenth century, a crisis in the sense that it would not afterward be the same. State power impelled demand for the military segment of the metals industry, so that the dramatic growth of the state insulated the industry from stagnant consumer demand. The growth of state power also shaped other industries, such as papermaking. As it had for Flemish textiles in the Middle Ages, the closing of borders to luxury products because of war hurt French paper in the seventeenth century. New competitors—in this case the English and the Dutch—were strengthened while their borders were closed to French products. The growth of the state and the rise of new forms of protectionism made the consequences all the more rapidly felt.

The conclusions we should draw reflect, first, the ways that demand evolved in different industries, and then, the ways that competition and industrial organization adapted to meet changing demand. While it would be an error to state that demand drove the economy in early modern Europe, its role in shaping the relative development of different industries was vitally important. Consumer industries, such as textiles (leather would be another example), were subject to changes in population and incomes. Therefore they grew in the sixteenth century. Political instability in the sixteenth century, moreover, concentrated much of that century's growth in certain cities—for example Leiden and Venice—that were relatively immune to war and other trade difficulties. In the seventeenth century a slackening in population growth and in the incomes of consumers of exported textiles limited demand. At the same time, as the international political and military climate changed, the conditions that had sustained Venice and Leiden (and even Nördlingen) changed. They were no longer protected against competitors who were not saddled with high labor costs, and eventually their industries succumbed to the combined pressures of reduced demand, lower prices, and competitors employing new organizational techniques.

In metalwork the same conditions were not yet ready to operate in the seventeenth century. Demand remained strong, so even potentially inefficient operators prospered. Only in the eighteenth century—as we will see—did some of them lose their markets to the more efficient and the makers of better products. Papermaking shows another side of the seventeenth century as economic turning point. It was free of the organizational and pricing pressures felt by the textile industry; but like much of French industry it was rocked by political forces at the end of the seventeenth century. As the state grew in power it was able in a variety of ways to shape economic life. The seventeenth century was a turning point because it was the time in which that strength became sufficient to really shape industrial development, for better or worse.

When major industrial cities lost markets for their products before the seventeenth century, they usually came up with something new to manufacture. The infrastructure that supported industrial production and trade was so strong that some new product was eventually found. Was this still the case in the seventeenth century? Admittedly, there are not many examples of earlier industrial decline, but those few seem reasonably clear. Leiden, of course, is one. Its traditional product unwanted in the sixteenth century, it found new products and prospered again. There are other examples in the Low Countries, including Brussels, Bruges, and Ghent.[49] We must believe that the infrastructure of craftsmen and traders remained strong enough to find new products and new markets.

This process of finding new products and new markets seems to end in the seventeenth century. The industrial crisis of the seventeenth century did not by itself eliminate all urban forms of industry; many industrial cities maintained and even expanded their production. But, for those cities that suffered some sort of industrial decline, it was nearly permanent, lasting until the advent of mechanized industry (in the nineteenth century in most of continental Europe). Industrial decline usually occurred because manufacturers were undersold by their competitors at the low-quality end of their line of products. The pressure this placed on them led gradually to concentration on higher-quality and higher-priced products, as they compensated for losses to regions with less skilled—and thus lower-priced—labor by turning their efforts to products for which they had no effective competition. From the late fifteenth century until the first third of the seventeenth century, this movement on the part of industrial cities toward luxury products was successful, as Europe grew and incomes became more concentrated in the hands of the elite. Luxury goods sold, and any industrial center skilled enough to produce them found ready markets for its output.

In the seventeenth century the markets for exported manufactured goods of high quality changed.[50] As mentioned earlier, incomes and population growth in the peripheral areas leveled off, so that any competition for those markets was felt very keenly. This is what happened to Venice, undersold by the English and Dutch in the Middle Eastern market for very high quality cloth. The producer's natural response was to shift upward once more in the kind of manufactured products he sold; but in the seventeenth century this shift was thwarted. First, and most simply, the gradual evolution of production had already pushed quality and cost to a level that severely limited markets. Only the truly wealthy could afford very expensive cloth or works of art, for example. Second, the population of the truly wealthy was increasingly to be found not scattered uniformly throughout Europe but more and more concentrated in the growing centralized states. These were exactly the states that in the seventeenth century were increasing their dependence on production at home, both because of mercantilist pressures to limit imports and increase exports, and because the presence of a large domestic market made domestic production worthwhile. Finally, much of the luxury industry that prospered in the cities of the Low Countries was focused on the production of Counter Reformation art objects. These markets were tiny, never capable of supporting an industrial population. As the Counter Reformation matured, and the baroque style gradually lost importance, these urban luxury industries lost what small markets they had.

Can we say that mercantilism and the intimately related growth of the state caused the death knell of urban industry for export in Europe? While it might be argued that the end of large export markets for luxury goods produced by urban craftsmen was part of a larger process that also included the growth of rural industries that produced low- and moderate-priced goods, even this explanation would make the story too simple.[51] First, most cities retained their relative importance within their regions, giving up some functions but retaining and even gaining others.[52] In most regions, towns and cities were organized into networks that provided services to their hinterlands. A hierarchical scale of urban places existed, each one providing more specialized services and goods to those further down the scale. At the top were the great capitals and international centers of trade and industry; they served the most specialized needs. At the bottom were very tiny towns of one or two thousand inhabitants; they served only a few nearby villages. Even rural industry needed an urban infrastructure to organize it.[53] Once the urban network was in place the advantages of rural industry could be exploited. The cities were built in the sixteenth century; in the seventeenth and eighteenth centuries rural industry could develop.

Although mercantilism and state power played important roles, the overall change that took place had much to do with larger cyclical changes, which transformed both supply and demand and encouraged early industrialists to concentrate their activities in new areas. The industrial crisis of the seventeenth century brought on the end of much, but not all, urban industry. Some of the older cities lost their prominence, but industry still existed and flourished in others. Moreover, the need for concentration, even before mechanization took complete hold, meant that new cities, such as Verviers, would grow up. What the seventeenth-century crisis of urban industry sounded was the death knell not of urban industry but of urban industry organized in traditional ways.

NOTES

1. Jan de Vries, *The Economy of Europe in an Age of Crisis: 1600–1750* (Cambridge: Cambridge University Press, 1976), p. 86.
2. The economic history of Leiden's woolen cloth industry has been extensively studied. Most of the information about Leiden in this chapter is drawn from N. W. Posthumus, *De geschiedenis van de Leidsche lakenindustrie* (The Hague: M. Nijhoff, 1939), vols. 2 and 3. On the competition between Leiden and the Verviers region, see N. W. Posthumus, "De industrieele concurentie tusschen noord- en zuid-nederlandsche nijverheidscentra in de XVIIe en XVIIIe eeuw," in *Mélanges d'histoire offerts à Henri Pirenne*, ed H. van der Linden and F. L. Ganshoff, 2 vols. (Brussels: Vromaut & Co., 1926), 2:369–379. On Leiden's evolution in comparison with that of Lille, see Robert S. Duplessis and Martha S. Howell, "Reconsidering the Early Modern Urban Economy: The Cases of Leiden and Lille," *Past & Present* 94 (1982): 49–84.
3. Emile Coornaert, *Un centre industriel d'autrefois: La draperie-sayetterie d'Hondschoote (XIVe–XVIIIe siècles)* (Paris: Presses Universitaires de France, 1930); and Posthumus, *Leidsche lakenindustrie*, vol. 2.
4. Coornaert, *Un centre industriel*, pp. 492–495; and Posthumus, *Leidsche lakenindustrie*, 2:6.
5. Coornaert, *Un centre industriel*, pp. 35–44.
6. Posthumus, *Leidsche lakenindustrie*, 2:40–104.
7. Ibid., 2:153–188, 3:879–924.
8. Ibid., 2:105–136.
9. D. C. Coleman, "An Innovation and Its Diffusion: The New Draperies," *Economic History Review*, 2nd ser., 22 (1969): 417–429.
10. Posthumus, *Leidsche lakenindustrie*, 3:930–931.
11. Ibid., 3:1098–1099.
12. Posthumus, "De industrieele concurentie"; and Henri Laurent, "La concurrence entre les centres industriels des provinces-unies et de la principauté de Liège au XVIIe et XVIIIe siècles et les origines de la grande industrie drapière verviétoise," *Revue d'Histoire Moderne* 2 (1927): 216–219.

13. Emile Fairon, *Les industries du pays de Verviers* (Verviers, 1922). Reprinted as "Histoire économique de pays de Verviers," *BSVAH* 43 (1956): 11–42.
14. Posthumus, *Leidsche lakenindustrie*, 3:883–924.
15. Posthumus, "Industrieele concurentie," p. 376; Jan de Vries, "An Inquiry into the Behavior of Wages in the Dutch Republic and the Southern Netherlands from 1580 to 1800," in *Dutch Capitalism and World Capitalism*, ed. Maurice Aymard (Cambridge: Cambridge University Press, 1982), pp. 37–61.
16. Posthumus, "Industrieele concurentie"; Laurent, "La concurrence entre les centres industriels"; and Fairon, *Les industries du pays de Verviers*.
17. Charles Wilson, "Cloth Production and International Competition in the Seventeenth Century," *Economic History Review*, 2nd ser., 13 (1960): 209–221; and Barry E. Supple, *Commercial Crisis and Change in England, 1600–1642: A Study in the Instability of a Mercantile Economy* (Cambridge: Cambridge University Press, 1959).
18. Pierre Lebrun, *L'industrie de la laine à Verviers pendant le XVIIIe et le début du XIXe siècle. Contribution à l'étude des origines de la révolution industrielle* (Liège: Faculté de Philosophie et Lettres, 1948).
19. For a bibliography of the crisis debate, see Theodore K. Rabb, *The Struggle for Stability in Early Modern Europe* (New York: Oxford University Press, 1975).
20. Geoffrey Parker, *The Thirty Years' War* (London: Routledge & Kegan Paul, 1984).
21. *The Random House College Dictionary*, rev. ed. s.v. "crisis."
22. Eric J. Hobsbawm, "The Overall Crisis of the European Economy in the Seventeenth Century," *Past & Present* 5 (1954): 33–53 (reprinted in *Crisis in Europe, 1560–1660*, ed. Trevor Aston [Garden City, N.Y.: Doubleday Anchor, 1967], pp. 5–62).
23. Rabb, *Struggle for Stability*, Chapter 9: "Economics, Demography, and Social Relations," pp. 83–99; and Niels Steensgaard, "The Seventeenth-Century Crisis," in *The General Crisis of the Seventeenth Century*, ed. Geoffrey Parker and Lesley M. Smith (London: Routledge & Kegan Paul, 1978), pp. 26–56.
24. De Vries, *The Economy of Europe in an Age of Crisis*.
25. H. R. Trevor-Roper, "The General Crisis of the Seventeenth Century," *Past & Present* 16 (1959): 31–64 (reprinted in Aston, *Crisis in Europe*, pp. 63–102); and J. H. Elliott, "Revolution and Continuity in Early Modern Europe," *Past & Present* 42 (1969): 35–56 (reprinted in Parker & Smith, *The General Crisis of the Seventeenth Century*, pp. 110–133). See also the discussion in Rabb, *Struggle for Stability*, and in Parker's introduction to *The General Crisis*.
26. There are two collections of essays, one including the original debate in *Past & Present* (Aston, *Crisis in Europe*, published in 1967) and one including later contributions (Parker and Smith, *The General Crisis of the Seventeenth Century*, published in 1978). The reader is well advised to begin with the Hobsbawm and Trevor-Roper essays in the earlier volume, and then turn to the more sophisticated essays

in the Parker and Smith collection. Rabb, *Struggle for Stability,* is useful for its synthesis and its attempt to put the terminological disagreements on a solid footing.

27. De Vries, *The Economy of Europe in an Age of Crisis.*
28. Paul M. Hohenberg and Lynn Hollen Lees, *The Making of Urban Europe, 1000–1950* (Cambridge: Harvard University Press, 1985), pp. 113–120.
29. I am indebted to Paul Hohenberg for suggesting this point.
30. Posthumus, "Industrieele concurentie"; and Laurent, "La concurrence entre les centres industriels."
31. Warren C. Scoville, *The Persecution of the Huguenots and French Economic Development 1680–1720* (Berkeley: University of California Press, 1960).
32. The literature on demand in early modern Europe is quite limited. For a general view, see Walter Minchinton, "Patterns and Structure of Demand 1500–1750," in *The Fontana Economic History of Europe,* ed. Carlo M. Cipolla, 6 vols. (London: Fontana, 1974), 2:83–176; or Frederic Mauro, *Le XVIe siècle Européen. Aspects économiques* (Paris: Presses Universitaires de France, 1966), pp. 152–208.
33. Roger Mols, "Population in Europe, 1500–1700," in *The Fontana Economic History of Europe,* ed. Carlo M. Cipolla, 6 vols. (London: Fontana, 1974), 2:15–82. There are somewhat more recent figures in Jan de Vries, *European Urbanization 1500–1800* (Cambridge: Harvard University Press, 1984).
34. Domenico Sella, "The Rise and Fall of the Venetian Woolen Industry," in *Crisis and Change in the Venetian Economy in the Sixteenth and Seventeenth Centuries,* ed. Brian Pullan (London: Methuen, 1968), pp. 106–126. Except where otherwise noted, I follow Sella's argument and evidence.
35. Ibid., p. 117.
36. Ibid., p. 120.
37. Myron P. Gutmann, "The Dynamics of Urban Decline in the Late Middle Ages and Early Modern Times: Economic Responses and Social Effects," in *Ninth International Economic History Congress, Bern, 1986: Debates and Controversies* (Zurich: Verlag der Fachvereine, 1986), pp. 23–56; and Sella, "The Rise and Fall of the Venetian Woolen Industry."
38. Paul Klep, "Urban Decline in Brabant: The Traditionalization of Investments and Labour, 1374–1806," paper presented at the Ninth International Economic History Congress, Bern, August, 1986. On the "traditionalization of investments" in Leiden, see Maartin Prak, *Gezeten burgers. De elite in een Hollandse Stad. Leiden 1700–1780* (Amsterdam: Bataafsche Leeu, 1985).
39. Supple, *Commercial Crisis and Change.* The section on the problems imposed by different rates of inflation and their impact on prices and competition is especially important.
40. Christopher R. Friedrichs, *Urban Society in an Age of War: Nördlingen, 1580–1720* (Princeton: Princeton University Press, 1979); Friedrichs, "Early Capitalism and Its Enemies: The Wörner Family and

the Weavers of Nördlingen," *Business History Review* 50 (1976): 265–287; and Friedrichs, "Capitalism, Mobility, and Class Formation in the Early Modern German City," *Past & Present* 69 (1975): 24–49.

41. Friedrichs, "Early Capitalism and Its Enemies," p. 279.

42. Domenico Sella, "The Iron Industry in Italy 1500–1650," in *Schwerpunkte der Eisengewinnung und Eisenverarbeitung in Europe 1500–1650*, ed. Hermann Kellenbenz (Cologne: Böhlau Verlag, 1974), pp. 91–105. On Milanese industry, see Sella, *Crisis and Continuity: The Economy of Spanish Lombardy in the Seventeenth Century* (Cambridge, Mass.: Harvard University Press, 1979), pp. 57–58. On the Spanish Road, see Geoffrey Parker, *The Army of Flanders and the Spanish Road* (Cambridge: Cambridge University Press, 1972).

43. Domenico Sella, "European Industries 1500–1750," in *The Fontana Economic History of Europe*, ed. Carlo M. Cipolla, 6 vols. (London: Fontana, 1974), 2:354–426.

44. Sella, "The Iron Industry in Italy," pp. 101–102; and Brinley Thomas, "Was There an Energy Crisis in Great Britain in the 17th Century?" *Explorations in Economic History* 23 (1986): 124–152.

45. See the map of the distribution of paper mills in England in D. C. Coleman, *The British Paper Industry 1485–1860* (Oxford: Clarendon Press, 1958), p. 57.

46. Ibid; and Scoville, *The Persecution of the Huguenots*, pp. 230–237.

47. This is the conclusion drawn by Scoville in *The Persecution of the Huguenots*.

48. Coleman, *The British Paper Industry;* Robert S. Duplessis, "Capital and Finance in the Early Modern Veluwe Paper Industry," *A.A.G. Bijdragen* 28 (1986): 185–198; and H. K. Roessingh, "Het Veluwse Inwonertal, 1526–1947," *A.A.G. Bijdragen* 11 (1964): 79–150.

49. Herman van der Wee, "De industriële ontwikkeling in de Nederlanden tijdens de 17de–18de eeuw. Enkele kritische bemerkingen naar aanleiding van het debat over de proto-industrie en poging tot aanvulling van het synthese-model," *Academiae Analecta* 46 (1984): 59–77; and van der Wee, "L'économie citadine dans les Pays-Bas méridionaux et dans la principauté épiscopale de Liège aux XVIe et XVIIe siècles," in *Splendeurs d'Espagne et les villes belges 1500–1700* (Brussels: Credit Communal, 1985), pp. 107–122.

50. Van der Wee, "L'économie citadine."

51. Steensgaard, in "The Seventeenth-Century Crisis," feels that the political aspects of the crisis, as a reaction to absolutism, are most important.

52. See the discussion and the papers cited in Myron P. Gutmann, "The Dynamics of Urban Decline in the Late Middle Ages and Early Modern Times."

53. De Vries, *European Urbanization*, pp. 240–241.

CHAPTER 5

Industry and Population Growth in Eighteenth-Century Europe

The events of the seventeenth century transformed European industry. Most dramatically in textiles, but also in other sectors, those transformations led in the eighteenth century to industrial growth, new industrial centers, and more rural industry. In a simultaneous change the European population grew, in both cities and villages. The approach taken in this book de-emphasizes the importance of population for seventeenth-century events, but in the eighteenth century we see how closely the processes of change were linked: population growth begot industry, and vice versa.

Where population and the growth of industry were most intimately linked, a new pattern of demographic and social behavior developed, which itself reinforced growth. The industrial growth of the eighteenth century was both cause and consequence of a great increase in rural industry and in agricultural production. Where these changes took place the part of the rural population that was made up of farmers diminished. A rural proletariat grew up, and this rural proletariat of agricultural wage laborers and industrial workers behaved somewhat differently from their neighbors and relatives among the peasant population. They were more inclined to marry early, which led them to have more children. This reinforced the basic pattern of population and economic growth. A reciprocal movement occurred in which population and economy reinforced each other, and eventually a new social system developed in the industrial villages and small towns.

The first key to understanding the process described in this chapter is the level of economic and industrial growth that took place in the eighteenth century. Spurred by the stimulus of seventeenth-century events, growth was strong during most of the eighteenth century. The industrial component of that growth was probably stronger than historians once thought, and cottage industry represented most of the difference. Once we see the important role played by traditional industry operated in established ways, we can turn to population growth. An enlarged rural proletariat explains a significant part of eighteenth-century population growth, and in the second part of this chapter we will see how that population grew.

Industry was important in the eighteenth century, but agriculture was still more important. Most people still lived in the countryside, even at the century's end. In 1800, only 9.4 percent lived in towns of 10,000 or more, and only 12.1 percent in towns of 5,000 or more (see Table 5.1).[1] In the most advanced regions of northern and western Europe (England, the Low Countries, and Scandinavia), the figure is only half again higher: 14.7 percent lived in towns of 10,000 or more. What this means is that at least 85 out of 100 Europeans lived in tiny towns and country villages at the end of the old regime. Still more had lived in the countryside 150 years earlier. In 1650, 8 percent of Europeans had lived in towns of 10,000 or more, and 10.6 percent in towns of 5,000 or more; in the developed north and west, only 10.7 percent had lived in towns of 10,000 or more. These percentages may hide the real number of urban Europeans in the last century of the old regime. Around 1800, some 12 million people lived in towns of 10,000 or more; around 1650, only 6 million did. While not considerable in comparison with today's urban agglomerations, the number of city and town dwellers indicates that many people earned their livelihood away from the land.

By the eighteenth century most Europeans still lived in the countryside, but there were a significant number of city and town dwellers. Moreover, while agriculture was still dominant, not even all those who lived in the countryside worked in farming. The role played by industry in the European economy of the eighteenth century was very important, and we see this importance in the few quantitative estimates that are available. In the past few years these estimates have been revised to increase the importance of industry at the beginning of the eighteenth century, and to lower growth rates during the years of the Industrial Revolution. We now see eighteenth-century development as a much more gradual process.

Table 5.1: Urbanization in Europe, 1650–1800

	1650	1800
PERCENT OF TOTAL POPULATION RESIDING IN CITIES OF 10,000 OR MORE		
All Europe	8.0%	9.4%
Northwestern Europe	10.7%	14.7%
CITIES OF 5,000 OR MORE		
All Europe	10.6%	12.1%

SOURCE: Jan de Vries, "Patterns of Urbanization in Pre-Industrial Europe, 1500–1800," in *Patterns of European Urbanisation Since 1500* (London: Croom Helm, 1981), p. 88.

INDUSTRY'S IMPORTANCE IN EIGHTEENTH-CENTURY EUROPE

Nowhere is the importance of eighteenth-century industry more striking than in the case of France. France lagged behind England—and even Belgium—in the adoption of mechanized industry in the late eighteenth and nineteenth centuries. Yet in the eighteenth century industry made up a large part of its total economy. At the beginning of the century, "industry and handicrafts" made up 26 percent of the gross physical product of France (the physical product is the "goods" part of the "goods, services, and investments" that make up gross national product).[2] By the 1780s the level of industry had risen to 39 percent, and by the first decade of the nineteenth century it had climbed to 43 percent (this despite the Revolution). England's economy was even more industrial than that of France.[3] At the beginning of the eighteenth century 37 percent of the total physical product of England was industrial.[4] By 1770 the figure had climbed to 42 percent. At the end of the Napoleonic Wars, in 1815, industry made up roughly half of the total physical output of the English economy.

Industry was already strong at the beginning of the eighteenth century. It then grew steadily. Whereas older estimates of growth rates for English industry would lead us to draw different conclusions, two sets of rates published in the 1980s make possible this new interpretation. Table 5.2 presents the estimates published by Deane and W. A. Cole in 1967, contrasted with the newer estimates by C. Knick Harley and N. F. R. Crafts. A jump in production came only after 1815. What is important and worth noting about these revised estimates is that the revisions are largely based on downward reevaluations of the role played by the cotton industry, usually seen as the most important part of the Industrial Revolution. A diminished cotton industry in the eighteenth century leaves us with the solid, if unexciting, tradi-

Table 5.2: Growth in English Industry—Various Estimates, 1700–1815 (% per annum)

ESTIMATES BY PHYLLIS DEANE AND W. A. COLE (1967)	
	Industry and Commerce
1700–1760	0.98
1760–1780	0.49
1780–1801	3.43

ESTIMATES BY N. F. R. CRAFTS (1983)			
	Industry	Commerce	Industry and Commerce
1700–1760	0.71	0.69	0.70
1760–1780	1.51	0.70	1.05
1780–1801	2.11	1.32	1.81

ESTIMATES BY C. KNICK HARLEY (1982)*		
	Industrial Production	Industrial Demand
1700–1770		0.8
1770–1815	1.4–1.6	1.4

*Harley estimates industrial growth in two ways, using estimates of industrial production and using estimates of demand for industrial goods.

SOURCES: Phyllis Deane and W. A. Cole, *British Economic Growth, 1688–1959: Trends and Structure*, 2nd ed. (Cambridge: Cambridge University Press, 1967), p. 78 (growth rates calculated by N. F. R. Crafts); N. F. R. Crafts, "British Economic Growth, 1700–1831: A Review of the Evidence," *Economic History Review*, 2nd ser., 36 (1983): 185; and C. Knick Harley, "British Industrialization Before 1841: Evidence of Slower Growth During the Industrial Revolution," *Journal of Economic History* 42 (1982): 276, 284.

tional industries, the largest of which were woolen textiles, iron, and leather. Per capita industrial production was higher in England than elsewhere, but we would expect to find the same distribution of production by industry in every other European country.

No other countries offer even the crude estimates available for England and France. But the Low Countries appear to have been as industrialized as England, if not more so. One often-cited figure reports that only one-third of the population of the Netherlands was employed in agriculture at the end of the seventeenth century, as opposed to two-thirds in England.[5] Estimates of the breakdown of gross physical product into agriculture and manufacturing are difficult to obtain for the eighteenth century, but it is safe to assume that what are now Belgium and the Netherlands were at least roughly equivalent to England—that 35 to 40 percent of their production was industrial in the eighteenth century.[6] It is clear, however, that the relative distribution of industry in the two was changing at that time, with the Netherlands becoming less industrialized and Belgium more so.[7] Table 5.3 shows comparative levels of industrialization in the eighteenth and nineteenth centuries, on a per capita basis, as a percentage of levels of United Kingdom industrialization in 1900. In 1750, Belgium, France, and the United Kingdom were almost equal—at 9–10 percent of the level of industrialization the United Kingdom would later reach. By 1800, the United Kingdom had jumped ahead, with Belgium and Switzerland second. The same was still true in 1860. The rest of Europe was less industrialized overall than England, France, Switzerland, and Belgium. Nevertheless, there were pockets of intense industrial activity in the western parts of what is now Germany, in the north of Italy, and elsewhere.

While Europe remained predominantly rural and agricultural in the eighteenth century, manufacturing had already become a major activity. Moreover, industrial production appears to have grown more rapidly than the economy as a whole, and more rapidly than did the population: per capita gross physical product grew, and per capita industrial product grew even more. This was the case in France, in England and the Low Countries, and for Europe as a whole. Finally, the size and growth of the industrial sector of the European economy was a characteristic of the entire

Table 5.3:   Per-Capita Industrialization Levels
in Europe, 1750-1860
(United Kingdom in 1900 = 100;
1913 boundaries)

	1750	1800	1860
Belgium	9	10	28
France	9	9	20
United Kingdom	10	16	64
Switzerland	7	10	26
Germany	8	8	15
Italy	8	8	10

SOURCE: Paul Bairoch, "International Industrialization
Levels from 1750 to 1980," *Journal of European Economic
History* 11 (1982): 281.

century, not just the last twenty-five years, when mechanized
factories were introduced in England for the spinning of cotton
thread.

The innovations of the Industrial Revolution made only a
small contribution in the eighteenth century. We can see this in
the evolution of various industries in England. Table 5.4 lists
the percentage contribution of various British industries to total
production in 1770 and 1815. Cotton, the first industry to
mechanize, represented only 1 percent of industrial production
in 1770, and only 8 percent in 1815. Metal products, the other
innovative sector, contributed only 5 percent in 1770 and 8 percent in 1815. On the other hand, older industries were still important: wool, linen, clothing, leather, and building. All these
were mechanized, and they changed technically much later than
cotton or metalwork. Not every historian will agree with the
exact figures presented in Table 5.4.[8] What they will agree with
is the continued growth and importance in the eighteenth century of the traditional industries, and the relatively light contribution made by the revolutionized industries before 1800.
Moreover, it is now clear that industrial growth in the eighteenth century was slower and more gradual than was previously thought. Levels of production at the beginning of the
century were fairly high, and they grew steadily but not geomet-
rically. The two very recent sets of estimates reported in Table
5.2 are set up alongside an older estimate, that published in

1967 by Phyllis Deane and W. A. Cole. The new estimates show that growth was substantial prior to the last two decades of the eighteenth century, and although great thereafter, not so great as had once been thought.

Industry prospered and grew before the Industrial Revolution because of the continued strength and expansion of the rural segment of traditional production. What large-scale industry had existed as early as the Middle Ages was largely confined to towns, which were the only places capable of sustaining dense economic activities such as manufacturing for export. Their strength was reinforced by government regulation. By the sixteenth century the growth of the central state as opposed to towns and principalities, and the development of better business communications, permitted new forms of industrial organization to challenge the corporate towns. The diminution of profits in the seventeenth century accelerated the process of change and gave a clear advantage to the new forms of industry that arose. These new organizational forms primarily used cottage industry organization, which lowered labor costs and centralized control of the

Table 5.4: Relative Importance of Various English Industries, 1770 and 1815 (in Percent)

	1770	1815
Textiles		
Cotton	1	8
Wool	15	11
Linen	8	6
Silk	4	2
Clothing	11	12
Leather	19	14
Metal	5	8
Food and drink	8	6
Paper and printing	1	2
Mining	5	8
Building	12	15
Other	12	9

SOURCE: C. Knick Harley, "British Industrialization Before 1841: Evidence of Slower Growth During the Industrial Revolution," *Journal of Economic History* 42 (1982): 269.

production process in the hands of an entrepreneur. These improvements spurred industrial production.

The strengthening of cottage industry in the eighteenth century links the industrial history of earlier periods to the later Industrial Revolution, which brought mechanization and social change. Its role as a connector between prior developments and subsequent changes is more important than its role as precursor of revolution. Some historians have given the name "protoindustrialization" to the rise of large-scale cottage industry in the late seventeenth and eighteenth centuries. To them, the renewed growth of rural industry in the eighteenth century is distinct from earlier rural industry and makes a contribution to the later process of industrialization in the factory.[9] Franklin Mendels is the most important among these historians, and this is his initial presentation of the role of "protoindustrialization":

> Well before the beginning of machine industry, many regions of Europe became increasingly industrialized in the sense that a growing proportion of their labor potential was allocated to industry. Yet, that type of industry—the traditionally organized, principally rural handicrafts—barely fits the image one has of a modernizing economy. There is, however, cognitive value as well as didactic advantage in thinking of the growth of "pre-industrial industry" as part and parcel of the process of "industrialization" or, rather, as a first phase which preceded and prepared modern industrialization proper.
>
> This first phase which, for lack of a better name, I will call protoindustrialization was not only marked by the rapid growth of traditionally organized but market-oriented, principally rural industry. It was also accompanied by changes in the spatial organization of the economy. . . . The second phase of modern, factory, or machine industrialization corresponded to mechanisms of economic change which were in sharp contrast with those of the first phase. In this context, the concept of "industrial revolution" could refer to the theoretical instant when an economy enters phase two.[10]

The growth of early industry is more than a way to move the beginning of the Industrial Revolution back by fifty or a hundred years. The rise of cottage industry connects earlier industrial growth with the advent of mechanization. The development of large-scale commercialized cottage industry for export, whether we call it protoindustrialization or something else, is important; but it is only one process among several in the long cycle of industrial change. This is no reason to dismiss the concepts that make up the idea of protoindustrialization. It is much more than a new way to describe large-scale cottage industry, or to stress its importance. The complete series of protoindustrialization hypotheses relates cottage industry to patterns of population growth and the emergence of new social forms, as well as to the later development of mechanized industry.[11] Needless to say, this formulation has been criticized.[12] Its contribution comes in reminding us of the strength of cottage industry before the Industrial Revolution and of the important links between population, social organization, and the economy.

We see the sustained strength of early industry in woolen textiles. In the eighteenth century, textile markets expanded almost everywhere. In England and France growth was episodic in the eighteenth century, but over the century as a whole both countries' industries expanded by a bit less than 1 percent per annum, on average (see Table 5.5).[13] Statistics for the Low Countries industry are difficult to find, but growth seems to have taken place at about the same overall pace. We can get an idea of this from the Verviers woolen industry. It did not grow without interruption, but it grew strongly in the eighteenth century.

It is difficult to quantify the growth of the Verviers woolen industry from 1650 to 1800. The region was divided among four sovereigns (Liège, Austria, the Dutch Republic and the German principality of Jülich), none of which kept very good records.[14] Each provides us with documentation for part of the period from the late seventeenth to the end of the eighteenth century, but none is complete or continuous. Even if more complete records had survived, we might doubt their validity. The region's manufacturers manipulated the system to minimize their taxes, and we should question whether they would have taken part honestly in any regulatory scheme that kept good records. The best evidence of their manipulation of the system was the division of the industry in Verviers between Verviers itself and Hodimont, its suburb (really only a street) on the other side of the Vesdre River.[15]

What evidence we have suggests that there were two distinct periods of growth in the Verviers textile industry. The first period was a "heroic age" of textile industry growth, which had begun by 1650 and ended in the 1740s; the second began around 1750 and continued until the construction of the first mechanized

Table 5.5:   Growth of Woolen Textile Production in Eighteenth-Century England and France (% per annum)

ENGLAND AND WALES
(measured in quantity of raw wool consumed)

1695–1741	0.78%
1741–1772	1.3 %
1772–1799	0.52%
1695–1799	0.87%

FRANCE

	Pieces of Cloth	Surface Area (in sq. *aunes*)*
1716/1718–1726/1728	0.15 %	0.60%
1726/1728–1748/1751	0.84	1.15
1748/1751–1775/1778	decline	0.09
1775/1778–1785/1787	1.81	2.56
1700/1702–1785/1787	0.72 %	0.93%

*The French data report both numbers of pieces of cloth and their volume, measured as square *aunes*, a surface measure. It is clear from the figures that while the number of pieces of cloth increased, so did the size of the average piece of cloth.
SOURCES: Phyllis Deane, "The Output of the British Woolen Industry in the Eighteenth Century," *Economic History Review*, 2nd ser., 17 (1957): 207–223; and Tihomar J. Markovitch, *Les industries lainières de Colbert à la Révolution* (Geneva: Librairie Droz, 1976).

factories after 1802. The first period was one of growth and conversion to large-scale early industry, punctuated by warfare and generally uncertain economic conditions from the 1670s until the 1700s. Although the quantitative evidence is sketchy, there is qualitative evidence to support these conclusions.[16] The industry was very strong in the peaceful years from 1650 until the early 1670s. Thereafter war brought on destruction and a long period of economic malaise throughout the region's economy. This malaise did not end until after the subsistence crises of the 1690s and 1700s. Then the textile business recovered before entering a level period, with a slight downward trend in the 1720s, that lasted until the 1740s. We can assume a growth rate above 1 percent per year for the half-century beginning in the 1680s.

The second period of growth in the Verviers textile industry took place after 1740 and was somewhat slower than the earlier period. Pierre Lebrun describes the growth of the Verviers-Hodimont industry as being at about 30 percent overall during the forty years from the late 1740s to the late 1780s.[17] That is a compounded annual growth rate of about .67 percent. If we add the additional—and more rapid—growth that took place in the secondary centers at Limburg, Herve, Eupen, and Monschau, the overall growth rate may have been as great as .8 to 1 percent, with most of the growth taking place during the last fifteen years of the old regime.[18]

PROLETARIANIZATION AND POPULATION GROWTH

Industry could not grow without consumers, but it was not yet large enough to generate its own. Rather, a general population increase sustained industrial growth. For western Europe as a whole, population had grown by 18 percent between 1550 and 1680. Between 1680 and 1820, the years of the eighteenth-century boom, it grew by 62 percent (see Table 5.6).[19] Historians have developed a number of theories to explain the growing populations of the eighteenth century. Some of these explanations depend heavily on local economic patterns, others cite broader economic development, and still others reflect a belief that a changing environment brought on the increases. Much of this discussion has centered on the growth of the English population, because England's growth was more rapid than that of any other European country.[20] Whereas some of the earliest discussions of this problem focused on rising fertility rates as an explanation for this phenomenon, most analysis done over the past forty years has cited lower mortality.[21] From the 1940s until the 1970s most historical demographers believed that Europe had an unvarying birth rate until the nineteenth century.[22] This belief in the "law of the constant birth rate" led historians to statements such as this one: "When birth- and death-rates are comparatively high, as they were at that time, it is very much easier to increase the population by reducing the death-rate than by increasing the birth-rate."[23] If the birth rate was constant, all the movement had to be in the death rate. For France, the tradition has emphasized the end of large-scale harvest failures after 1730, which in turn ended the periodic mortality crises.[24] This brought an end to the era of crises for France, and population could grow. For England, two explanations of the mortality decline have competed for attention, without any real resolution.[25] One of these explanations emphasizes the introduction of smallpox inoculation in the eighteenth century, which purportedly reduced the death rate. The other explanation rests on the improvement of diet, with the argument that improved agriculture, more nutritious crops such as the potato, and higher levels of general prosperity gave people better food, which subsequently lowered the death rate.

By the eighteenth century, population growth was more subject to change as a result of new marriage patterns and higher levels of fertility. We know this as a result of research published in the 1970s and 1980s, and now widely accepted. The population grew because a new social group developed that had fewer ties to the land and thus was more likely to marry even when its members could not expect to acquire a farm. The behavior of this group, a rural proletariat supported by piecework or daywork wages, depended on a Malthusian linkage of economic conditions with marriage, a linkage in which couples were more likely to marry in good times than in bad. Sustained prosperity lowered the age of marriage; and women who married younger bore more children. Some of the members of this group were agricultural workers. The rest were employed in cottage industry, so that they

Table 5.6: Population Growth Rates in Europe, 1550–1820 (in percentages)

	1550–1680	1680–1820
England	64	133
France	29	39
Netherlands	58	8
Spain	−6	64
Italy	9	53
Germany	0	51
Western Europe	18	62

SOURCE: E. A. Wrigley, "The Growth of Population in Eighteenth-Century England: A Conundrum Resolved," *Past & Present* 98 (1983): 122.

had few or no ties to agriculture. The size of both groups grew in the eighteenth century, while the size of the rural landowning population grew hardly at all, and the urban population grew rather more slowly.[26]

Any time we use the words "proletariat" or "proletarian" we risk confusion and intellectual prejudice. The proletariat was that part of society supported by wage labor. It had, by the nineteenth century, an identifiable social character—whether one agrees with Marx or not about its political aspirations. A rural proletariat made up of both agricultural and industrial workers grew up in the sixteenth, seventeenth, and eighteenth centuries, identified in part by contrast with its neighbors, the farm-operating peasantry. The proletarian model says that this social group had its own patterns of demographic behavior. Any circumstances that reduced economic constraints by offering new economic opportunities simultaneously reduced constraints on marriage and led to more marriage and higher levels of fertility. Charles Tilly proposes the following hypothesis:

> On the average, proletarians responded to economic expansion with greater declines in mortality and greater increases in fertility than nonproletarians did and responded to economic contraction with greater increases in mortality but no greater declines in fertility than nonproletarians did. The consequence was a disproportionate natural increase of proletarians in good times, not completely compensated by the natural decrease of bad times. Since the period we are considering was on the whole an era of economic expansion, such a system would have produced a significant tendency for the proletariat to increase more rapidly than the rest of the population.[27]

Seen in the light of the growth of this rural proletariat, the social and demographic component of Mendels's protoindustrialization hypothesis becomes a subset of a larger process.[28] The proletarianization model says cottage industry dissolved the social inertia and ended the practice of late marriages among European peasants.[29] Young men and women no longer needed to delay their marriage until they could inherit a farm or save enough money to establish themselves as farmers. The income they earned as protoindustrial spinners, weavers, or nailmakers would allow them to set up housekeeping in their own small cottage or even in a room in someone else's house. Free to marry earlier because they had their own regular incomes, they bore children who were able to help them with the work, and the process reinforced itself. The only times the process did not work was when no work was available; then the rate of marriage declined and growth slowed.

This perspective on the demographic outcome of cottage industry is not novel. As early as the eighteenth century, observers noticed that regions in which industrial work supplemented or replaced agricultural work grew very quickly. These observations formed the basis for Rudolf Braun's work on the cotton-spinning regions of the Zurich highlands. His description of this territory shows that the highland districts grew by a stunning 85 percent during the period 1700–1762, while the farming districts grew by only 16 percent.[30] Contemporary observers, writing in the 1790s, saw the scale of the growth and concluded that a number of factors caused it. First, the Zurich highlands were miserably poor, and before industrial growth many of their residents had been forced to emigrate to secure a living. There was no established peasant culture in which to incorporate social changes gradually. In this environment cotton spinning offered opportunity. As Braun writes, "It is no exaggeration to state that for these people the cottage industry proved . . . a medium which could guarantee a rooting in the land of their ancestors, permanent settlement in a home, as small and scanty as it might be, and the united family."[31]

Early industry improved the standard of living. Braun continues:

> Putting-out industry gave girls and boys the material prerequisites for marriage, and this possibility did away with any hesitation or fears that the young might have about knowing and getting to love each other. With no material considerations to stand in the way, one could yield to the attraction of the other sex. "The young lad," wrote Johan Schulthess [an early-nineteenth century Swiss professor of theology], "begins, as soon as he is confirmed—as though it were a veritable initiation ceremony—to steal after one or more girls." These maidens, however, the writer continued, "knowing that they cannot get a man any other way, open their chambers to these night boys and abandon themselves to the certain or uncertain hope that, in case of pregnancy, they will not be abandoned to shame." "This picture," protested Schulthess, is not "the fantasy of an ivory-tower

scholar; oh no, it is drawn from life." Reared in the countryside, he tells us that "he had witnessed as a young boy many an example of this scandalous behavior, which had become much more serious and common in the four decades since." Schulthess referred to the inspection records of the rural pastors and cited from them a report: "The so-called practice of bundling gets to be looked upon as a right and freedom, and to be considered as nothing sinful. Marriage is always the sequel of pregnancy."[32]

The Swiss writers of the late eighteenth and early nineteenth centuries were convinced that industrial prosperity led to earlier marriage. Moreover, fewer people never married.[33] Earlier marriage and little permanent celibacy increased fertility and swelled the population. The change was clear in the regions of peasant farming, but the growth there was moderate when compared to that which took place in the poor, sparsely settled highland regions. There, no farming intervened in the workers' lives, and there were no traditions of waiting for land before marrying. These "beggar weddings" received the most opprobrium from middle-class observers, who saw the moral code of the spinners as a dangerous attack on conventional patterns of behavior.

Wherever economic change created salaried employment the same process seems to have occurred: nuptiality increased because marriage ages and the proportion of the never-married declined, leading to higher fertility. In Switzerland the rural proletariat was largely industrial, but it could just as well have been agricultural. Recent research emphasizing how higher fertility can cause population growth has supported this way of looking at the causes of population growth in the eighteenth century. E. A. Wrigley and Roger Schofield reconstructed the size and composition of the English population between 1541 and 1871, before the first reliable censuses.[34] In the process they estimated levels of fertility, mortality, and nuptiality, and evaluated the relative contribution of each to growth in the eighteenth century. Their analysis clearly shows that both fertility and mortality changed dramatically between about 1680 and 1820, with the gross reproduction rate rising from about 2 to nearly 3, and the average expectation of life at birth rising from around 35 years to around 40 years. The gross reproduction rate is technically the number of daughters born to a hypothetical cohort of women.[35] Raising it from 2 to 3 means the average family would increase from four to six children (because a woman has both sons and daughters), a substantial increase. The expectation of life at birth is a measure of mortality. An increased expectation of life means fewer deaths in a given period of time, hence a larger population. The combination of lower mortality and higher fertility raised the overall growth rate in the English population from zero at the bottom of the seventeenth-century trough to more than 1.5 percent per annum at the peak of population growth around 1820.[36]

In England the contribution of fertility to eighteenth-century growth was more important than that of mortality. The change that affected fertility was a reduction in the age at which women married and an increase in the proportion who eventually married. The age-specific rates at which married women bore children did not change. This means that a married woman of a given age had a consistent likelihood of bearing a child. For women aged 25 to 29, this rate was about 34 per 100; in other words, of 100 married women aged 25 to 29, about 34 would bear children during any single year.[37] That likelihood hardly changed at all between 1550 and 1799. What did change was the proportion of all women who married and the age at which they married. Thus the proportion of all women in any age group who were married increased during the eighteenth century, as the age at marriage declined. The combination of stable marital fertility rates and increasing numbers of married women in each age group led to more births—higher fertility. Table 5.7 shows how this might have worked, for two hypothetical populations in which there were 600 women aged 20–49. All that distinguishes the two populations are different assumptions about the proportion of women married in each age group. The second assumption shows women marrying younger and a smaller proportion of women never marrying than does the first assumption. It produces 141 births per year instead of 104—an increase of almost 40 percent in a change from one to the other.

We can generalize from the English results, but we need to do so cautiously. Fertility made a large contribution to population growth only where there was strong economic growth that produced a population no longer linked to the land. Only rapid industrial growth and some kinds of agricultural change could do so.[38] There are not yet many sets of national figures with which we can compare the English. Data for France and Sweden suggest

Table 5.7: How a Change in Marriage Age Affects Overall
Fertility

Age Group	Marital Fertility Rate per 1,000‡	Total No. of Women	ASSUMPTION 1*		ASSUMPTION 2†	
			No. of Married Women	No. of Births	No. of Married Women	No. of Births
20–24	500	100	24	12	43	22
25–29	430	100	55	24	81	35
30–34	375	100	70	26	94	35
35–39	300	100	81	24	95	29
40–44	195	100	82	16	96	19
45–49	25	100	83	2	96	2
TOTAL				104		141
Singulate mean age at marriage				27.2		23.9

*Based on Verviers region, "Other" category, females.
†Based on Verviers region, "Industrial" category, females.
‡Based approximately on René Leboutte, "La transition démographique: Un changement culturel?" paper presented at a meeting of the Social Science History Association, November 1985, Table 10.

that the English pattern was not universal. France had relatively slow population growth in the period from 1680 to 1820.[39] During the part of that period for which fertility and mortality data are available, it appears that both fertility and mortality were declining, keeping the rate of growth relatively stable. For Sweden, still a different pattern emerges. Its strong growth was almost exclusively the result of changes in mortality, levels of fertility remaining almost unchanged.[40] Both these conclusions are consistent with what we would expect. France had balanced economic growth in the eighteenth century, and Sweden had a largely agricultural economy.

Overall, however, there is reason to believe that the growth of the proletariat made a major contribution to the growth of European population in the eighteenth century. De Vries's work on European urbanization between 1500 and 1800 shows that what he calls the "rural nonagricultural" part of the population grew very rapidly in the eighteenth century.[41] Its growth was greater than that of both large and small cities as a proportion of the European population. What is especially interesting about this line of reasoning is the relationship between urban and rural population growth and the rise and fall of urban industrial strength. De Vries concludes that rural nonagricultural populations grew because cities in the late seventeenth and eighteenth centuries lost some of their dominance in industry, a point that links our conclusions here with those in Chapter 4.[42] This should not suggest that the protoindustrial or the proletarian model of behavior always worked well, or worked all the time. Historians today are skeptical of any process that requires people to have automatically adjusted their behavior in a specific way to certain economic conditions.[43] Human behavior and the force of tradition are too complex and too powerful to perform in that way.

The processes of early industrial growth and population growth began almost simultaneously in the late seventeenth and early eighteenth centuries. They began for different reasons. Population growth started because of a number of causes, the most important being an improvement in European agriculture, a reduction in disease, and after 1710 a reduction in warfare.[44] Industrial growth started because of changes in the production process that led to lower-cost goods. Once started, the process might have become perpetual, with population fueling demand and demand spurring the population; but we know that all these new people had to be fed. The overall agricultural economy had to keep growing too, which it did, and there was a floor beneath which marriage ages could not go. The social outcome was a growing rural proletariat until after 1800, which increased more rapidly than the population as a whole, because of the fixed quantity of land and traditional jobs, and the increasing quantity of nontraditional jobs in agriculture, in cottage industry, and in the cities.[45]

INDUSTRY AND POPULATION AT THE LOCAL LEVEL

Thus far we have dealt with big population aggregates. We looked at Europe as a whole and its nations: England, France, Belgium, the Netherlands, Sweden. The results tell us that population and industry grew, and we suspect they grew by the creation of a much larger proletariat by 1800. The hypothesis is that earlier marriage and higher fertility spurred this growth. The task now is to look at smaller areas, where these propositions can be more effectively tested. A lot of local history work has already been done on industrial and proletarian populations in the seventeenth and eighteenth centuries. We will begin by looking at population change in the Verviers region in the eighteenth century, and then draw conclusions from it and a number of other local studies.

To follow the growth of population we need series of documents, ones in which the same question is asked repeatedly over a long period of time. Regular censuses are the best source for population size, but we do not have any. We must turn to other documents instead. Two kinds of sources are available to us, the number of taxpayers in certain communities who paid regularly collected taxes and the number of baptisms that took place each year. Neither source is perfect, but taken together (and with some reservations) they can give us a good idea of what was happening.

The problem with taxpayer lists is that not everyone paid taxes. While it might be argued that the number of taxpayers is a fixed proportion of the total population, we know this is not the case. People who do not pay any taxes are the poorest members of any community; the rise and fall of their number follows a different rhythm than does that of the number of taxpayers. Still, as we can see by looking at the total number of taxpayers in Limburg (shown in Chapter 6, Table 6.2), the number of taxpayers gives us a sense of the community's evolution—from around 175 taxpayers in the late seventeenth century to 300 or more by the end of the eighteenth century. Limburg, on this basis, nearly doubled in size between 1670 and 1780, with especially strong growth between 1710 and 1740, and after 1760.

The registers of baptisms (see Table 5.8 and Figure 5.1) echo the evidence we can draw from the lists of taxpayers. In Limburg the relationship is especially noticeable in the eighteenth century. In the seventeenth century the number of baptisms declined, even though the number of taxpayers increased. The explanation is the presence of a military garrison of several hundred men, which was at its largest before 1680 and from 1701 to 1715.[46] The garrison temporarily swelled the town's population with soldiers, who married local women or brought their wives and mistresses. Their children were baptized in the town, but none

Table 5.8: Decennial Average Number of Baptisms in Five Verviers Region Parishes, 1650–1790

	Ensival	Limburg-Bilstain	Soiron	Thimister	The Four Parishes	Verviers	Total
1650–1660	46	70	71	57	244	283	527
1661–1670	41	59	81	61	242	314	556
1671–1680	31	53	88	43	215	295	510
1681–1690	39	33	98	52	222	286	508
1691–1700	34	35	86	50	205	242	447
1701–1710	46	54	97	54	251	256	507
1711–1720	59	52	107	65	283	283	556
1721–1730	78	56	105	65	304	343	647
1731–1740	98	55	128	75	356	419	775
1741–1750	80	53	122	78	333	396	729
1751–1760	62	51	122	76	311	332	643
1761–1770	62	53	138	87	340	389	729
1771–1780	68	56	128	96	348	384	732
1781–1790	80	70	137	97	384	424	808

SOURCE: AEL, Parish Registers.

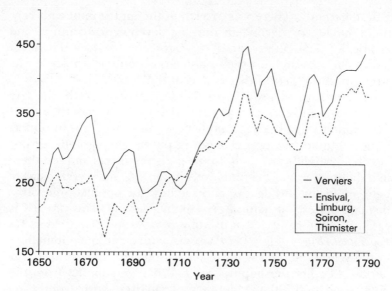

Figure 5.1. Annual Number of Baptisms in Five Verviers Region Parishes: 1650–1790 (five-year moving means)*
SOURCE: AEL, Parish Registers
*Graph shows even-numbered years only.

of the soldiers paid taxes. Verviers (which had troops in winter quarters but no garrison) and Limburg follow roughly the same pattern. The number of baptisms per year in Verviers was almost level in the late seventeenth century, grew from 1690 to about 1740, and grew again after 1760. As we might expect for a much larger town, its rate of growth was less than that of Limburg. The average number of baptisms per year in Limburg doubled between its low point in the 1680s and its high point in the 1780s, while that of Verviers increased by about 50 percent over the same span of time.[47]

In addition to Verviers and Limburg, Table 5.8 includes the average annual number of baptisms for Thimister, Ensival, and Soiron. Like Limburg, these three rural parishes roughly doubled their number of baptisms between the late seventeenth century and the end of the eighteenth century. And like both Verviers and Limburg, they show very strong growth in the early eighteenth century, which ended with a peak in the 1730s. What we have then is a pattern, albeit one in which each parish behaves a bit differently. There was growth in the mid-seventeenth century, stability or decline in the late seventeenth century, and erratic but clear-cut growth in the eighteenth century. The most noticeable feature of the eighteenth-century growth is its strength in the period that ended in the 1730s.

The pattern of growth we see around Verviers in the late seventeenth and eighteenth centuries is what much of the rest of this chapter will attempt to explain. We need to begin by understanding the population changes in purely demographic terms. To do so we will turn again to the parish registers and use them in a different way. This time, we will look at the overall balance between births and deaths, and see how the population evolves through periods of natural growth and decline. This process is essentially the same as that used by Wrigley and Schofield in *The Population History of England.* We start with a specific population, in the year 1790, and work backward through time in five-year periods. To get the population in 1785, we subtract from the population in 1790 the number of children born from 1785 through 1789 and add to it the number of people who died during those years. We also need to make an adjustment for the quantity of net migration in those years. The process of making these population estimates is complicated, but the results provide a good—if approximate—guide to the size of the population, its age structure, and the components of change.[48] We can learn from these estimates to what extent population growth depended on changes in nuptiality and fertility, and to what extent on mortality and migration. That will be a big help in understanding how industrial growth affected both producing and consuming populations.

Figure 5.2 shows the evolution of population size in Verviers and in Thimister, Ensival, and Soiron. Tables 5.9 and 5.10 report quinquennial population totals as well as the associated period migration rate, the gross and net reproduction rates, and e_0, the average expectation of life at birth. The Verviers population grew strongly from the 1650s until the 1670s, and then grew more slowly from the 1690s until the 1730s, before a new burst of growth between 1735 and 1750. Its population was more or less stable thereafter. For the three villages we only have figures beginning in 1675, and the estimating process is not nearly as certain for the villages as it is for Verviers. From the 1680s until

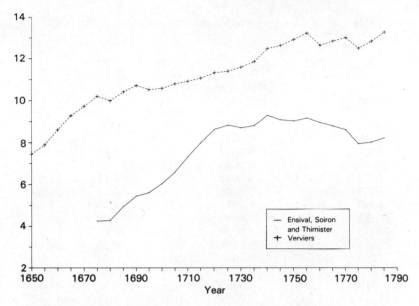

Figure 5.2. Estimated Population Size in Four Verviers Region Parishes, 1650–1790 (in thousands)
SOURCE: Tables 5.9 and 5.10.

1720, their population grew sharply. They grew very slowly in the 1720s and 1730s, before beginning to decline slowly after 1740.

The components of population change in Verviers and the three villages, and the relationship of population change to economic change, should interest us as much as the timing of growth and decline. The chronology in Verviers and the villages is not exactly the same, but its phases are: a period of more rapid growth from the mid-seventeenth century until some time in the first half of the eighteenth century, followed by a period of slower growth and then stability or slight decline. This coincides with the periods of economic development in the textile industry: it was growing and changing from before the mid-seventeenth century until the mid-eighteenth century, and mature thereafter.

Fertility, mortality, and migration contribute to population change. The three panels of Figure 5.3 show the evolution of these three basic population characteristics. The first panel shows e_0, which is the average expectation of life at birth in the population. An e_0 of 40 (which is normal for the eighteenth

Table 5.9:   Estimating the Verviers Population, 1650–1765

Year	Estimated Population Size	Period Migration Rate	Gross Reproduction Rate	Net Reproduction Rate	e_o
1650	7,438	0.0016	NA	NA	43.68
1655	7,876	0.0014	2.51	1.72	46.95
1660	8,600	0.0011	2.26	1.61	48.73
1665	9,269	0.0008	2.48	1.40	37.94
1670	9,714	0.0002	2.51	1.41	37.85
1675	10,192	−0.0003	1.74	0.74	28.65
1680	9,971	−0.0011	1.77	1.16	44.44
1685	10,398	−0.0020	1.72	1.02	40.06
1690	10,701	−0.0028	1.40	0.65	31.20
1695	10,499	−0.0036	1.31	0.78	39.91
1700	10,562	−0.0034	1.51	0.94	41.97
1705	10,774	−0.0031	1.47	0.92	42.09
1710	10,893	−0.0029	1.48	0.97	44.44
1715	11,043	0.0000	1.83	1.17	43.45
1720	11,294	0.0027	2.03	1.16	38.39
1725	11,366	0.0065	2.24	1.34	40.54
1730	11,557	0.0110	2.41	1.49	41.97
1735	11,813	0.0182	2.84	1.94	46.87
1740	12,436	0.0191	2.36	1.51	43.38
1745	12,583	0.0240	2.61	1.67	43.40
1750	12,863	0.0252	2.14	1.57	50.65
1755	13,167	0.0216	1.79	0.87	32.82
1760	12,573	0.0213	2.05	1.35	44.77
1765	12,781	0.0172	2.15	1.27	39.73
1770	12,942	−0.0035	1.88	0.66	23.69
1775	12,427	−0.0099	2.12	1.09	34.41
1780	12,758	−0.0319	2.14	0.96	30.16
1785	13,183	−0.0734	2.16	0.99	30.86

SOURCE: Myron P. Gutmann, "How Do Urban and Rural Industrial Populations Grow? Migration and Natural Increase in Verviers and its Hinterland," paper presented at the International Union for the Scientific Study of Population Meeting on Urbanization and Population Dynamics in History, Tokyo, January 1986, Table 6.

century) means that on average people lived 40 years. It is heavily influenced by infant mortality, so that it does not mean that most people died at age 40, or were prematurely senile. Based on the average number of years lived in the population, the expectation of life groups everyone together. Both for an infant who died and for a woman who reached age 80 the average is 40 years. Thus in an environment where about one-fourth of all infants died in the first year of life and adults on average lived into their sixties, the average expectation of life was about 40 years. The gross reproduction rate (GRR) is a measure of fertility. It tells us the average number of daughters born to a hypothetical group of women. The measure of migration is the annual migration rate, the proportion of the population that would move in a given year. A negative value indicates immigration; a positive value indicates emigration.

During most of the seventeenth and eighteenth centuries, the expectation of life in Verviers was moderate, averaging about 40 years. Only briefly—in the 1670s, 1690s, and 1750s and for a longer time beginning in 1770—was life expectancy lower, between 23 and 34 years. Most of these were periods of epidemic mortality and warfare, and they served to brake temporarily the

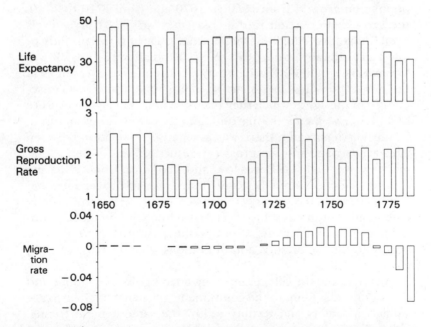

Figure 5.3. Components of Population Change, Verviers, 1650–1790 (five-year period beginning in year shown)
SOURCE: Table 5.9.

growth of the population. Beginning in the 1770s, however, high mortality became persistent, and it reflects the transformation of population dynamics in Verviers—from those of a village or very small town (despite the fact that it was neither) to those of a city, which had a perpetual deficit caused by more deaths than births. The graph of migration confirms this. Net migration was never high in Verviers, except at the end of the old regime. During the seventeenth century there was almost no net migration. During the years from 1720 to 1770, low positive net migration compensated for stable mortality and generally high fertility. After 1770, net migration became negative, as mortality increased and fertility failed to compensate. At the end of the old regime, the demographic behavior of Verviers was like that of a big city with a mature population structure: mortality exceeded fertility, and a stable or growing population demanded immigrants.[49]

The gross reproduction rate tells us more about the causes of population change in Verviers. During the periods of strong population growth, from 1650 to 1670 and from 1710 to 1740, the gross reproduction rate increased or stayed at high levels (well above two daughters per woman). During the periods of lower growth rates, from 1675 to 1710 and after 1740, GRR was lower. Changes in GRR are largely a consequence of changes in the proportion of women married at any time, which is a consequence of the age at which they marry. When marriage ages were high, fewer women were married, and they bore fewer children. In the Verviers region there was a negative correlation between ages at marriage and the gross reproduction rate. When age at marriage was high, GRR was low, and vice versa. Confirming the English evidence, nuptiality contributed strongly to fertility, and fertility contributed strongly to growth. Until the last third of the eighteenth century, fertility was the predominant driver of population growth and decline. After that time, a more balanced equation of fertility, mortality, and migration—characteristic of a big city—evolved.

Verviers and the villages made up an integrated economic and demographic system, so the components of change in the two are similar. Mortality and fertility follow the same general trends, although the estimation model for Verviers is more stable, and therefore values change less (Table 5.10 and Figure 5.4). Overall, both fertility and mortality were higher in the villages than in Verviers. The biggest difference between the three villages and

Table 5.10:   Estimating the Population of Thimister, Ensival, and Soiron, 1675–1785

Year	Estimated Population Size	Period Migration Rate	Gross Rate	Net Rate	e_0
1675	4,246	−0.0683	NA	NA	18.78
1680	4,282	−0.0672	2.60	1.63	42.48
1685	4,942	−0.0640	2.18	1.26	38.91
1690	5,439	−0.0650	2.15	0.74	22.99
1695	5,603	−0.0662	2.16	1.03	32.15
1700	6,027	−0.0591	2.01	1.15	38.67
1705	6,577	−0.0481	1.88	1.25	45.24
1710	7,291	−0.0400	1.55	1.07	47.26
1715	7,959	−0.0272	1.65	1.11	45.70
1720	8,606	−0.0156	1.68	0.86	34.22
1725	8,798	−0.0052	1.77	0.75	28.18
1730	8,669	0.0070	2.15	1.15	36.09
1735	8,776	0.0174	2.67	1.83	46.77
1740	9,256	0.0187	2.45	1.22	33.55
1745	9,041	0.0241	2.77	1.55	37.60
1750	8,986	0.0288	2.54	1.81	48.98
1755	9,123	0.0283	2.25	1.39	41.62
1760	8,908	0.0269	2.35	1.37	39.30
1765	8,743	0.0261	2.58	1.28	33.28
1770	8,561	0.0049	2.24	0.56	16.77
1775	7,896	0.0115	2.63	1.21	30.72
1780	7,971	0.0034	2.74	1.24	30.35
1785	8,173	−0.0218	2.55	1.31	34.59

SOURCE: Same as Table 5.9.

Verviers was in migration. As in Verviers, the level of net migration in the three villages was never very high, but the villages experienced strong net in-migration in the seventeenth century, feeding their growth between 1675 and 1720 with migrants. By the 1730s the direction of migration was outward, where it stayed until just before the end of the old regime.

Although related, the means by which population grew and declined in Verviers and in the villages differed. This was especially so during the crucial years from the 1670s until the 1730s, in which the textile industry grew and the region was buffeted by invasions. In these years the population of Verviers increased by means of an excess of fertility over mortality. The villages grew more rapidly, because of immigration. They attracted migrants

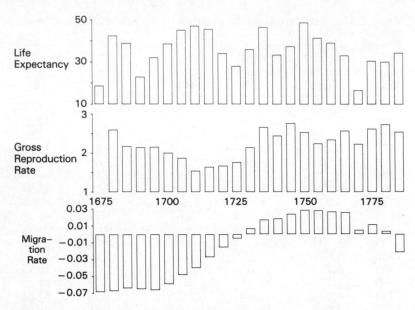

Figure 5.4. Components of Population Change, Ensival, Soiron, and Thimister, 1675–1790 (five-year periods beginning in year shown)
SOURCE: Table 5.10.

prior to the 1730s because they must have had available increasing quantities of work in cottage industry. After that time the industry had matured, and increases in the number of jobs were much harder to sustain. Migration from the region as a whole was outward by the mid-eighteenth century (probably in the direction of the city of Liège), only to reverse when mortality conditions changed—after 1770 in Verviers and after 1785 in the villages.

EARLY INDUSTRY AND MARRIAGE IN THE VERVIERS REGION

We see that population growth in the Verviers region followed the pattern expected from a proletarianizing population. It grew in the eighteenth century, largely because fertility increased— which it is surmised was caused by a declining marriage age. To find out whether that surmise is correct, we will look at a collection of women's first marriage ages for five parishes. The women are divided into two groups, those for the town of Verviers and those for four other parishes (Thimister, Ensival, Soiron, and Limburg), so that we can distinguish between the more urban population of Verviers itself, and the more rural populations of the villages in its hinterland. The ages are reported as decennial averages in Table 5.11, and as five-year moving means in Figure 5.5.

The marriage ages show that, in general, women who lived in the Verviers region waited a long time before marrying; moreover, they waited about as long in the town of Verviers itself as in the four nearby parishes. This alone suggests that they were not increasingly eager to marry as industry developed in the region. Although there was no overall decline in marriage ages over time, they were not static. In the early eighteenth century marriage ages declined, reaching the bottom of a trough in the

Table 5.11: Mean Age of Women at First Marriage in Five Verviers Region Parishes, 1650–1790

	VERVIERS		ENSIVAL, LIMBURG, SOIRON, THIMISTER	
	Mean	Number of Women	Mean	Number of Women
1650–1659	25.54	142	24.89	63
1660–1669	25.79	187	26.26	86
1670–1679	25.87	167	25.67	106
1680–1689	26.61	213	26.75	121
1690–1699	27.06	188	26.63	130
1700–1709	27.22	235	27.83	198
1710–1719	26.73	245	27.57	186
1720–1729	26.47	243	26.21	215
1730–1739	25.79	281	25.93	298
1740–1749	26.74	237	26.73	267
1750–1759	26.00	234	26.65	262
1760–1769	27.03	383	27.03	355
1770–1779	27.92	396	26.84	377
1780–1789	27.16	420	27.11	417
1650–1790	26.71	3,571	26.74	3,081

SOURCE: AEL, Parish Registers: Verviers, Thimister, Ensival, Soiron, Limburg.

decade of the 1730s. Thereafter they rose, peaking in the late eighteenth century.

There may have been two protoindustrial models of marriage behavior, instead of one, which we can call short-term and long-term. The short-term model says that there was an almost immediate correlation between economic conditions and marriage, so that when times were good the marriage rate increased. This is the hypothesis taken up by Franklin Mendels in his original work on protoindustrialization.[50] He showed that Flemish linen spinners were more likely to marry when times were good. This produced population growth. Few other historians have been able to replicate Mendels's results, so it is possible that the phenomenon he described existed only in eighteenth-century Flanders.[51] Christian Vandenbroeke has gone so far as to challenge Mendels even for Flanders.[52] An attempt to replicate Mendels's statistical procedures for the Verviers region produced ambivalent results.[53] There is not a strong short-term relationship between nuptiality and the economy.

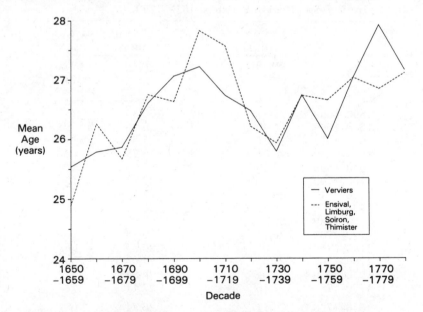

Figure 5.5.   Age of Women at First Marriage in Five Verviers Region Parishes, 1650–1790 (decennial means)
SOURCE: AEL, Parish Registers.

The alternative to the short-term approach is a long-term model. It was suggested by the work of Braun and seemingly confirmed by David Levine.[54] It tells us that at one time a stable peasant community existed in some localities, but that these communities were vulnerable to change because local law and custom did not prohibit the division of property and the construction of new houses. As industrial work became available the absence of restrictions permitted the formation of industrial households. The consequence was a lower marriage age, higher fertility, and overall population growth.

The Verviers region shows no such long-term trend; rather, marriage ages stayed high in the eighteenth century, and they continued to be high until the middle of the nineteenth century.[55] The one phenomenon worthy of comment is the trough in marriage ages recorded in the middle of the eighteenth century. We might speculate that the industrial economy was especially strong then, relative to earlier and later, and that the greater availability of work, or higher wages, led people to marry at younger ages during a two- or three-decade period. We can formulate a hypothesis which predicts that an improvement in economic conditions between 1720 and 1760 led to a parallel decline in marriage ages. The economic evidence does not readily confirm this hypothesis. According to the figures published by Pierre Lebrun, the textile industry did not grow between the 1720s and 1748, the period in which marriage ages hit bottom.[56] The industry was expanding during the second half of the eighteenth century, when marriage ages were increasing.

Our analysis will look different if we take a longer view. There was a heroic age of industrial growth from before 1650 until 1720, punctuated by wars. The 1720s, 1730s, and 1740s were not a period of strong growth. Later, growth was steady but slower. Marriage ages were low from the 1650s through the 1670s, reflecting the economic growth of the heroic age. They rose in the period from the 1680s until the 1700s, during which war and high food prices reduced prosperity. Business growth renewed after the wars and peaked in the 1720s before sliding back slightly in the 1730s and 1740s. During these years marriage ages fell, reaching bottom in the 1730s. This was the end of the era of growth and marks a transition to the more stable period of maturity that began before 1750. There was a time lag between changing economic conditions and changing values (such as decisions to marry), which makes this hypothesis believable. It took the people of the Verviers region some time to appreciate fully the prosperity that the end of the wars brought after 1720.

The proletarian model of marriage behavior works in the Verviers region, but the results are complicated. First, marriage ages stayed very high, even for the part of the population that married the youngest. For the region as a whole, mean marriage ages never fell much below 26 years, except during the very first years we are studying, the 1650s.[57] These are very late ages at marriage. What we have here is a population in which the creation of a new labor force succeeded in reducing marriage ages, but it did so in a context where marriage ages were very high and stayed high. This was true in almost all of eastern Belgium, including large cities.[58] We need to see the persistence of high marriage ages as something that grew out of people's basic attitude toward life and the family, part of that amorphous entity called "culture." It is not quickly modified by economic change.

The second theme we need to remember is the two-phase history of early industry in the Verviers region. The first phase—which spanned the years from before the mid-seventeenth century until the 1730s or 1740s—was a period of overall growth and development in industry, in both metalwork and textiles. This period of growth was punctuated by warfare and recession that lasted from the mid-1670s until about 1710. In this period of growth and development, marriage ages were low when times were good. In all likelihood they were declining from high levels in the early seventeenth century. Times were not good during the years of war and depression, which led to increasing ages at marriage.

The idea that the growth of industry created a single proletariat needs to be clarified before going further. This point is dealt with in greater detail in Chapter 6, but it is safe to say that three industrial populations coexisted in the Verviers region. One of them, made up of weavers, teaselers, and shearmen, was thoroughly industrialized. These people constituted a distinct subpopulation that was not simultaneously participating in agriculture, trade, or the traditional crafts. The peasants, on the other hand, used industrial work (mostly spinning) by some family members to supplement their incomes. The full-time spinner families were a third group. They were very poor, socially isolated, and socially disadvantaged. The better-off industrial workers (especially the weavers) seem to have adopted a set of marriage strategies that permitted lower marriage ages. The peasants and others did so to a much lesser extent. The spinners were too poor to take much advantage of industrial prosperity for marriage. As the number of industrial workers became a larger proportion of the total population, marriage ages declined. But when their numbers stabilized in the mid-eighteenth century, they no longer made a difference. Times were good; but the really industrial population had already formed, and marriage ages were unlikely to decline further for the total population. Only a relatively small proportion of workers can be accurately described as part of the industrial proletariat: they made up fewer than one-fourth of the population in the villages and less than one-half of the population of Verviers. Even if their marriage ages had been *very* low (which they were not), the overall marriage age for the whole community would not have declined significantly.

This chapter has been about population growth and its causes, and their relationship to the development of industry. Population growth in the Verviers region in the eighteenth century was similar to that in England. Natural increase—an excess of births over deaths—contributed most to population growth, and higher birth rates rather than lower death rates fueled most of that growth. Birth rates rose when people married at younger ages. In the villages around Verviers there was more growth by migration, probably because their economies grew proportionally more than did that of the town. These industrial villages attracted immigrants from more remote villages, coming in search of jobs in a kind of stepwise migration.

Economic change provided the motor for population change, and the development of the textile industry was the dominant economic change. In effect, the creation of textile jobs in a mixed economy of dairying, metalwork, and trade made it easier to marry, made more children affordable and desirable, and led to population growth. This appears to be the same sequence of events that took place on a much larger scale in England, and it is the same story that other local studies have shown.[59] Paul Deprez's work on Flanders (seconded by Franklin Mendels's) showed that the districts with sandy soils, small landholdings, and the linen industry had much higher rates of population growth than did the more heavily agricultural districts.[60] Karl-heinz Blaschke's research on Saxony gives us a rare opportunity to examine clearly differentiated social groups. There, gardeners and cottagers—the rural proletariat—grew much more rapidly than any other group in the population, both before and after 1750.[61] What is important about the Saxon findings is the confirmation, in a population that was not purely protoindustrial, of the role played by the proletariat in population growth.

Rudolf Braun's research on the region around Zurich shows the influence of a proletarianized population in the eighteenth century in the most dramatic way.[62] He separates the area into "highland" and "farming" districts. During the period from 1700 to 1762, when the cotton-spinning business grew strongly, the population of the highland districts grew by 84.5 percent, while that of the farming districts grew by 15.6 percent. The fragility of growth is shown by the fact that after 1762 growth in the highland districts exceeded that in the farming districts by much less. What growth there was resulted from generally low mortality, with somewhat higher marital fertility and much earlier marriage in the industrial districts as compared with the farming districts.

We need to think about the European population in the eighteenth century as being made up of a producing population and a consuming population. Much of the discussion in this chapter has been about the creation of producers, but we should not forget the consumers. Virtually all the sustained population growth that took place in Europe in the eighteenth century led to the creation of consumers who had little or no chance of producing for themselves. Many of these were city dwellers, but many—like those of Verviers and its hinterland—were still in or near the countryside. Industrial growth led to population growth, by providing jobs, but the process was circular. Industrial workers were good consumers, because they had little time to produce for themselves and because they were paid in cash. They spawned a large service sector, which we will see in the occupational distributions in Chapter 6. This entire population, produced by industrial growth, led to further industrial and economic growth. The gradual spread of commercialization in the eighteenth and nineteenth centuries has long been seen as associated with the growth of mechanized industry. We must also associate it—both economically and demographically—with the substantial growth in industry that took place in regions like Verviers before the first factories were built.

There are two important elements to this chapter. The first is the discovery of more gradual economic and industrial growth in the eighteenth century, built at least in part on the growth of cottage industry. This in turn was propelled by seventeenth-century economic changes, and by population changes too. The second important element in this chapter is the emergence of a rural proletariat. Where it grew up, this social group transformed demographic behavior and sparked dramatic growth. We identify members of the proletariat, and contrast them with the peasants among whom they lived, both by the amount of land they owned and by their occupations. They performed different work and had a different attitude toward the land. The way to see these differences is by an examination of the society that grew up along with widespread early industry in the eighteenth century.

NOTES

1. These figures come from Jan de Vries, "Patterns of Urbanization in Pre-Industrial Europe, 1500–1800," in *Patterns of European Urbanisation Since 1500*, ed. H. Schmal (London: Croom Helm, 1981), p. 88. For cities of 10,000 or more they are also given in de Vries, *European Urbanization 1500–1800* (Cambridge: Harvard University Press, 1984).

2. Jan Marczewski, "Some Aspects of the Economic Growth of France, 1660–1958," *Economic Development and Cultural Change* 9 (1960–1961): 369–386.

3. There is at the moment considerable disagreement among scholars about the level of production in the English economy in the eighteenth century. A good summary of this debate can be found in the Harley article cited in note 4 and in Jan de Vries, "The Decline and Rise of the Dutch Economy, 1675–1900," in *Technique, Spirit, and Form in the Making of the Modern Economies: Essays in Honor of William N. Parker, Research in Economic History*, supplement 3 (1984): 149–189; and N. F. R. Crafts, *British Economic Growth During the Industrial Revolution* (Oxford: Clarendon Press, 1985).

4. These figures were obtained by multiplying Harley's output indices for agriculture and industry, which are scaled to 1841, by Cole and

Deane's 1967 estimate of 1841 production in the two sectors. C. Knick Harley, "British Industrialization Before 1841: Evidence of Slower Growth During the Industrial Revolution," *Journal of Economic History* 42 (1982): 286; and Phyllis Deane and W. A. Cole, *British Economic Growth, 1688–1959: Trends and Structure,* 2nd ed. (Cambridge: Cambridge University Press, 1967), p. 166.

5. Angus Maddison, *Phases of Capitalist Development* (Oxford: Oxford University Press, 1982), p. 163.

6. On the structure of the Dutch economy in the eighteenth century, see Johan de Vries, *De economische achteruitgang der Republiek in de achttiende eeuw* (Amsterdam: J. van Campen, 1959). The evolution of the Dutch economy has, like the English, generated a considerable amount of debate recently. For one side, see de Vries, "The Decline and Rise"; for the other side, see James Riley, "The Dutch Economy After 1650: Decline or Growth?" *Journal of European Economic History* 13 (1984): 521–569. There are, to the best of my knowledge, no comparable figures for Belgium.

7. For a comparison, see Joel Mokyr, *Industrialization in the Low Countries, 1795–1850* (New Haven: Yale University Press, 1976).

8. The figures presented in Table 5.4 are drawn from Harley, "Evidence of Slower Growth." His estimates tend to minimize the growth of industry, in contrast to some economic historians whose estimates maximize the growth of industry. For a discussion of the possibilities, see de Vries, "The Decline and Rise"; and N. F. R. Crafts, "British Economic Growth, 1700–1831: A Review of the Evidence," *Economic History Review,* 2nd ser., 36 (1983): 177–199.

9. Franklin F. Mendels, "Proto-industrialization: The First Phase of the Industrialization Process," *Journal of Economic History* 32 (1972): 241–261.

10. Ibid., p. 241.

11. For the best current statement of how he sees the problem, see Mendels, "Proto-industrialization: Theory and Reality," in *Eighth International Economic History Congress, Budapest, 1982: "A" Themes* (Budapest: Akademiai Kiado, 1982), pp. 69–107. See also the prospectus for the 1982 meeting by Mendels and Pierre Deyon, "Proto-industrialisation: Théorie et réalité," *Revue du Nord* 63 (1981): 11–19.

12. Some of the criticisms are noted in Mendels's general report, "Protoindustrialization: Theory and Reality." There have been two largely negative review essays dealing with the subject: Pierre Jeannin, "La protoindustrialisation: développement ou impasse?" *Annales ESC* 35 (1980): 52–65; and D. C. Coleman, "Proto-Industrialization: A Concept Too Many," *Economic History Review,* 2nd ser., 36 (1983): 435–448. See also the contributions to a conference published as Maxine Berg et al., eds., *Manufacture in Town and Country Before the Factory* (Cambridge: Cambridge University Press, 1983).

13. Phyllis Deane, "The Output of the British Woolen Industry in the

Eighteenth Century," *Economic History Review*, 2nd ser., 17 (1957): 207–223; and Tihomir J. Markovitch, *Les industries lainières de Colbert à la Révolution* (Geneva: Librairie Droz, 1976).

14. The settlement of the War of the Spanish Succession in 1714 transferred the Spanish Netherlands to Austrian control by the Treaty of Rastatt.

15. See above, pp. 75. Pierre Lebrun, *L'industrie de la laine à Verviers pendant de XVIIIe et le début du XIXe siècle* (Liège: Faculté de Philosophie et Lettres, 1948), pp. 66–75.

16. See the general discussion of the evolution of the economy of eastern Belgium in Myron P. Gutmann, *War and Rural Life in the Early Modern Low Countries* (Princeton: Princeton University Press, 1980). The quantitative evidence begins with the 1720s and is published in Lebrun, *L'industrie de la laine*, and Paul Servais, *La rente constitueé dans le ban de Herve au XVIIIe siècle* (Brussels: Credit Communal, 1982). The *aunage*, or tax on cloth production in Verviers, begins its series for the years 1734–1735. The only quantitative figures about production that exist for the preceding period are those for the cloth turned over by Verviers merchants for sale in the communal sales hall in Liège. These lists exist for much of the period from 1685 to 1735, and their interpretation is extremely difficult. What one can conclude is that production in Verviers was at least 4,000 cloths per year by 1685, and was certainly higher. A growth rate of 1 percent per year from 1685 to 1785 is not inconsistent with the level of production indicated by sales hall receipts. For the records of the sales hall, see AV, F.172–F.173, F.269–F.275.

17. Lebrun, *L'industrie de la laine*, p. 332.

18. On the strength of growth at the very end of the old regime, see ibid.

19. E. A. Wrigley, "The Growth of Population in Eighteenth-Century England: A Conundrum Resolved," *Past & Present* 98 (1983): 122.

20. Ibid.

21. J. T. Krause, "Changes in English Fertility and Mortality, 1781–1850," *Economic History Review*, 2nd ser., 11 (1958): 52–70; and more recently, Michael W. Flinn, "The Stabilization of Mortality in Pre-Industrial Western Europe," *Journal of European Economic History* 3 (1974): 285–318.

22. Myron P. Gutmann, "Historical Demography Twenty Years After Ariès," paper presented at the Annual Meeting of the American Historical Association, December 1980.

23. J. D. Chambers, *Population, Economy and Society in Pre-Industrial England* (London: Oxford University Press, 1972), p. 122.

24. The classic works are Jean Meuvret, "Demographic Crisis in France from the Sixteenth to the Eighteenth Century," in *Population in History*, ed. D. V. Glass and D. E. C. Eversley (London: Edward Arnold, 1965), pp. 507–522; and Pierre Goubert, "Historical Demography and the Reinterpretation of Early Modern French History: A Research Review," *Journal of Interdisciplinary History* 1 (1970): 37–48.

25. T. McKeown, R. G. Brown, and R. G. Record, "An Interpretation of the Modern Rise of Population in Europe," *Population Studies* 26 (1972): 345–382.

26. Charles Tilly, "Demographic Origins of the European Proletariat," in *Proletarianization and Family History*, ed. David Levine (Orlando: Academic Press, 1984), pp. 1–86.

27. Ibid., p. 39.

28. Rudolf Braun, *Industrialisierung und Volksleben: Die Veränderungen der Lebensformen in einem ländlischen Industriegebiet vor 1800 (Zürcher Oberland)* (Erlenbach: Eugen Rentsch Verlag, 1960); Braun, "Early Industrialization and Demographic Change in the Canton of Zürich," *Historical Studies of Changing Fertility*, ed. Charles Tilly (Princeton: Princeton University Press, 1978), pp. 289–334; Franklin Mendels, "Industrialization and Population Pressure in 18th-Century Flanders," (Ph.D. dissertation, University of Wisconsin, 1970); Mendels, "Industry and Marriages in Flanders Before the Industrial Revolution," in *Population and Economics*, ed. Paul Deprez (Winnipeg: University of Manitoba Press, 1970), pp. 81–93; Mendels, "Proto-Industrialization: The First Phase"; and Mendels, "Proto-industrialization: Theory and Reality".

29. David Levine, *Family Formation in an Age of Nascent Capitalism* (New York: Academic Press, 1977).

30. Braun, "Early Industrialization and Demographic Change," p. 328.

31. Ibid., p. 310.

32. Ibid., pp. 315–316.

33. Ibid., p. 317.

34. E. A. Wrigley and R. S. Schofield, *The Population History of England, 1541–1871: A Reconstruction* (Cambridge: Harvard University Press, 1981); their findings are summarized in Wrigley, "The Growth of Population."

35. The gross reproduction rate is the hypothetical number of female daughters born to a cohort of women if females do not die before age 45 or 50. See James A. Palmore and Robert W. Gardner, *Measuring Mortality, Fertility, and Natural Increase: A Self-Teaching Guide to Elementary Measures* (Honolulu: East-West Population Institute, 1983).

36. Wrigley and Schofield, *The Population History of England*, p. 243.

37. Ibid., p. 254.

38. For a list of conditions that would produce proletarianization and hence the kind of growth conditions suggested here, see Tilly, "Demographic Origins of the European Proletariat," pp. 23–26.

39. Wrigley, "The Growth of Population," p. 122.

40. Wrigley and Schofield, *The Population History of England*, pp. 246–248.

41. De Vries, *European Urbanization*, pp. 217–246.

42. These relationships are demonstrated by Paul Klep, "Urban Decline in Brabant: The Traditionalization of Investments and Labour,

1374–1806," paper presented at the Ninth International Economic History Congress, Bern, August 1986.

43. Myron P. Gutmann and René Leboutte, "Rethinking Protoindustrialization and the Family," *Journal of Interdisciplinary History* 14 (1984): 607–621; and Paul Spagnoli, "Industrialization, Proletarianization, and Marriage: A Reconsideration," *Journal of Family History* 8 (1983): 230–247.

44. James C. Riley, "Insects and the European Mortality Decline," *American Historical Review* 91 (1986): 833–858; and Gutmann, *War and Rural Life.*

45. Tilly, "Demographic Origins of the European Proletariat."

46. On the Limburg garrison and its impact, see J. Thisquen, "Histoire de la ville de Limbourg," *BSVAH* 9 (1907): 184–205.

47. The number of baptisms is deceiving as a measure of population size in a different way than is the number of taxpayers. For baptisms to be a proxy for population size, the birth rate must remain constant over time. While we know that the birth rate in Belgium before 1800 had not yet begun to decline, it was not constant. Nonetheless, over fairly long periods of time, spanning a decade or longer, the average birth rate was fairly stable. We can begin by assuming that the changing number of births generally reflects the overall population size.

48. This estimation process is described in Myron P. Gutmann, "How Do Urban and Rural Industrial Populations Grow? Migration and Natural Increase in Verviers and Its Hinterland," paper presented at the International Union for the Scientific Study of Population Meeting on Urbanization and Population Dynamics in History, Tokyo, January 1986.

49. De Vries, in *European Urbanization 1500–1800,* bases his models on the assumption that in cities of 5,000 to 10,000 inhabitants "births and deaths . . . just suffice to generate the observed growth of such cities, i. e. they are neither net sources nor recipients of migrants" (p. 202). Migrants were needed in larger places. The results presented here seem to confirm his speculation.

50. Mendels, "Industrialization and Population Pressure."

51. See, for example, Rab Houston and K. D. M. Snell, "Proto-industrialization? Cottage Industry, Social Change, and Industrial Revolution," *The Historical Review* 27 (1984): 473–492; and G. Hohorst, "Protoindustrilisierung im Übergang zum industriellen Kapitalisms: Die demoökonomische Entwicklung im Kreis Hagen 1817 bis 1863," in *La protoindustrialisation: Théorie et réalité. Rapports,* ed. Pierre Deyon and Franklin Mendels (Lille: University of Lille, 1982).

52. Christian Vandenbroeke, "Le cas flamand: Evolution sociale et comportements démographiques au XVIIe–XIXe siècles," *Annales ESC* 39 (1984): 915–938. For Mendels's response, see pp. 939–956.

53. Myron P. Gutmann, "Protoindustrialization and Marriage Ages in Eastern Belgium," unpublished paper, October 1983. A revised

version of this paper will be published in the *Annales de Démographie Historique* in 1987.

54. Braun, *Industrialisierung und Volksleben;* Braun, "Early Industrialization and Demographic Change"; and Levine, *Family Formation.*

55. On Verviers, see George Alter, "Family Economy and the Timing of Marriage," in *Family, Fertility, and the Demographic Transition* (Madison: University of Wisconsin Press, in press); and Alter, "The Influence of Social Stratification on Marriage in Nineteenth Century Europe" (Ph.D. dissertation, University of Pennsylvania, 1978). On a nearby region, see Gutmann and Leboutte, "Rethinking Protoindustrialization and the Family."

56. Lebrun, *L'industrie de la laine.* For a good summary, see Paul Servais, *La rente constituée,* pp. 240–241.

57. These results are at least partially affected by truncation bias, because during the early years of registration it is sometimes difficult to find the baptisms of women baptized long before their marriage. Thus we are more likely to find the baptisms of women who married for the first time at 20 years of age than of women who married for the first time at 35 years.

58. René Leboutte, "Réconversions industrielles et transition démographique dans la Basse-Meuse Liégeoise 1750–1976" (Ph.D. dissertation, University of Liège, 1985); Gutmann and Leboutte, "Rethinking Protoindustrialization and the Family"; and Alter, *Family, Fertility, and the Demographic Transition.*

59. Wolfram Fischer, "Rural Industrialization and Population Change," *Comparative Studies in Society and History* 15 (1973): 158–170; and Tilly, "Demographic Origins," pp. 29–36.

60. Paul Deprez, "The Demographic Development of Flanders in the Eighteenth Century," in *Population in History,* ed. D. V. Glass and D. E. C. Eversley (London: Edward Arnold, 1965), pp. 608–630; also discussed in Fischer, "Rural Industrialization," p. 166.

61. The growth rates are derived by Tilly and reported in "Demographic Origins," p. 32. They were drawn from Karlheinz Blaschke, *Bevölkerungsgeschichte von Sachsen bis zur Industriellen Revolution* (Weimar: Bohlhaus, 1967), pp. 190–191.

62. Braun, "Early Industrialization and Demographic Change."

CHAPTER 6

A Hybrid Society

The economic and demographic changes that took place in Europe in the eighteenth century helped create a new population of producers and consumers. A rural population grew up that derived much of its income from industrial work. Over time, fewer and fewer of these families owned agricultural land or even worked in agriculture except for seasonal labor in the harvest. They became proletarianized.

The proletarianization of the rural industrial labor force did not give its members immediately the characteristics of late nineteenth and early twentieth centuries industrial workers. Rather, in the Verviers region and elsewhere, they lived in a hybrid society, somewhere between a perfect peasant society and a perfect industrial society. It was part urban and part rural; part agricultural and part industrial; part traditional and part modern; part socially harmonious and part socially discordant.

New forms of personal life and new forms of social life emerged. These forms of personal and social life made neighbors of peasants and industrial workers, and often created hybrid families, where some members worked in farming and others in industry. It also made hybrid individuals, who split their time between agricultural and industrial activities. They found new living arrangements, in which many people lived in houses that contained more than one family. And they began the process of making social classes, by differentiating workers socially and making them vitally conscious of their disagreements with their employers.

This chapter talks about the community and the lives lived within the community. Early industrial society is a new subject of study among historians, and its characteristics have not been the subject of nearly enough research. We have fewer examples than we would desire. Moreover, much of the research on these societies deals with the nineteenth century, after a great deal of change had already occurred. The risk we face is one of excessive uniformity and simplicity. European society was complex even before eighteenth-century growth; it became still more so in the eighteenth and nineteenth centuries. There is no single pattern of early industrial society, even if this chapter suggests one with its broad strokes. We need to keep in mind the extraordinary diversity of European society.

Work, land, and family are the keys to understanding the structure of society in early industrial communities. The existence of cottage industry did not mean that it was organized in a single way. In some places everyone—men and women, adults and children—were employed in it. In others only a select group—often women—found industrial work, while the rest of the population worked in agriculture or traditional crafts. Still elsewhere people worked in a wide variety of tasks—in agriculture and industry, crafts and services—with men and women, adults and children, moving easily from one activity to another. Every labor force was organized in its own way. Once we know how, we can make sense of the relationship between people and the land. Where industry shared the labor force with farming, we will see that land continued to play an important role in people's lives. Where industry monopolized workers, land became less and less important. Work and the land help us learn about the family. The nature of the labor force, the persistence of farming, and the ownership of land are the crucial components that shaped the rural proletariat. They did so through marriage, the mechanism by which families were formed. We will look at work, land, and the formation of families as our starting points for understanding how early industry worked together with an agricultural environment to shape a hybrid society.

THE STRUCTURE OF THE COTTAGE INDUSTRY LABOR FORCE

Every community in which cottage industry became widespread had its own specially formulated labor force, based on the economic needs of industry and on the social environment in which it grew up. In the earliest modern discussions of protoindustrialization, the authors selected for study communities in which a large proportion of the labor force worked as families in cottage industry, and compared them with communities in which cottage industry had penetrated little. These communities shared a social pattern. Rudolf Braun's work on the cotton-spinning communities of the Zurich highlands, already discussed in Chapter 5, fits this model.[1] Braun found two kinds of communities, ones in which it was legally possible to divide up a family's land and ones in which it was not. In the divisible communities, cottage industry became established because it was possible to cut up a single parcel of land and build several cottages on it, each inhabited by a spinner family. Men, women, and children worked, and little of the older agricultural base of these communities remained. It was in these communities that marriage ages fell and social commentators spoke of "beggar weddings." In the other kind of community, where it was very difficult to divide property, agriculture remained the principal activity, marriage was later, and the population grew less rapidly.

David Levine's work on four English parishes followed the pattern established by Braun.[2] He contrasted two starkly different parishes, Shepshed and Bottesford. Shepshed was poor and largely independent of control by a dominant landowning family; Bottesford was more prosperous and under the strong control of the Manners family, dukes of Rutland. Shepshed became the most industrial village in Leicestershire, whereas Bottesford remained agricultural. The consequence for the industrial parish was striking growth based on lower ages at marriage and high fertility. A majority of its families were involved in the knitting trade. Bottesford stayed agricultural and grew only slowly. Marriage ages remained high. The conclusion historians drew from the work of Braun and Levine was that cottage industry led inevitably to a single kind of social change, where it took over whole communities and transformed relationships within them. The visible form of the change was in greater poverty, low marriage ages, and high rates of population growth. Now we know that this was only one kind of social and economic development among several possibilities. The key is the extent of participation in the cottage industry labor force, and the relationship that had to agriculture and the land.

A second, contrasting model of cottage industry society has been described by Gay Gullickson.[3] In the village of Auffay in

France hand cotton spinners were almost exclusively women in the eighteenth century. Most men worked in agriculture or crafts, while a few were weavers. Here, population grew but marriage ages stayed very high until the industry was transformed after 1785. Hand spinning was replaced by machine spinning. The number of weavers increased rapidly in the early nineteenth century. The new economic opportunities for men gave many couples the opportunity to marry, and marriage ages declined. Auffay developed as it did because before 1786 cottage industry work was limited to women, and although it supplemented the incomes of many families, it did not rapidly change the opportunities to marry and establish a new household. Only when large numbers of men became weavers after 1786, and were no longer tied to agriculture and traditional crafts, did the pattern change.

The labor force of the Verviers region fits somewhere between that of the fully industrialized communities—such as the divisible Swiss villages and Shepshed—and Auffay prior to 1786. Like Auffay, it had in its population a strong and independent sector containing agriculture and traditional crafts. Like the other places, it had an equally strong group of industrial workers. It shared social characteristics of both patterns. The first modern censuses of the Verviers region were taken between 1795 and 1810. They came about after the region was incorporated into France in 1794, a consequence of the French Revolution and its wars. Table 6.1 reports the occupational structure of Verviers and some of the villages around it, in the first usable censuses taken after the beginning of the French regime. The table gives occupations of household heads, to provide comparable data about both the structure of employment and the social status of households. By the early nineteenth century the region around Verviers was heavily industrial (see Figure 6.1).[4] Verviers was a large industrial town, and its residents worked in industry, crafts, and services.[5] The other places ranged from more rural to more urban, but none of them was overwhelmingly agricultural. In Thimister about one-third of the household heads were employed in agriculture, but more than half were employed in textiles. Herve, which was an administrative center for a small territory, had the most traditional employment structure, with large craft, trade, hospitality, administrative, and professional sectors. It had a bit less industry (mostly spinners), but it still had

Table 6.1: Occupational Structure of the Verviers Region, About 1800

	Herve	Limburg	Ensival	Soiron	Thimister	Charneux	Verviers
Number of households	699	234	341	193	521	559	2,396
PERCENTAGE OF HOUSEHOLD HEADS EMPLOYED IN:							
Administration	1.9	0.9	1.2	1.0	1.0	0.4	1.3
Professions	3.0	1.7	0.6	3.1	1.0	1.6	1.7
Landowners	1.6	0.0	0.9	0.0	1.2	1.1	1.0
Agriculture	18.3	24.8	12.9	13.5	33.6	29.7	0.8
Day laborer	12.0	10.7	7.3	0.0	10.9	2.9	13.7
Farmer	3.4	14.1	5.6	9.9	22.3	26.8	0.8
All other	2.9	0.0	0.0	3.6	0.4	0.0	0.0
Crafts	17.2	7.3	9.4	15.0	3.3	7.7	11.2
Food & lodging	8.0	6.8	4.7	4.7	0.8	2.0	4.0
Trade	10.4	0.4	2.9	4.7	2.1	3.9	6.0
Textile industry	26.4	50.8	62.4	23.8	51.3	46.0	47.9
Spinners	21.3	5.6	3.2	18.6	18.1	30.2	3.6
Teaselers	0.3	6.4	12.6	0.0	0.2	0.0	8.8
Weavers	2.9	25.2	24.6	3.6	28.8	13.6	14.8
Shearmen	0.3	4.3	13.5	0.5	0.0	0.0	10.3
Draper	1.4	9.0	2.3	0.0	2.9	1.8	3.0
Other	0.3	0.4	6.1	1.0	1.3	0.4	7.4
Metalwork	2.6	0.0	0.0	25.4	0.0	0.7	1.1
Mining	0.3	0.0	0.0	0.0	2.5	5.7	0.0
None	9.9	6.4	4.1	7.3	3.1	1.3	10.3
Unknown	0.6	0.4	0.0	0.0	0.6	0.0	1.2
All industry	29.3	50.8	62.4	49.2	53.7	52.4	49.0

SOURCES: Herve: AEL, FFP, 224/2; Limburg: AEL, Communes, Limburg, 571; Ensival: AEL, FFP, 246; Soiron: AEL, FFP, 247/12; Thimister: AEL, FFP, 225/7; Charneux: AEL, FFP, 223; Verviers: AV, Relève des habitants de la ville de Verviers, 1806.

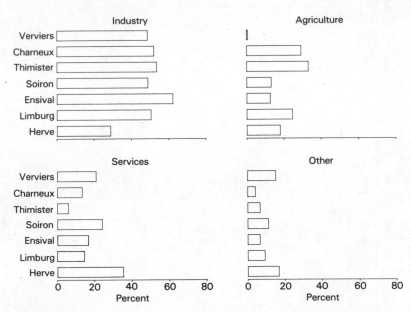

Figure 6.1. Occupational Distribution in the Verviers Region, About 1800
SOURCE: Same as Table 6.1.

little agricultural work. Overall, the evidence suggests that by the late eighteenth century half of all workers were employed in industry, and one-fifth or less were employed in agriculture. By Paul Servais's calculation, spinning work alone produced an annual income equal to one-third that of milk production.[6] When combined with other forms of industrial income, from nailmaking and weaving, industry made a substantial contribution to rural incomes in the region around Verviers.

Ages at marriage stayed high in the Verviers region, but we have seen that they followed the long-term development of cottage industry. When times were very good in the textile industry, and many men were moving into industrial work, marriage ages declined. The population grew. Overall, however, marriage ages stayed high because there were limits to the amount of industrial work, and because agriculture maintained its underlying importance. Couples waited to marry because they still hoped to obtain land. The Verviers region was not unique in its intermediate labor force, which included farmers and craftsmen in addition to cottage industry workers. Wherever agriculture remained a viable alternative to industry, mixed social environments grew up. We find another mixed society in the tiny town of Comines in French Flanders.[7] There intensive agriculture, practiced on small parcels of land, flourished alongside industry. The age at marriage stayed high, especially among the more agricultural part of the population.

The theoretical ground on which our model of proletarian growth stands offers one way to understand the impact of the change of employment and the new relationships between men and land. Occupations and land ownership ran parallel to industrial growth. As more and more people were employed in industry, their ties to the land were weakened and the importance of property to them diminished, both inside the family and within the larger community. This is the logic: if the possession of land was required to establish a household, a substitute source of income would disrupt the social system built around land. The community's discipline would be diminished, because land gave parents power with which to control their children. The members of a rural proletariat, employed in industry or even in agriculture, had no control over the land and thus were not subject to the land's discipline.

This argument has been criticized because it rests on implausible assumptions and because it is difficult to verify empirically.[8] The most improbably assumption lies at its core: the idea that land provided discipline, when we know that a very large part of the population had very little land and very little prospect of ever getting enough land to be self-sufficient. If the social discipline (such as late marriage ages) we find prior to industrial development had no basis in land, there is little reason to expect that the creation of an industrial proletariat destroyed it. There are two problems with the verification of this hypothesis. First, the extremely detailed research bringing together patterns of land ownership and family characteristics has yet to be done. Second, it is difficult to show in any population that the availability of land determined individual decisions about specific actions such as marriage and childbearing; the absence of its relationship in an industrial population does not prove very much.

Variations in the structure of the industrial labor force interacted with the role of land and agriculture in the economy to shape the society that was formed. Even in the developing proletariat, people did not readily give up their allegiance to the land. Put another way, only where industry seemed to offer an unrestricted path out of the limits of peasant society did it lead people to change their behavior. The proletariat was not completely formed by the end of the eighteenth century.

LAND AND SOCIAL STRUCTURE IN THE VERVIERS REGION

Land Ownership

As the rural population grew, the average amount of land controlled by each family declined, but the level of concentration increased: a smaller number of peasant farmers each had more land, while a larger and larger category of landless or almost landless workers developed. From the relatively landless population came the industrial workers. For Limburg we can readily differentiate the part of the population which had farmland from that which had only a garden, and that which had no land at all.[9] In 1670, about 40 percent of all taxpayers in the two most important sections of Limburg paid tax on farmland (Table 6.2). The remaining 60 percent had only a garden or no land at all. Those with only a garden or no land were employed by others; many of them worked as farm laborers, while the rest worked in industrial jobs. By the end of the eighteenth century the number of taxpayers with land declined to about 18 percent. In 1670 about half the families in Limburg worked in industry; by 1780 more than two-thirds of them did. Limburg was less industrialized than Verviers, but more so than most other places.

Thimister was less industrial than Limburg. Its tax rolls show that by 1682, the year for which we have our earliest data, some 24 percent of taxpayers paid tax on one-half *bonnier* or less, just enough for a garden.[10] Another quarter of the taxpayers had between one-half and two *bonniers*. This one-half of the taxpaying population, plus the untaxed, constituted the candidates for industrial employment. Those with larger farms would have been

Table 6.2: Taxpayer Characteristics in Limburg, 1670–1780

Year	Total Number Taxpayers	% No Land	% Garden Only	% With Land
1670	184	20.1	37.0	42.9
1700	165	28.5	29.7	41.8
1710	243	46.5	25.5	28.0
1720	250	41.6	31.6	26.8
1730	269	44.2	31.1	25.7
1740	290	46.6	29.0	24.5
1750	278	47.1	29.5	23.4
1760	271	48.0	31.4	20.7
1771	331	54.4	26.6	19.0
1780	297	52.9	29.0	18.2

SOURCE: AEL, Communes, Limburg, 238 (1700), 246 (1710), 254 (1720), 266 (1740), 276 (1750), 286 (1760), 294 (1771), and 299 (1780); and AEL, Thisquen, 139 (1670), and 141 (1730).

too busy with farming to be very occupied with industrial work, and even wives and children would have been short of time. By 1787 some 39 percent of Thimister's taxpayers had one-half *bonnier* or less and were likely industrial workers, while the intermediate category had shrunk to 19 percent. In all likelihood, one-third of all households were involved in industry in Thimister in the late seventeenth century, while half or more were doing industrial work in the late eighteenth century. The same was the case in Soiron and Ensival, although the latter became much more urban (and therefore more like Limburg) by the end of the eighteenth century.

One striking fact about the region between the Meuse and Vesdre rivers was the large proportion of the land owned by families whom we can classify as part peasant and part industrial worker.[11] While farms were small in the second half of the eighteenth century (more than 40 percent were less than one hectare, enough to feed only one or two cows), more than 80 percent of the land was owned by residents of the village in which it was located or by residents of neighboring villages. City dwellers from Verviers, Liège, Aachen, or Maastricht owned very little land. The dominant local landowners were dairy-farming peasants: farmers with five or more cows may have controlled as much as 60 percent of the land in combination dairying-textile villages such as Thimister, Charneux, or Clermont.[12]

That peasants had been the main landowners in the mid-seventeenth century, before the rapid growth of industry, should not surprise us.[13] What might be unusual is their continuing ownership of most of the land in the eighteenth century. Declining farm size and the growth of rural industry should signal poverty. Yet there was an active local land market in which small parcels of land were traded. This land helped round out the middle-sized farms that were so crucial to the peasant character of the villages. These pieces of land were purchased with the income produced by rural industry, specifically the income of women and children working part-time at spinning.

We must not underestimate the importance of the land market and the income that supported it. In most communities between the seventeenth and nineteenth centuries, the market for credit and for land made more peasants sellers than buyers and concentrated landownership in the hands of a few rich peasants or in the hands of rich city dwellers. The mechanism that led to this is simple. Peasants were vulnerable to all sorts of economic shocks: high taxes, bad weather, and poor harvests, as well as more extreme forms of bad luck such as the death of a husband or wife, or the arrival of an army to spend a few days or to winter in the region.[14] For those without large reserves of cash (which meant almost everyone), the only response was to borrow from wealthier neighbors or from urban lenders. The kind of shocks that caused the initial problem came far too often, so that rather than paying off the loans, peasants found themselves first further in debt and later forced to give up the collateral—usually land—that they had given as security.

This pattern was normal in the seventeenth century, especially during and after the wars of Louis XIV (which ended in 1713). The credit market worked to transfer cash from the city to the countryside, and the ownership of land from the peasantry to the bourgeoisie. It would do so again in the nineteenth century, after factories replaced cottage industry around Verviers.[15]

But in the eighteenth century a different pattern operated, because incomes from industrial work allowed peasants to pay off the loans they needed to cope with calamities, and let them purchase small parcels by borrowing the money to pay for them. City dwellers became net sellers rather than net buyers of rural land. Land and agriculture thus retained much of their importance to the people of the Verviers region. This was reflected in the kind of rural industrial society that developed in the eighteenth century.[16]

Rural social structure in the countryside around Verviers merged the hierarchy of land ownership and the hierarchy of occupations. At the very top were businessmen, municipal officials, professionals, and the small number of large landowners, *les plus adhérités* (to use the Walloon term; in French it would be *coqs de village*). Next came the more substantial peasants, those with several hectares of land and a number of cows. Even these families, we can be sure, were involved in the industrial part of the economy. If we look in detail at the censuses taken around 1800, a number of farmers had wives who were spinners. In Thimister in 1803, 22 of 82 farmers' wives (27 percent) were spinners.[17] Among the farmers who did not have a wife who spun or children who were spinners or weavers, many were related to people who worked in the textile industry. When looking into this it was assumed that people who lived in the same village and had the same surname were related. In Thimister 34 of 51 kin groups (67 percent) that included at least one farmer family were related to a family headed by a spinner or weaver.[18]

At the bottom of the social ladder were beggars and the settled poor, but just above them were workers who owned a small piece of land, or rented a cottage, or lived with someone else. These families earned practically all their income from industrial work, but they were not a homogeneous group. We can divide them into one group made up of agricultural laborers; a second consisting of weavers, teaselers and shearmen; and a third group made up of spinners (Figure 6.2). While all three of these groups were thoroughly integrated into the community (they were related to members of almost every other group), they were still distinct—by wealth, by function, and by composition.

Figure 6.2.   The Proletariat in the Verviers Region

---

1. Agricultural Workers
2. Spinners
3. Other Industrial Workers
   a. Weavers
   b. Teaselers
   c. Shearmen

The region's social structure was not strictly divided into agricultural and industrial elements. The social and political elite of the villages around Verviers included prosperous farmers, merchants, and protoindustrialists. All held local political office, all served as special representatives, all signed petitions. Similarly, if we could examine the occupations of the parents of brides and grooms, we would see that there was a significant amount of intermarriage between the traditional crafts, farmers, and the skilled textile occupations. Silvana Patriarca, Etienne Hélin, and René Leboutte have shown this for the early nineteenth century, but for the earlier period the sources with which to examine this do not exist.[19]

The only exceptional group was the spinners, who were a bit outside the integrated village society. Spinner households were different from other households. They were more likely to be headed by women, and more likely to be headed by single or widowed people, than other households. They were almost certainly poorer than other households. In Herve, Soiron, Charneux, and Thimister, they made up a minority of about one-fifth of the population, and it was a minority apart. Even their living conditions differed. Most families in these villages lived in their own houses, however small.[20] In Thimister about one-third of all households lived in houses with other families, with about 20 percent being the secondary family, or tenant. Spinner families and agricultural worker families were overrepresented in this group.

Kinship and Friendship

We need to push our social analysis beyond the limits imposed by occupations and land. The village consisted of groups of allies, linked by kinship or friendship, and organized along lines of patronage and clientage rather than along class lines. Bruno Dumont's recent work on the political and social life of the communities of the duchy of Limburg shows this.[21] Each circle of allies included some richer and more powerful members, and some poorer and less powerful ones. The more respected gave the others support and protection in material form; the weaker gave the stronger access to manpower—during the labor intensive times of the agricultural calendar, for special projects such as construction, and for the general strength to be found in numbers: the bigger the circle of allies you have, the stronger you appear.

These overlapping circles of kinship and friendship gave meaning to the social relationships of individual and family life cycles. These were the people who participated in a family's important events: baptism, communion, marriage, burial. From the circle came godparents for a baptized child or a confirmee. If marriage partners should not be close kin, they could be and often were members of the family's circle of friends. However, we should not inflate the importance of concepts such as kinship and circles of allies, at the expense of older proven ideas such as property and occupation. For one thing, identifying these circles in old-regime villages is hardly easy. We see keys in marriage alliances, and in godparentage and the witnesses present at weddings; but the network is so complex that deciphering it is very difficult.[22] These relationships come to the surface most readily in legal documents that record antisocial behavior, in the investigation of quarrels, or in the litigation over property and inheritance. Le Roy Ladurie exploits these sources in his work.[23] They are also used by David Sabean in a book about German village and small-town society.[24] But these sources are not always available to the historian, and their interpretation is tricky.

Kinship, property, and wealth determined social relationships. This was not a society of classes, based merely on access to the means of production. Groups of friends and kin sustained themselves with a system of emotional and material support based on reciprocity and patronage. There was social discipline in this too. This social discipline is what kept young adults from marrying earlier than they did, more than the mere allure of future property and more than the risk of parental disapproval. Marriage did not only mean property, it meant continued access to the family's circle and all it offered in the form of patronage; this was especially important for younger children (or any children not destined to inherit a large share of their parents' estate), and for the children of poor parents.[25] The social discipline of the family's circle must be added to what we know about the social discipline of a youth culture that controlled the marriage market through courtship processes and "rough music."[26] Only by bearing in mind this kind of social discipline can we understand the persistence of late marriage in western Europe despite the growing importance of individualism.

NUPTIALITY PATTERNS AND SOCIAL STRUCTURES

The relative social isolation of the spinners and day laborers and the relative integration of the weavers should not mask for us the social distinctiveness of these groups within the mature early industrial society of the Verviers region. In no way is this more apparent than in the nuptiality patterns of the different social groups. We can measure the age pattern of nuptiality by occupation at the end of this era, by calculating the singulate mean age at marriage (SMAM). This is a measure based on census information about the age, sex, and marital status of a population. The distribution of men and women by their age and marital status is used to calculate the proportion single in each five-year age group between the ages of 15 and 55. These proportions are then placed in a formula created by the demographer John Hajnal to imply the average age of marriage for the population recorded in the census.[27]

Table 6.3 reports the singulate mean age at marriage by occupation, for six rural communities. These figures are based on censuses taken around 1800, but we should recall that people aged 50 had been married twenty years, so that the ages are reflective of earlier social conditions. Because many adults had no occupation listed in these censuses, the table reflects what we can call the family's occupational status, based on that of the

Table 6.3: Singulate Mean Age at Marriage, by Occupation: Six Verviers Region Communities, ca. 1800*

	Males	Females
Proletarian Occupations	28.22	29.01
Spinners & Low-status textile	29.87	29.84
Servants & laborers	26.26	27.30
Industrial Occupations	25.43	23.76
Weavers	25.59	23.89
All others	25.24	23.66
Other Occupations	29.20	26.71
Farmers	30.57	27.78
Crafts	26.77	26.56
Food & lodging	28.50	27.46
Trade & transportation	26.02	24.07
All others	32.07	27.47
Total population	27.71	26.64

*The communities are Charneux, Thimister, Herve, Limburg, Ensival, Soiron.
SOURCE: Same as Table 6.1.

household head. To calculate singulate mean ages at marriage by occupation I put everyone in the occupational category of the head of household if they were related to him or her. I placed unrelated members of the household (professional assistants, servants, lodgers, and simply "unrelated" people, for example) in the category of their own occupation. Thus the wife of a farmer or weaver who was herself described as a spinner would be classified among the farmers or weavers, whereas an unrelated woman spinner who lived with them would be classified among the spinners. I did this not only to be able to give occupations to people who had none but also to take into account that the wife and children of a farmer or weaver, no matter what they worked at, should be grouped with him.

Marriage ages were high in the Verviers region, for men as well as women. The differences between occupational groups are highlighted in Figure 6.3. Men in farmer families had the highest singulate mean age at marriage, followed by spinners and members of the food trades.[28] All these were above 28 years. Below them came a second group, who married between the ages of 26 and 27 years: servants and laborers, craftsmen, and members of the transportation and trading occupations. Finally, men in industrial households married when they were about 25.5 years old. For women, the pattern is similar. Women in spinning households had a much higher singulate mean age at marriage than any other group, nearly 30 years. Beneath them came farmers, the food trades, servants and laborers, and crafts, all between 26.5 and 28. Then there was a second big jump, to women in industrial families and in trading and transportation families, with mean marriage ages at or below 24 years.

The marriage ages of the spinners, weavers, and other industrial occupations are the most important data in the table. That farmers had relatively high marriage ages, and that other traditional occupational groups (such as crafts and the preparation and sales of food) fall in intermediate places, should not surprise us. But we might wonder why the spinner families had such high ages at marriage, and why industrial families had such low ages at marriage. In the case of spinners the protoindustrialization hypothesis says that the ready availability of work and income made them likely to marry very young.[29] That was not the case in the Verviers region, as it was not in Auffay before 1786, because spinning was work for women and for the very poorest members of the community.[30] The origin of the word "spinster" is not without importance.[31] Unmarried women who had no other means of support worked at spinning, and if they could not live with relatives who had other occupations, they would be classified in these data as spinners. These women raise the singulate mean marriage age for females in spinner families. The poverty of those who used spinning as anything other than supplemental income meant that we cannot see them in an advantaged position that would make them more inclined than the population as a whole to marry; if anything they were less so.

The weavers and holders of other industrial jobs present us with the opposite problem of interpretation. If these people were better integrated into the rural society of the Verviers region, they should have been more like the farmers in marriage behavior too, and not married so early. Obviously, that is not true. It is likely that the weavers used their relative prosperity not to buy

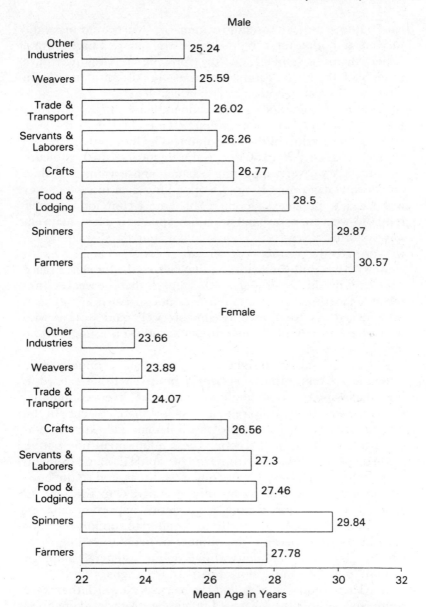

Figure 6.3.   Singulate Mean Age at Marriage, by Occupation: Six Verviers Region Communities, c. 1800
SOURCE: Table 6.3.

land but to set up a household and marry. This would make the weavers and other industrial workers, while more a part of rural society than the spinners, the true proletariat. They may have resembled their occupational cousins, the English handloom weavers, more closely than anything else.[32]

The economic and social vulnerability of the weavers becomes apparent in other evidence. One element is the size, cost, and ownership of the broadloom. The loom was large and expensive, costing 20 to 50 florins during most of the eighteenth century.[33] A weaver supporting a family and earning less than one florin a day would have to work a long time to save money with which to purchase a loom.[34] Much more common was their rental to weavers by urban and rural capitalists. The usual rent was 4 florins a year, the equivalent of four days' wages for a weaver.[35] In the Verviers region we see looms changing hands among fairly wealthy individuals, who treated the loom as a piece of income-producing property.[36] It suggests that the weaver himself (for most weavers were men) was not so much a craftsman who owned his tools as a reasonably well paid worker who worked either at home or in a draper's workshop using tools he may have rented.

We can get another insight into the social and economic place of textile workers from the system of poor relief that existed in the villages and towns of the Verviers region.[37] Every community had some way of providing for its less fortunate citizens. In the best situation the village or the parish had an endowment dedicated to providing for the poor. These endowment funds were made up of income earned from land or capital donated by members of the community. The income was distributed to the poor by the parish priest or by an official assigned to the task, in response to recommendations from clergy, important citizens, and public officials. When the funds required to support the poor were inadequate, because the number of people needing them had increased, the community would conduct a general campaign to raise money from its more prosperous citizens.

We know about the poor and the means with which they were supported because the towns of Limburg and Verviers kept good records, and because the French regime collected statistics about poverty beginning around 1800.[38] While we must guess that nearly half of the population was poor in the sense of not living well, the statistics of the early nineteenth century tell us that contemporaries considered between 8 and 15 percent of the population to be poor under the definition set by Antoine-François Desmousseaux, prefect of the department of the Our-the, in November 1800: "those who, being incapable of work and without relatives capable of assisting them, can absolutely not exist without the aid of national charity."[39] The letters written by the clergy of Limburg in the eighteenth century tell us that the poor who received regular assistance were those too old to work, the ill and injured, and widows and widowers supporting young children.[40]

In terms of occupation, most of the recipients of aid were laborers, textile workers, or members of the families of laborers and textile workers. Relatively few came from farmers' families. We can confirm this for the early nineteenth century when we compare the list of recipients of aid with the census, which included occupation.[41] Not everyone mentioned in the list of poor can be found in the census.[42] We can find fifteen out of a list of forty-five. Among these fifteen, none were farmers or members of other traditional crafts. Four were weavers, two were spinners (there were not many spinners in Limburg), three worked in other industrial jobs in the textile industry, two were day laborers, one was an *epicier* (a petty retailer), two were crippled, and one had no occupation at all. The conclusion to draw is that the textile trades—and especially the weavers—were very vulnerable to hardship. The weavers were not elite but rather part of a growing industrial proletariat. Marriage ages, loom prices and ownership, and the data on poor relief confirm this.

Poor relief was not reserved for the agricultural population in Limburg. We do not get the sense that industrial workers were outsiders and their requests for assistance went unanswered. Obviously there is much we do not yet know about the recipients of assistance in Limburg, and the process by which they received aid. But when we speak of a hybrid society between agriculture and industry, we can say that the system for supporting the poor recognized the roles played by both the agricultural and the industrial parts of the population.

It is difficult to judge how people perceived their social status and that of their neighbors, without direct evidence about values. Despite this caveat, we can conclude that in the late eighteenth century, rural society in the Verviers region valued both the real and the symbolic importance of land, on the one hand, and the income that came from industrial work, on the other.[43] The two were inextricably mixed. We can see the value they put on land in its relatively broad distribution among the area's inhabitants, and in their willingness to sustain a busy market. In the eighteenth century, at least, even peasants with modest holdings were not being pushed off the land by a middle class of yeomen and businessmen eager to possess their land and subject them as workers. Yet we should not underestimate the rural population's commitment to industrial work. Overall, half of all adults were employed directly in industry in the region, and the income from it was used not merely by the poorest members of the community for subsistence but by their more prosperous neighbors as an income supplement that allowed the acquisition of property and the preservation of peasant status.

The preservation of the peasantry does not contradict the growth of an industrial proletariat in the Verviers region. There was only a limited amount of land, and only limited opportunities for peasant dairy farmers. As the population grew, most of the growth took place at the bottom of the social scale, among workers employed in the lowest level of industrial work, as nailmakers and spinners. Their parents and some of their relatives, however, were weavers and shearmen. This is how the occupational data confirm the growth of the proletariat.[44] Our local data about the occupations of household heads, shown in Table 6.1, tell us that by 1800 between one-fifth and two-fifths of all households were led by a person with a proletarianized job. This proportion had probably doubled in a century. This was taking place in a region where social conditions in settings of rural industry were relatively favorable, so that industry continued to exist as a supplement, rather than becoming everyone's source of income. In poorer regions the proletariat must have grown faster and become economically and socially disadvantaged all the more quickly.

Limburg and Ensival were tiny towns, socially somewhere between the more rural village and the more urban Verviers. Their occupational structures show this. These tiny towns had larger numbers of weavers and smaller numbers of spinners than the rural villages and Herve. The other difference is in the presence in both communities of larger numbers of teaselers and shearmen (especially in Ensival), and of drapers (in Limburg). But we should not make too much of these differences. The textile industry's occupational structure made weaving and finishing processes (such as teaseling and shearing) predominant in places closer to Verviers. Limburg, which was a secondary center, not only had more weavers, teaselers, and shearmen, it also had more drapers, the industry's leaders. Moreover, Limburg had a significant number of people occupied in agriculture, while Ensival had almost as many as Soiron. The social organization of all these more rural communities was substantially the same, with an agricultural and traditional commercial sector and a balancing industrial sector of roughly the same size.

Poverty was also different in the small industrial towns. In Limburg, weavers were the occupational group most likely to be receiving assistance. Looking at housing patterns, in both Limburg and Ensival we find weavers, teaselers, and shearmen all more likely to be sharing a house than farmers, tradesmen, and craftsmen. The spinners characterized such places as Charneux and Thimister, by providing a large and distinctive occupationally defined set of families at the bottom of the social hierarchy. The spinners in those communities were poorer and more socially isolated than the weavers in Limburg and Ensival, but all these industrial families were operating at some level of social disadvantage.

MOBILITY AND RESIDENCE IN THE HYBRID SOCIETY

The break from the land and the conversion to new occupations brought new patterns of behavior. In general, the populations of heavily industrialized rural areas were far more mobile, both geographically and socially, than peasant populations still closely tied to the land.[45] In this industrial setting workers became more like another mobile group, the poor, who moved around because they were unable to support themselves on the land.[46]

In the literature of the eighteenth century we find a number of autobiographies of successful literate industrial workers. There are enough of them to think of a genre, from which we can cautiously generalize. The caution derives from the extent to which these lives were exemplary but not representative. Only the most successful wrote autobiographies. One well-known autobiography of this type is that of the Swiss Ulrich Bräker, author of *Life Story of the Poor Man of Toggenburg.*[47] Bräker's father was a saltpeter-maker who longed to be a farmer. The family faced many difficulties as the father attempted to fulfill that dream, only to sink hopelessly into debt and emerge again as a saltpeter-maker. Bräker moved frequently during his childhood and adulthood. He served as a soldier and at a variety of other jobs before settling in as a cotton merchant. Like his father, he had aspirations higher than the conditions in which he found himself. He wanted to be an author and even won a literary prize. Bräker never became rich, and he did not like the social conditions that accompanied his literary success. But he succeeded as merchant and author. He was mobile, both socially and geographically.

The Verviers region has its own analogue to Bräker. Henri-Joseph Delilez was born in 1745 in the town of Pepinster, a village located about six kilometers west of Verviers.[48] The son of an agricultural worker, he was sent at the age of 11 to work as a shepherd for one of his uncles. At age 15 he began work as an agricultural servant, which he continued for eight years. This looks like the normal agricultural work life, one likely to continue. Yet Delilez was different. He learned the rudiments of reading; by the time he was 18 he chose employers by the size of their libraries and their willingness to lend books to him.

At the age of 24, this agricultural worker without any capital (his widowed father was far from comfortable, the father of five children) easily made himself into an industrial craftsman. Delilez returned from a pilgrimage to Rome and apprenticed himself to a fuller, one of the smallest occupational groups in the Verviers region.[49] Less than four years later he was confident enough to tramp as a journeyman, finding work in Italy, Austria, and Czechoslovakia (Moravia). He returned to Ensival only in 1777, at the age of 32, married to a woman from nearby Eupen whom he met in Czechoslovakia. Once home, however, his normal process through life was again disturbed. He did not continue long as a textile-trade journeyman. Beginning in 1780 he devoted more and more of his time to teaching, so that by the late 1780s he did so full-time. In the 1790s he served first as municipal secretary and then, in 1796, as public school teacher.[50] He continued to teach until his death in 1816 at the age of 71.

As with Bräker, the main pattern we can draw from Delilez's life is mobility. We must be cautious about drawing sweeping generalizations, but we can conclude from his memoir that many other natives of the Verviers region moved around. He encountered them almost everywhere he went. That he was literate, became a teacher, and wrote a memoir places him among a minority. Yet his story echoes enough facts confirmed by other kinds of documents to suggest that Delilez's is one model of life in the industrial-agricultural communities that became widespread in the eighteenth century.

We should conclude from Delilez's narrative that all forms of mobility were possible in the growing industrial communities of the eighteenth century. He moved easily from agriculture to industry to teaching. He also moved easily from place to place. Villages and towns lay close enough together to make movement from one to another easy, and the slight social and economic differences among them kept few individuals from relocating. Finally, he was socially mobile. He started as a shepherd, worked as a textile craftsman, and became a minor functionary and schoolmaster. In the process he acquired some land. Self-improvement was possible. Moreover, his origins did not keep him from being accepted by the village elite in Ensival.

The flexibility and mobility we see in Delilez's life reflect a general structure that mixed agriculture and industry and made movement easy. The communities in which he lived lay between a purely agricultural peasant society dominated by landlords, lawyers, and wealthy farmers and a factory society as created in the nineteenth century. These eighteenth-century industrial communities had their own form of social bond, because industrial jobs were not really new and because the peasant base was not so exclusively the source of income as it had been in the past.

The settlement pattern in which Delilez and his contemporaries lived is remarkable and worth understanding. Map 6.1 reproduces some elements of a map drawn in the 1770s by Austrian military engineers.[51] Like many military maps drawn in the eighteenth century, the original is remarkably detailed, showing individual buildings and fields. This detail provides an extraordinary view of the nature of physical living and communication arrange-

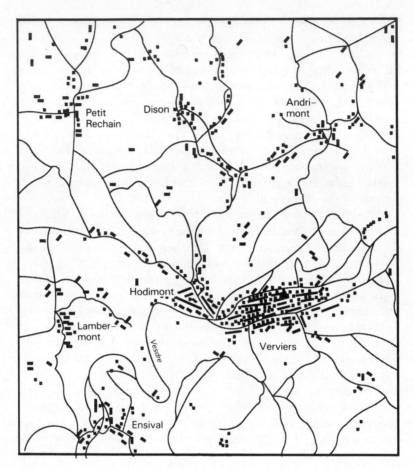

Map 6.1.   Settlement Patterns in the Verviers Region

ments. Verviers lies near the center of the part of the map repro-
duced here. The Vesdre runs from center right to lower left. We
see clearly the densely populated industrial region north of the
Vesdre.

The pattern of settlement encouraged the kind of geographical and occupational mobility experienced by Delilez. The region
east of Liège and north of the Vesdre was made up in the eighteenth century of communities strung out along a dense network
of roads, rather than concentrated in nucleated settlements. If we

look at any of the roads on the map, we find houses along much of the way. This is so from Hodimont to Andrimont and Dison, and from Hodimont to Ensival and Lambermont. Communities lay close together. There were many roads and paths. Walking from one place to another—in search of a new place to work, a new kind of employment, or a farm or house to rent—was a matter of spending a single day or just a single evening on the road. Among places mentioned often in this book (not all of them located on Map 6.1), the road from Verviers to Limburg is about eight kilometers; from Verviers to Ensival three kilometers; from Ensival to Pepinster four kilometers; from Verviers to Herve ten kilometers; and from Verviers to Thimister eight kilometers. Moreover, the number of houses and farms along the road made this a relatively safe journey, even at night. These distances were easily traversed.

Most of the houses our traveler would have found along these roads were small, built of wood or stone, heated with fireplaces, and illuminated with relatively small, square windows. Many of the stone buildings are still standing, so we can get a very good sense of what they looked like and how they were used in the eighteenth century.[52] There were a few large farm buildings, large not in their residential sections but in the parts of the building used to house livestock or store supplies and tools. And by the late eighteenth century each of the villages had a center in which stood a few attractive multistoried houses, of the kind one would have seen in a town like Verviers or even Liège.

All the houses, in Verviers and in the villages, were intensively used by their owners and tenants. Verviers in the seventeenth and eighteenth centuries collected taxes based on the value of real estate and on the number of families. The records show that a large number of houses, even the most valuable ones inhabited by some of the wealthiest families, contained more than a single family.[53] That should hardly surprise us, since Verviers was already a substantial town. We find a similar pattern in the village censuses taken around 1800. These censuses were taken house by house, and we can see how many houses were inhabited by more than one family. In Thimister, for example, 174 families out of 521 (almost exactly one-third) shared a house with other families.[54] We find the same pattern in almost all the villages.

SOCIETY IN THE EARLY INDUSTRIAL TOWN: URBAN, SEMIURBAN, OR RURAL?

Cottage industry spawned early industrial towns, just as it engendered several kinds of villages. The bustling small town, inhabited by fewer than 20,000 residents, was an ideal location in which to center an industry that had a great deal of contact with the countryside. Verviers was one of these. There were many others. The French town of Sedan—about which more later—was a bit larger than Verviers, but it had much the same social milieu.[55] These towns had close commercial relationships with larger cities, but they differed from them in significant ways. We saw in Chapter 5 that Verviers had a characteristic demographic pattern throughout much of the seventeenth and eighteenth centuries. This was probably typical of many towns its size. These towns also had their own social characteristics.

One clear way that the small industrial town differed from the villages in its hinterland was in its size. It was significantly larger. Verviers was five times as large as a big village such as Thimister, Charneux, or Herve. Gullickson describes Auffay, with its 1,250 inhabitants, as a large village; but the towns nearby were much larger.[56] Among the towns mentioned earlier, only Comines was tiny, with about 2,000 inhabitants.[57] In fact, a multiple of five is an understatement. Verviers was a single urbanized settlement, whereas the villages all had a central core with a number of hamlets. Verviers probably grouped together eight times as many people as lived in the biggest village. Along with size came density. Verviers's 12,000 people in 1789 were crowded into an area not much bigger than that of a village, with a density four or five times as great. If one-third of all families in Thimister shared houses with other families, two-thirds or more did so in Verviers, dividing a small two- or three-story house.[58] With size and density came dirt. The town government struggled hard against dirt, authorizing official manure collectors (who had the right to sell what they collected) and fining the worst violators of ordinances against dumping dirt. The villages too had problems with dirt; but the much larger population, and the amount of dirt contributed by industry, made the problem all the more difficult in Verviers.

In addition to larger size, the small towns had a different kind of population, although not so different that we can ignore the similarities between them and neighboring places. Figure 6.1 highlights the different occupational structures of Verviers and Limburg. In many ways their structures are similar: about half the population directly involved in industry; about one-tenth described as *journaliers* or day laborers; relatively small numbers in the high-status occupations: the professions, administrative tasks, and *rentiers* (those who lived off the income from their investments). Their differences stand out, however. The most notable difference is the almost total absence of farmers in Verviers, where they make up less than 1 percent of household heads, compared to nearly 14 percent in Limburg. On the other hand, Verviers had a higher proportion of household heads working in services, and its industrial structure differed from that of both Limburg and the more rural industrial centers such as Thimister. Verviers was the center of the textile industry. Its workers were concentrated in cloth finishing. It had few spinners, a substantial number of weavers, and even more teaselers and shearmen.

The differing proportional spread between the three large skilled textile groups—weavers, teaselers, and shearmen—does not reflect a different social structure so much as a different economic structure in the small town in contrast to the villages. These three groups had the same general level of social status; all three fared well in good times and were vulnerable to hardship in difficult times. What made Verviers different socially from Thimister and Charneux, and even from Limburg and Ensival, was the complete absence of agriculture. Verviers had an industrial and commercial elite; its social leaders came from the industrialists and to a lesser extent from bankers, notaries, and lawyers. Its responsible citizens were all craftsmen and small businessmen. In the villages, part of the elite and a significant part of the second tier of socially respectable citizens came from among the farmers. This gave a completely different cast to influence and to the general tone of social relations.

Government

It is not easy to grasp completely what made Verviers different from the villages around it, and the reason is that it was like those other places in some ways and unlike them in others. The proximity of one place to another, the freedom of movement possessed by everyone, the integration of the economy—all these things made a unit of the region. We have a difficult time breaking it up. Yet Verviers was decidedly different and decidedly urban—economically, socially, and environmentally. We can see this in the way the town was governed and in the concerns of its governing body: the minutes of the Verviers town council are a living record of a group preoccupied with the problems of a town.[59] In volumes of minutes and orders, and in file after file of correspondence, we find a small number of decidedly urban themes repeated again and again.

The first concern of the *échevins* and *burgermasters* of Verviers was their political and economic environment: how to govern the town and how to deal with other governmental bodies (such as other towns in the region, the principality of Liège, and the government of the Austrian Netherlands in Brussels) in order to maintain their autonomy and guarantee the unhindered conduct of their principal industry, textile manufacturing. Preserving their freedom to do business without great restrictions and heavy taxes was the main subject of the town leaders' actions. Their second subject of concern was management of the town's physical environment, especially the Vesdre River. Town life and the textile industry demanded the construction and management of physical facilities, about which the council decided. Where to put the cemetery? How to provide enough room for stretching out cloth to dry after fulling? How to provide a public water supply? Water was always crucial to old regime towns, but it was even more so in the textile industry, where fresh water was needed for cleaning and dyeing, and where water power was needed for fulling. Diverting water to these uses with dams and canals restricted its flow, led to flooding around the diversions, and fouled it for human consumption, causing a constant stream of complaints to the council and a stream of orders and concessions from it.

The last major concern of the council was public order. Its members had many reasons to worry. All urban populations are disruptive, and in this Verviers was no exception. The city government provided police and a guard service in times of danger, although crime was still a problem according to the complaints it received. Public demonstrations and riots seemed a constant risk. Even in good times, when food and wages were adequate or abundant, the carnival season or other times of religious celebration (in Verviers, for example, the moment the so-called "Cross of Verviers" was carried to Liège) could lead to riot. In bad times, when unemployed workers found food impossible to buy or when troops were occupying the town—which happened all too often between 1650 and 1800—matters could get out of hand even more quickly. Industrial relations between workers and employers gave the council still more reason to worry and to act. These relations help us pin down the kind of society that existed in Verviers even before the factories, and show just how the transition to mechanization was going to work.

Worker-Employer Relations

Relations between workers and employers in Verviers appear to have been relatively smooth most of the time.[60] There were few regulations governing either side's conduct, which gave everyone great flexibility to act as they wished. With many employers and many skilled workers, we get no sense of monopoly or monopsony. This confirms the sense of social and economic flexibility described earlier and the sense of mobility we get from reading Delilez's journal. Nevertheless, disagreements arose. In 1739 the weavers complained that the drapers were employing "foreign" workers.[61] They were sufficiently serious to go on strike. The prince-bishop of Liège forbade the sending of yarn to the countryside, a rule relaxed as soon as the economy recovered in 1746.

The shearmen were always the most militant of the textile workers, probably because it was they who worked in the relatively large shops the drapers were operating in the eighteenth century. Working together, and paid by the day instead of by the piece, they most closely resemble modern factory workers. They were the first to organize and among the earliest to strike against their employers. There were early strikes in 1719, 1722, and 1762 at Eupen, in 1739 and 1740 in Verviers (simultaneous with the weavers' strike), and in 1742 in Hodimont. The Hodimont strike led to a ruling in 1743 from the Brussels government that set wages and limited the employment of "foreign" shearmen to those with two years' apprenticeship.[62] None of these strikes could be called a workers' success, since employers retained almost complete freedom to hire whomever they wished.

These events in the Verviers region took place almost simultaneously with similar workers' uprisings in Sedan. Sedan had an industry whose products were similar to those of Verviers. It produced high quality wool cloth for the international market, protected by special royal concessions. Moreover, there was a constant stream of interraction between Sedan, Verviers, and Monschau. The most mobile workers, especially the shearmen, moved back and forth freely among these and other textile centers.[63] And the employers themselves had very good business relationships. The main difference between the two textile centers was the presence in Sedan of a number of Protestant manufacturers, the decendants of families that had been permitted to remain even after the revocation of the Edict of Nantes. The textile industry in Sedan was wracked in the eighteenth century by strikes called when the shearmen felt that their independence and professionalism were called into question.[64] This happened more frequently as the manufacturers built larger workshops in which they attempted to control production and reduce costs. When the workers thought they could gain an advantage, or when they felt conditions were untenable, they called a strike—an event they named a *cloque*. This is how Gérard Gayot describes the beginning of a strike:

> Someone cried *cloque* in one or several shops; an assembly was held in a public hall, or perhaps in the town square, to restate the demand that would be presented to the police lieutenant by the representatives of the shearmen—they called themselves "deputies" in 1750. During the lengthy wait while the sentence was heard, the striking workers visited all the shops of the city to obtain the general cessation of work, which they judged the most effective means of putting pressure on the town's political authorities and the businessmen. Thus, for a complaint limited to a single shop in 1713, nearly 100 factories went on strike for a week.[65]

The Sedan conflict of the 1730s and 1740s arose over the obligation to carry pieces of cloth from the workshop to the drying racks. Not only was this hard work, but the manufacturer wanted to require it from the shearmen in addition to the quantity of production required of them daily. It was, in effect, an addition to their workday without pay, something that "since time immemorial" they had not been required to do. The problem arose mostly during times of labor shortage, because at those times a shearman asked to do extra work could simply quit and move to another employer. During most of the 1740s both shearmen and employers attempted to maintain the old fiction of relations between near equals. They tried, without much success, to negotiate their differences. By April 1750, in the wake of a royal decree issued in reaction to strikes in Carcasonne, Lyon, and Le Mans, as well as in Sedan, the employers (led by the Protestants among them) began to stand firm. On August 3 the workers began a general strike, which lasted until September 14. On that day royal troops arrested the leaders of the strike, ending it.

The manufacturers were in control. They were able to defeat the workers because they had the support of the state and because they had access to labor from other textile centers. During the final forty-three-day strike, they brought in workers from Verviers and Paris. The mobility of skilled labor in early modern Europe, something that was hardly new in the eighteenth century, this time worked in the interest of the employer.[66] They also appear to have had the support of their nominal competitors in Verviers and Monschau, although the ways in which this support worked is not yet fully apparent. The result, nonetheless, was a victory for the employers and a transformation of relationships between workers and employers that would be crucial for later developments.

The last big strike in Verviers occurred in the summer of 1759, when the Verviers shearmen struck. Theirs was not a complaint about poverty but an attempt to organize workers, to raise wages at a time when conditions were good and labor supplies short. The industry had at least nominally regulated wages, with the rate for shearmen set at 20 sous per twelve-hour-and-forty-minute day. Employers systematically evaded this rule by buying low quality German coins at a discount in Aachen and then forcing workers to accept them at face value.[67] The workers struck over this practice, and the employers responded by refusing to change their way of doing business. The initial outcome shows the shape of relations among workers, employers, and the city council. The city council issued an edict that set exchange rates, at a level that benefited the employers. This is what we would expect, given the domination of the Verviers city government by the industrialists, and given the obvious determination of the council to maintain as free an economic environment as possible.

The parties in the dispute were not necessarily governed by this solution. The shearmen continued to strike and went so far as to establish a "Confraternity of Shearmen of Verviers, Ensival, Hodimont, and the Francomont" that set wages at 20 sous per day.[68] It opened membership to those with two years of apprenticeship and a certificate of good conduct. This was a sort of labor union, with a treasury, the theoretical provision of strike benefits, and efforts at alliance with shearmen in nearby Aachen and Eupen. It indicates the sense of solidarity among the several hundred workers in this trade—the kind of solidarity between skilled workers one finds elsewhere in the eighteenth century and earlier, especially among skilled textile workers, printers, and others like them.[69] Rather than exploited employees pitted against ferocious industrialists, we find a kind of stand-off between two well-matched groups. Yet despite the strength and solidarity of the workers, they eventually had less power than their employers.

No one had enough power to resolve the situation unilaterally. The prince-bishop of Liège refused to approve the ordinance of the town council and the employers' agreement that had preceded it, because of the continuing danger to public order. He made no other rule, however, and the dispute finally settled down after a certain amount of time, largely because of the exhaustion of the parties. We can guess that some employers offered better rates, which got work going again. This was not an isolated case; small disagreements took place every few years in the 1760s and 1770s. In 1781 a new period of prosperity in the industry brought on a new strike by the shearmen, signaling their continuing sense of power and solidarity.

The question was posed at the beginning of this section about the ways in which the industrial town differed from the more rural communities near it. It was bigger and denser, of course, and it had no agriculture. But the behavior of the shearmen, and the similarities between Verviers and the other places in which there were significant numbers of them, suggests that we should not exaggerate the differences. Verviers, Hodimont, Ensival, and Limburg in the French-speaking area, and Eupen and Monschau in the German-speaking region, shared a lot of social characteristics. These shared characteristics confirm the continuum that existed between the most rural and the most urban parts of this hybrid society.

In April 1750 the Sedan shearmen justified their unwillingness to do certain tasks by saying that they "were not village workers."[70] By identifying themselves as skilled craftsmen who had undergone an apprenticeship, they declared that they were not like the poor and unskilled cottage industry workers who could be pushed around by their employers. The shearmen of Sedan were mistaken. In the eighteenth century the industrial town and the countryside converged in many ways, so that workers in the one lived lives similar to workers in the other. The density of settlement that arose in areas where early industry was strong is one element in this evolution. Dense settlement led to easy movement and communication; easy communication made for similarities between the small towns and the villages around them.

Despite the convergence of town and hinterland, the development of early industrial communities had not yet led to a homogenous society in the eighteenth century. Land and agriculture were still important to many families in industrial villages, especially in areas—such as Normandy and the Verviers region—where farming continued to employ a significant number of people. We find a layered society, in which there were peasant farmers, somewhat skilled industrial workers such as weavers, and a rural proletariat of laborers and spinners. These groups had different attitudes toward the land and toward the formation of families, at least insofar as we can judge by examining marriage patterns and the land market. Where these layered societies existed, society was less subject to the kind of rapid transformations that occurred in some places in Switzerland, Flanders, and England. There, industrial work became almost the only source of income available and a more homogenous rural society may have developed.

Early industrial society in small town and countryside was a hybrid. It shared characteristics with old-fashioned peasant villages and with the industrial society of the nineteenth century. It was part traditional and part modern. This was especially so in areas such as that around Verviers—where it grew up slowly and steadily. There it built on a long traditional of industrial work, and a long evolution of land occupation adapted to industrial work.

NOTES

1. Rudolf Braun, *Industrialisierung und Volksleben: Die Veränderungen der Lebensformen in einem ländlischen Industriegebiet vor 1800 (Zürcher Oberland)* (Erlenbach: Eugen Rentsch Verlag, 1960); and Braun, "Early Industrialization and Demographic Change in the Canton of Zürich," *Historical Studies of Changing Fertility*, ed. Charles Tilly (Princeton: Princeton University Press, 1978), pp. 289–334.

2. David Levine, *Family Formation in an Age of Nascent Capitalism* (New York: Academic Press, 1977). But see also his disclaimer, in Levine, "The Decline of Fertility in Europe: Review Symposium," *Population and Development Review* 12 (1986): 340, n. 6.

3. Gay L. Gullickson, "Proto-industrialization, Demographic Behavior and the Sexual Division of Labor in Auffay, France, 1750–1850," *Peasant Studies* 9 (1982): 106–118. Gullickson argues her point of view with a mass of interesting evidence in her subsequent book, *Spinners and Weavers of Auffay* (Cambridge: Cambridge University Press, 1986).

4. The conclusions drawn here from individual communes are confirmed by Servais's compilation of occupational statistics for larger administrative units. They appear accurate despite the economic collapse that took place during the early years of the Revolution. See Paul Servais, "Industries rurales et structures agraires: Le cas de l'entre-Vesdre-et-Meuse aux XVIIIème et XIXème siècles," *Revue Belge d'Histoire Contemporaine* 13 (1982): 185.

5. For more data on Verviers, see Claude Desama, "La population active à Verviers pendant la révolution industrielle," *Population et Famille* 47 (1979): 45–67, and 48 (1979): 45–75; also his monograph, Desama, *Population et révolution industrielle. Evolution des structures démographiques à Verviers dans la première moitié du 19e siècle* (Liège: Faculté de Philosophie et Lettres, 1985).

6. Servais, "Industries rurales," pp. 188–190.
7. D. Terrier and P. Toutain, "Pression démographique et marché du travail à Comines au XVIIIème siècle," *Revue du Nord* 61 (1979): 19–25.
8. Myron P. Gutmann and René Leboutte, "Rethinking Protoindustrialization and the Family," *Journal of Interdisciplinary History* 14 (1984): 607–621; Paul Spagnoli, "Industrialization, Proletarianization, and Marriage: A Reconsideration," *Journal of Family History* 8 (1983): 230–247; and Christian Vandenbroeke, "Le cas flamand: Evolution sociale et comportements démographiques au XVIIe–XIXe siècles," *Annales ESC* 39 (1984): 915–938.
9. These documents can be found in AEL, Communes, Limburg, 238–299, and in AEL, Thisquen, 139 and 141.
10. A *bonnier* is about 2.5 acres. Joseph Ruwet, *L'agriculture et les classes rurales au Pays de Herve sous l'ancien régime* (Liège: Faculté de Philosophie et Lettres, 1943), p. 247.
11. Servais, "Industries rurales et structures agraires"; and Servais, "Les structures agraires du Limbourg et des pays d'Outre-Meuse du XVIIe au XIXe siècle," *Annales ESC* 37 (1982): 303–319.
12. Servais, "Structures agraires," pp. 304–309.
13. For a list of the lords of these (and other Belgian) communities, see Eugene de Seyn, *Dictionnaire historique et géographique des communes belges*, 3rd ed., 2 vols. (Turnhout: Brepols, 1947); and Bruno Dumont, "Les communautés villageoises du duché de Limbourg" (Ph.D. Dissertation, University of Liège, 1987).
14. See Olwen Hufton, *The Poor of Eighteenth-Century France* (Oxford: Oxford University Press, 1974), for the risks faced by the poor. On the risks of war in the larger region, see Myron P. Gutmann, *War and Rural Life in the Early Modern Low Countries* (Princeton: Princeton University Press, 1980). See also Claude Desama and André Blaise, "Comment les communautés villageoises avaient recours au crédit au XVIIe siècle," *Credit Communal de Belgique* 21 (1967): 55–65; and P. Servais, "Le poids économique d'une occupation militaire," *Annales de la fédération archéologique et historique de Belgique* (1975), pp. 141–144.
15. The nineteenth century evolution is discussed by Servais, "Industries Rurales," as well as in Silvana Patriarca, "Farmers, Spinners, Weavers, and Their Families: Protoindustry and the Factory System in Charneux, Belgium, 1770–1870" (M.A. thesis, University of Texas at Austin, 1986).
16. The strength of peasant attitudes among cottage industry workers is the main subject of the work of Hans Medick, especially as it restates Chayanov's "theory of peasant economy." See Hans Medick, "The Proto-Industrial Family Economy," in Peter Kriedte et al., *Industrialization Before Industrialization* (Cambridge: Cambridge University Press, 1981), pp. 38–73; also A. V. Chayanov, *A. V. Chaya-*

nov on the Theory of Peasant Economy, ed. Daniel Thorner et al. (Homewood, Ill.: Irwin, 1966).
17. The distribution was as follows:

Housewife	14	17%
Spinner	22	27
Farmer	37	45
Milkmaid	4	5
None	5	6
Total	82	100%

SOURCE: Same as Table 6.1.

18. I identified 98 groups in Thimister as having two or more households headed by persons with the same surname.
19. Patriarca, "Farmers, Spinners, Weavers, and Their Families," p. 46; and Etienne Hélin and René Leboutte, "Le choix du conjoint," paper presented to the Chair Quetelet Meeting, "Au delà du quantitatif: Espoirs et limites de l'analyse qualitative en démographie," Louvain-la-Neuve, September 1985.
20. This analysis is drawn from the early nineteenth-century censuses cited in Table 6.1.
21. Dumont, "Les communautés villageoises."
22. For one example of how this might be done on the basis of marriage records, see George Alter, "The Influence of Social Stratification on Marriage in Nineteenth-Century Europe: Verviers, Belgium, 1844–1845" (Ph.D. dissertation, University of Pennsylvania, 1978).
23. See, for example, Emmanuel Le Roy Ladurie, *Montaillou, village occitan de 1294 à 1324* (Paris: Gallimard, 1975; translation, New York: Braziller, 1978).
24. David W. Sabean, *Power in the Blood: Popular Culture and Village Discourse in Early Modern Germany* (Cambridge: Cambridge University Press, 1984).
25. The property-poor are now the subject of study. For England, see Richard M. Smith, "Some Issues Concerning Families and Their Property in Rural England, 1250–1800" in *Land, Kinship and Lifecycle,* ed. Richard M. Smith (Cambridge: Cambridge University Press, 1984), pp. 68–85. The classic work is Hufton, *The Poor of Eighteenth-Century France.*
26. Natalie Z. Davis, "The Reasons of Misrule: Youth Groups and Charivaris in Sixteenth-Century France," *Past & Present* 50 (1971): 41–75; E. P. Thompson, " 'Rough Music': Le Charivari anglais," *Annales ESC* 27 (1972): 285–312; and John Gillis, *Youth and History* (New York: Academic Press, 1974), pp. 1–36.
27. John Hajnal, "Age of Marriage and Proportion Married," *Population Studies* 7 (1953–1954): 111–136.

28. I do not discuss the residual category of "All Others" in the "Other Occupations" panel of Table 6.3 because it includes clergy, who distort nuptiality figures.

29. Much of the discussion in the classic works that develop the protoindustrialization hypothesis as it applies to nuptiality—Braun and Mendels, for example—discuss rural spinners, albeit in the cotton and linen industries, respectively.

30. Gullickson, "Proto-industrialization."

31. See the interesting articles by Susan Watkins and Olwen Hufton in a special issue of the *Journal of Family History* on the subject of "Spinsterhood" 9 (Winter 1984): 310–325, 355–376.

32. See E. P. Thompson, *The Making of the English Working Class* (New York: Random House, 1963), pp. 269–313. There are also interesting parallels in Auffay. See Gullickson, "Proto-industrialization" and, more important, *Spinners and Weavers*.

33. See, for example, A.E.I., Notary J. L. Nizet, October 6, 1714, "Transport d'un metier fait par le sir Joseph Clement de Goer de Herve en faveur du Sr. Capne Pironet"; and Nicole Haesenne-Peremans and Etienne Hélin, "La naissance d'un prolétariat industriel," in *La Wallonie. Le pays et les hommes. Histoire-économies-sociétés*, ed. Hervé Hasquin, 2 vols. (Brussels: La Renaissance du Livre, 1975), 1: 425.

34. Pierre Lebrun, *L'industrie de la laine à Verviers pendant le XVIIIe et le début du XIXe siècle* (Liège: Faculté de Philosophie et Lettres, 1948), pp. 321–325.

35. Haesenne-Peremans and Hélin, "La naissance d'un prolétariat," p. 425.

36. This is the case in the documents from Notary Nizet cited in Note 33.

37. Nicole Haesenne-Peremans, *La pauvreté dans la région liégeoise à l'aube de la révolution industrielle. Un siècle de tension sociale (1730–1830)* (Liège: Faculté de Philosophie et Lettres, 1981).

38. On the French regime, see ibid., pp. 217–229. The documents about Limburg are in AEL, Communes, Limburg, 794–837, 895–900, 924; those about Verviers are in AV V. 84, F. 276; F. 119.

39. Haesenne-Peremans, *La pauvreté*, p. 218.

40. AEL, Communes, Limburg, 895.

41. The census is for the year 7 of the French Revolution (1798). It is found in AEL, FFP 244/30. The poor relief documents are lists of recipients of weekly assistance in the years 11 and 12 of the Revolution. AEL, Communes, Limburg, 897.

42. The reasons for the absence of two-thirds of the names from the census are that there was considerable mobility in four years, and the area included for poor relief administration was larger than the town of Limburg as defined by the census.

43. Paul Servais, *La rente constituée dans la ban de Herve au XVIIIe siècle* (Brussels: Credit Communal, 1982).

44. Charles Tilly, "Demographic Origins of the European Proletariat,"

in *Proletarianization and Family History,* ed. David Levine (Orlando: Academic Press, 1984), pp. 1–86.

45. Franklin F. Mendels, "Social Mobility and Phases of Industrialization," *Journal of Interdisciplinary History* 7 (1976): 201–207.
46. Hufton, *The Poor of Eighteenth-Century France,* pp. 69–106.
47. U. Bräker, *The Life Story and Real Adventures of the Poor Man of Toggenburg* (Edinburgh: University Press, 1970).
48. H. Carton de Wiart, "La vie et les voyages d'un ouvrier foulon du pays de Verviers au XVIIIe siècle d'après un manuscrit inédit," *Academie Royale de Belgique. Classe des Lettres. Mémoires* (in-8⁰) 2nd ser., 13 (1921): 1–59. This account claims to be based on an autobiography, which Carton de Wiart quotes extensively. I have not been able to locate the original autobiography, although there is no reason to doubt the authenticity of the account.
49. Lebrun, *L'industrie de la laine,* p. 265.
50. Delilez is listed in the 1799 census of Ensival as a teacher. AEL, FFP 246.
51. This map is derived from section 192 in the *Limbourg* portfolio of *Carte de Cabinet de Pays-Bas Autrichiens levée à l'initiative du comte de Ferraris* (Brussels: Credit Communal, 1965). For another view of the same area, see Map 5 *(planche V)* in Claire Lemoine-Isabeau and Etienne Hélin, *Cartes inédites du pays de Liège au XVIIIe siècle* (Brussels: Credit Communal, 1980).
52. Belgian planning officials have made an excellent study of housing types and communal geography in Soiron. See F. Peters et al., *Soiron: Un village du pays de Herve* (Brussels: Ministère de la Culture Française, n.d.).
53. See, for example, AV, F 218, Property Tax 1780, which shows how many families lived in each house.
54. AEL, FFP 225/7.
55. Gérard Gayot, "La longue insolence des tondeurs de draps dans la manufacture de Sedan au XVIIIème siècle," *Revue du Nord* 63 (1981): 105–134.
56. Gullickson, "Proto-industrialization," p. 107.
57. Terrier and Toutain, "Pression démographique," p. 19.
58. I draw this conclusion from an analysis of the property tax collected in Verviers, which shows how many families lived in each house. See, for example, AV, F 218, Property Tax 1780.
59. Part of the Verviers municipal archive has been catalogued in a cardfile index. This index can give any user a good introduction to the kinds of topics dealt with by even a small city in the seventeenth and eighteenth centuries. Unless otherwise noted, the discussion that follows is based on the volumes of minutes and files of letters and decrees in the Verviers Municipal Archive.
60. There is a growing literature on relations between workers and employers in the eighteenth century. See John Rule, *The Experience*

of Labour in Eighteenth-Century English Industry (New York: St. Martin's Press, 1981); Maxine Berg, *The Age of Manufactures, 1700–1820* (London: Fontana, 1985); William Reddy, "Modes de paiement et contrôle du travail dans les filatures de coton en France, 1750–1848," *Revue du Nord* 63 (1981): 135–146.

61. See E. Fairon, "La question ouvrière dans la vallée de la Vesdre au XVIIIe siècle," *Chronique SVAH* (1906): 43–52; and Lebrun, *L'industrie de la laine,* pp. 257–268.

62. Lebrun notes that this is the only example of a guildlike rule in the modern history of the Verviers industry. *L'industrie de la laine,* p. 259, n. 5. An attempt to set up craft guilds in Verviers in 1684–1685 failed. See Fairon, "Question ouvrière," p. 47, and AV, F 96/91.

63. Gayot, "La longue insolence," p. 114.

64. This section is based on Gayot, "La longue insolence."

65. Ibid., p. 115.

66. On the mobility of workers and the problems of recruiting, see Robert Darnton, *The Business of Enlightenment: A Publishing History of the* Encyclopédie *1775–1800* (Cambridge, Mass.: Harvard University Press, 1979), pp. 203–212.

67. Fairon, in "Question ouvrière," justifies this action on the part of the employers by arguing that they themselves received the money for their German trade and had to do something with it. He is not convincing.

68. *Ibid.,* pp. 261–262; and AV, V 15, pp. 677–681.

69. Natalie Z. Davis, "A Labor Union in the Sixteenth Century," *Economic History Review,* 2nd ser., 19 (1966): 48–68.

70. Gayot, "La longue insolence," p. 123.

CHAPTER 7

Early Industry in Its Prime

By the eighteenth century European industry was very well developed, even if it had not yet become mechanized. From the middle of the seventeenth century until at least the end of the eighteenth, it produced large quantities of goods; and it did so with a mixture of urban and rural workers, under old and new patterns of organization, using old and new techniques. This was early industry in its prime, and some elements of it are the subject of this chapter.[1] We will see how early industry operated by looking at a set of very specific situations: the early industrial businesses that grew up in the seventeenth and eighteenth centuries in the region around Liège and Verviers.[2] A pattern develops in these industries over the course of the seventeenth and eighteenth centuries. Both the nailmaking and the textile industries at that time employed a form of cottage industry: a small number of entrepreneurs distributed raw materials to rural workers, who completed part of the operation before it was passed on to someone else. In the seventeenth century the industry was fairly well concentrated geographically, but most of the entrepreneurs were small operators who performed a variety of tasks and were involved in a number of businesses. Few were simply nail suppliers or textile operators. Rather, they devoted much of their time to a core activity (such as organizing the production of cloth and then arranging for its sale); but they were still heavily occupied in subsidiary or tangential occupations. A nail merchant might also own farms and urban property, lend money, and accept all sorts of payment in kind: cloth, hardware, even foodstuffs, which he then sold. An aristocratic landlord might sell textiles or nails or something else. While industry was growing in the late seventeenth century, in the Liège region it was still in the midst of a heroic age—an age when money was to be made by the adventuresome, and those who tried attempted a bit of everything.

A century later, by the end of the eighteenth century, the

industries of the Liège region had changed. The region lost its early monopoly on nail production, in the face of competition; but the production of more sophisticated metal goods and the textile industry blossomed and compensated for the loss. As the local industries grew, some of their operations spread over the countryside while others became more and more heavily concentrated in the emerging towns, especially the suburbs of Liège and the towns of Verviers and Eupen. The new scale of operations brought concentration to business activities, just as it did to their distribution in town and countryside. The major entrepreneurs of the late eighteenth century still owned land and houses and still occasionally lent money; but they were increasingly specialized in the operation of their business, especially if that business was the manufacture and sale of woolen textiles. The demand for their product, and the consequent demand for the manager's time to operate his business, simply meant that tangential operations were left to other specialists.

THE ORGANIZATION OF COTTAGE INDUSTRY IN THE SEVENTEENTH CENTURY: NAILMAKING

In past chapters we have concentrated on the organization of the textile industry, especially its techniques and operations. Here we will begin with the metalwork industry and see how that industry worked in the seventeenth century. Like textiles, it grew to prosperity in the Liège-Verviers region by employing dispersed workers in the countryside. The largest operation was nailmaking, and the individual nailmakers worked in the villages, on their own or in small groups. Their employers were the nail merchants, who paid them piecework wages. The Liégeois nailmaking industry produced a variety of grades of nails.[3] Smaller nails were used for construction and furniture making, while the larger grades of nails were used for shipbuilding. The merchants who produced the largest nails were the wealthiest, and they were primarily concentrated in the city of Liège itself. The merchants who arranged the manufacture of smaller nails were more numerous and more likely to live in the smaller towns, such as Verviers or Limburg. The merchants who specialized in large nails worked on the basis of orders from major Dutch shipbuilders or their suppliers. To obtain such a contract called for a significant marketing effort, which only one of the better-connected and richer nail merchants could undertake. The rewards for these ventures were substantial and made the operations worthwhile. This was the second reason why the production of larger nails was controlled by the city merchants: large nails produced much greater profits than did small nails.

The nail merchant arranged for the production of the nails, and he owned most of the equipment needed to make nails from iron. The raw material the merchant purchased was forged iron, in the form of bars. While there were supplies of iron ore in the Liège region, and a few forges in the seventeenth century, the iron produced around Liège was not exactly what the merchants and their workers wanted, so most of the raw material for nails was imported from Luxembourg. The Luxembourg iron was softer and easier to work than Liégeois iron. Until the late eighteenth century, when the Liégeois were forced by competition to shift to harder iron, this imported iron was used.

Nailmaking was done in two stages, each stage performed in a different kind of workshop. In each case the workshop was owned by the merchant, who contracted with a master to operate the shop for him. The nail merchant first arranged to have the bars converted to iron rods in a rolling and slitting mill (there were nine in the region by 1700). While not every merchant owned his own slitting mill, all were owned by nail merchants. The rods that were produced were square and the thickness of the desired nail. They were of various lengths. These the nail merchant delivered in "bundles" to the master nailmaker, who operated the nailmaking forge for him.

Some individual nailmakers worked at home in a tiny workshop. But as the industry evolved most of the production took place in small workshops in which a group of nailmakers shared a single source of heat. The nailmaking forge was an uncomplicated place, resembling a blacksmith's shop. At the center of a shedlike building was a small forge, fired with coal; the draft was provided by a bellows operated by a child (although by the early twentieth century, when the last hand-made nails were made near Liège, the bellows was being powered by a dog running in a cage). Around the forge were several work stations, each equipped with a large block for pounding, a small anvil, and the other tools of the nailmaker's trade.

The nailmaker first heated a rod in the forge. He then fashioned its end into a point for the nail and cut off a length sufficient for the nail by placing the rod against a notched block—called a "scissor"—and striking the rod sharply with his hammer. He fashioned the head of the nail by first bending the unpointed end, then placing it in a special anvil that allowed the nail to be held securely in a vertical position, then pounding the bent end into a neat, square head. After every second nail, the nailmaker reheated the rod. When the rod became too short to handle, what was left was discarded and a new rod begun. In this way, some 30 percent of the total weight of the rods was lost, to be sold by the master of the nailmaking forge (as opposed to the nail merchant) for his own profit.

Productivity varied. A maker of small nails might produce twenty pounds of nails per week. At eight pounds per 100 nails, this represents 250 nails. On the other hand, a producer of large nails might produce one hundred pounds per week. At sixty pounds per 100 nails of this size, this worker is producing 167 nails per week. The maker of small nails was more productive than the maker of large nails, but not much more productive. Because the price of the nails was based largely on their weight, with only a slight advantage in the price of small nails over large ones, the production of large nails was much more profitable. In other words, as the size of the nails increased, the proportion of the sale price that was spent on labor diminished. In one set of available figures, salaries represented 26 percent of the price of eight-pound nails (8 pounds per 100 nails), whereas it represented only 20 percent of the sale price of twenty-four-pound nails.[4] Still larger sizes must have been even more profitable.

Nailmaking represents one variety of cottage industry, a kind in which a hierarchy of managers and small operators exists. Rather than dealing directly with each of the individual workers engaged in one stage or another of nailmaking, the merchant works with managers—one at the slicing mill and another at the nail forge. The merchant supplies the equipment and the raw material, and pays the master a piecework rate for each nail (or pound of nails) produced. The master then finds a group of workers (about ten in the slicing mill, about five in the nail forge) and pays them, either by the day worked or, as was probably more common, by the amount produced. His profit is the difference between what he is paid per piece, and what he pays his employees per piece, plus the value of the leftover raw materials he is allowed to keep.

In the Liège region, the master, rather than the merchant, was usually responsible for transportation. He picked up the raw material from the rolling and slitting mill, and carried it to the workshop. When his workers were finished, he carried the nails back to the merchant's warehouse and exchanged them for a cash payment and a new load of iron rods. The transportation of raw materials and finished product became a heavy burden on the master's time, keeping him from supervising his crew and from working himself. This burden led by the eighteenth century to the appearance of another sort of entrepreneurial figure in the countryside around Liège and Verviers, men who served as intermediaries between merchants and workers, either at the level of the nail masters or at the level of the individual spinners and weavers in the textile industry. Such an intermediary, called a *martchoté* in the nail industry (a *façonnaire* in the textile industry) arranged the transportation of raw materials and finished products between the towns where the merchants lived and the villages where the workers lived. He was paid by the master nailmakers out of their small profit from operating the nail forge (by the individual workers in the textile industry).

We have identified a cast of characters here. At the top of our business hierarchy are the nail merchants. They employed the masters of the slitting mills and paid the masters of the nail forges. They often dealt with intermediaries (the *martchotés*), who provided transportation services. At the bottom of the hierarchy were the workers—those in the slitting mill or the nailmakers—and their wives and children. These are the members of our early proletariat, and they were subject to the kinds of pressures faced by all early industrial workers: they were engaged in part-time and seasonal work and were basically expendable. By the eighteenth century there were more nailmaking facilities around Liège than demand for Liégeois nails warranted. Nail merchants, especially those who produced for the high-profit trade in nails for the Dutch shipbuilding industry, were very competitive. If they failed to get a contract in a given year, their operation, including their nailmakers, sat idle. This was less of a problem for the slitting mill, which might be leased out to another merchant, but it was clearly a problem for the nail forge and the nail workers. The nail forge represented a trivial investment for the merchant and could easily be allowed not to work until another high-profit order could be found. The workers, on the other hand, might not have any work until the master and merchant with whom they were associated received another order. They faced a considerable risk of unemployment and poverty.

The Family de Fays

Although all the contributors to the early nail industry around Liège are interesting, we will gain most here by spending some time with the merchants who controlled the industry. We can look at the business from their point of view because we have some records that belonged to a family of nail merchants in the seventeenth century. The family, called de Fays, was prominent in Verviers in the seventeenth and eighteenth centuries.[5] As early as 1578 we find a mention of Gille de Fays, a nail merchant, who married Marguerite Louroux. Gille died in 1585 and was succeeded in the business by his son Renson, who died in 1646. Renson was in turn assisted and succeeded by his son Lambert. Some of the account books and correspondence of Renson and Lambert have survived, and we can use them to see the world of a seventeenth-century nail merchant and that of his son, who traded in wool and a few other commodities.

Two of Renson de Fays's journals survive, one dating from the very beginning of the seventeenth century and covering roughly the period 1601–1610, the second beginning in 1618.[6] These registers show his relations with nailmakers or master nailmakers. He works, in the ten-year span covered by the main register, with a number of nailmakers—ninety-five different names appear—spread out over a large region around Verviers.[7] Their dispersion is shown by Map 7.1.

In his journal, de Fays reports that he gives each nailmaker a quantity of iron (the normal quantity was one thousand pounds at a time, although the amounts varied greatly). After a certain amount of time the nailmakers return the iron in the form of

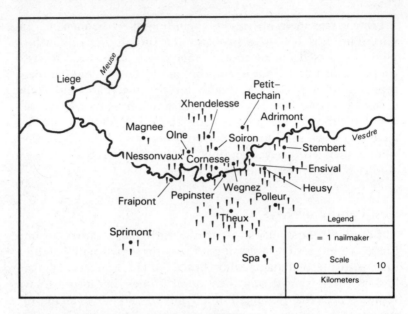

Map 7.1. Renson de Fays's Nailmakers

nails, which he records by category of nail and weight. When they return the nails, de Fays pays them in cash for their work and provides them with a new load of iron. In simplified form, Table 7.1 presents a series of de Fays's transactions with a nailmaker, Jean Colla le Marichalle, who lived in the *ban* of Olne.[8]

De Fays's transactions with le Marichalle illuminate a number of interesting characteristics of the nailmaking business. First, the business is seasonal.[9] Le Marichalle works much more quickly in the winter than in the summer, probably because he and whoever works with him devote their time in the summer to other activities—farming or crafts or construction.[10] Second, it seems likely that le Marichalle employs others in his shop. Between November 1619 and February 1620 he produces about seventy-five pounds of nails per week. These are not very large nails, and seventy-five pounds per week was probably more than one nailmaker could produce. His family and other nailmakers must have assisted him. Third, we see that a significant portion (15 to 20 percent) of the iron de Fays gives the nailmaker is not returned. The sale of the surplus iron from the ends of rods supplements the relatively modest amounts paid to the nailmakers. Finally, we see that de

Table 7.1:   Renson de Fays's Account Book, 1619–1620

Transactions with Jean Colla le Marichalle

NOVEMBER 9, 1619

Delivered 1,000 pounds of iron and gave him 193 florins (a unit of money).

FEBRUARY 5, 1620

Received 810 pounds of nails (4 kinds)
Add to le Marichalle's account: 250 fl.
Charge to his account a 7 daller (= 10.5 florins) owed by
   someone else
Gave him 1,000 pounds of iron
Gave him 7 rix Dallers (= 21 florins)

AUGUST 21, 1620

Received 822 pounds of nails (4 kinds)
Add to le Marichalle's account: 265 florins
Gave him 1,000 pounds of iron
Gave him 48 fl.

DECEMBER 10, 1620

Received 817 pounds of nails (1 kind)
Gave him 1,000 pounds of iron
Gave him 3 rix dallers (= 9 florins)

SOURCE: Adapted from H. Angenot, "Un marchand cloutier verviétois aux XVIIme siècle," *BSVAH* 13 (1913): 150.

Fays serves as a moneylender to the nailmakers and others, because he accepts part of le Marichalle's work as payment for someone's debt.

The full diversity of de Fays's activities is apparent in his journal. Beyond manufacturing and selling nails, he traded a variety of other products. Often he paid his nailmakers in kind: cloth, butter, cheese, bacon, and so on.[11] And he lent them and others money. By 1625 his loans totaled 9,314 florins, not an inconsiderable sum.[12] De Fays's wealth permitted him to acquire an important place in the Verviers community. He served as *burgermaster* twice, from 1614 to 1616 and from 1622 to 1624. Alongside the traditional elite of the villages and small towns—

the landowners, lawyers, and notaries—a merchant-of-all-goods such as de Fays was able to make a name for himself.

Rich as he appears, we should not make Renson de Fays into a modern industrial capitalist. None of his activities was especially large, and none of them took up so much of his time that he was occupied by it to the exclusion of the others. A few years later, at the middle of the seventeenth century, Renson de Fays's son Lambert was engaged in a different and rather more specialized business. In the middle of the seventeenth century Verviers was already becoming a major center in the textile industry, and Lambert de Fays was an active wool merchant. Although the documents in our possession are incomplete, those we do have allow us to follow the evolution of his business.[13] In the 1630s, Lambert de Fays was already an active wool trader, although he was not yet limiting his business to this activity. His account books show him trading at the German fairs—in Frankfurt and Strasbourg as well as elsewhere—primarily to buy wool but also occasionally to buy wine and sell nails. There is no evidence that he followed his father into the large-scale nailmaking business, but the two men obviously worked together. In the 1630s, Renson de Fays appears extremely often in the books of his son, in both financial and commercial transactions. Lambert's main business in the 1630s, however, was to break up the bales and sacks of wool he bought in Germany into smaller units, which he sold to local drapers. The woolen cloth he received from the drapers as payment he traded to Germany. The two most common transactions in his account book in this period were with his German correspondents for fairly large sums of money and with local drapers for fairly small sums.

By the 1640s, Lambert's business was more specialized and he operated it on a larger scale. Obviously this was still the family business, and we should suspect that the transformation from nail trading, lending, and general commerce to the wool trade was undertaken by father and son together. In the account book we see an evolution from a majority of entries being de Fays's accounts with Verviers drapers (the wholesale side of the business) to the majority of entries being de Fays's accounts with his suppliers of wool. These suppliers are no longer at the German fairs but instead primarily in Amsterdam. Individual transactions rise in value, and he rarely deals with individual drapers in Verviers.

We can confirm the evolution of de Fays's activities in his letter books. These are the books in which he wrote drafts of letters to send. Unfortunately they contain only one side of the correspondence, and what they do contain is in a very abbreviated form, since these are the drafts from which the final letters were copied. Still, we see de Fays moving from a situation in which he writes always in French to his local correspondents and to his agents at the German fairs, to a situation in which he corresponds in French and in Dutch to the same correspondents as well as to his new suppliers in Amsterdam. The scale and concentration of his business was growing along with the scale and concentration of the Verviers textile industry.

MATURING PREFACTORY INDUSTRIES

Nailmaking

By moving to textiles, the younger de Fays avoided the later deterioration of the nailmaking industry. Nailmaking grew around Liège in the late seventeenth century; but by the end of the first quarter of the eighteenth century its growth had slowed and an increasing pool of workers and entrepreneurs found themselves competing for a limited market. In the face of the mature industry's stagnation, its character did not change. It adapted to slack demand and competition from other regions by shifting from cannibalism to cooperation, and back again. By turns, the participants in nailmaking either consumed one another or acted together to discourage competition.[14]

The Liégeois nailmaking industry was not defeated by a technological breakthrough, either at home or elsewhere. It had prospered in the sixteenth and seventeenth centuries because of its early adoption of the slitting mill and of coal as a heat source, its reputation for dependable craftsmanship, and its proximity to the growing Dutch shipbuilding industry. Over time, coal and the slitting mill were adopted elsewhere, and Charleroi, a city farther up the Meuse, developed a labor force sufficiently skilled to produce nails. Still more important, the Dutch shipbuilding industry's lead diminished in the eighteenth century, as its ships lost their technical advantages and Dutch shipping lost its preeminent position to England. As Dutch traders shipped fewer cargoes and English traders shipped more, the market for Dutch-built ships eroded. By the late eighteenth century Dutch shipbuilding was greatly reduced, the number of wharves dropped from a peak of perhaps 300 to a level only half that by 1794.[15]

As Dutch shipbuilding fell off, the demand for Liégeois nails declined. By the middle of the eighteenth century, the only large shipbuilding yards that remained in the Netherlands were those operated by the trading companies and the admiralties.[16] The contracts to supply these wharves were what the largest nailmakers in the region of Liège competed for, both among themselves and against new competitors from Charleroi. As the competition heightened, a number of crises rocked the industry and its structure was partially changed to adapt to new circumstances.[17] The most important conclusion to draw from this situation is that nailmaking matured but failed to find new innovations (either technical or organizational), so that it lost its leading role in the region's economy.

The first sign of difficulty in the nailmaking industry appeared around the year 1700, in the wake of an effort by the government of the Spanish Netherlands to encourage and protect its metal industry against the neighboring Liégeois industry. Brussels encouraged the construction of two slitting mills in its duchy of Limburg, by freeing them from import duties on Liégeois coal and Luxembourg iron, and by allowing their rods and nails to be exported duty free. Manufacturers of nails produced in the duchy of Limburg could undersell their Liégeois counterparts. The impact of this on the economy of the whole region is difficult to assess, since it merely shifted the balance slightly within a largely unified industry. Nonetheless, the manufacturers and workers in Liégeois territory felt pressure. Selling an identical product, they faced nearby competitors who had a solid price advantage. The Liégeois merchants had very little ground on which to compete, since they paid as much for raw materials, used the same technology, and sold in the same markets, which were not expanding rapidly. The only part of their costs they could manipulate easily was wages, and after 1700 they squeezed the amounts they paid their workers.

Discontent festered among the workers during the first two

decades of the eighteenth century, breaking out in a strike—one of the earliest in European history—in 1719. The strike of 1719 was resolved in 1721 by a form of collective bargaining agreement imposed by the prince-bishop of Liège. The industry remained vulnerable, and it faced severe difficulties after 1735 as new tariff squabbles combined with severe economic difficulties in 1739 and 1740. Merchants and their workers were exposed to difficulties because of overall economic distress, increasing competition from elsewhere, and the danger of monopolies emerging inside the local industry. This last risk became clear in 1740, when a single Liégeois merchant, the widow Malaise, combined with three Dutch merchants to grab the entire order from the Dutch East India Company, some 158,000 pounds of nails. Each year, this order constituted perhaps as much as 30 percent of Liégeois production, and its placement with a single merchant risked depriving other merchants and their workers of employment for an entire year.

The merchants and the government of Liège responded to the new risks they faced after 1735 by creating an imperfect cartel they called the "Society of Merchants." It existed from 1743 until 1759 before disbanding and was reconstituted from 1770 to 1795. The purpose of the Society of Merchants was to ensure work for everyone, both merchants and workers. It did this by dividing orders among the merchants who were members of the society, and by providing a constant stream of iron to be made into nails, even when orders were not in hand and during the slow winter months. This, coupled with regulated wages, was designed to guarantee an income to the workers. The system never included all the merchants and was hardly perfect in its operation. The workers were rarely paid according to the official rates, and fraud in their payments was common. The workers went on strike repeatedly, but the industry managed to survive until the end of the century.

The real success of the Society of Merchants was the maintenance of peace in the Liégeois nailmaking industry in the face of stagnant markets and increasing competition from outside. The competition from the duchy of Limburg, although it disrupted relations between merchants and workers, was never overwhelming, since the Limburg industry was really part of the Liégeois industry. But by mid-century genuine competition was coming from two new centers, Charleroi and Charleville.[18] Located farther up the Meuse, these towns had access to a better grade of iron and were often supported by the tariff policies of the Austrian Netherlands and of France. The society protected the industry from decline until after 1780, but the slow, steady growth that took place from 1700 to 1780 was not enough to keep pushing it forward.

Textiles

As the Liégeois nailmaking industry reached one form of maturity in the eighteenth century, the woolen textile industry, which had grown up nearby, was maturing in a different way. Both industries experienced dramatic growth in the seventeenth century. This expansion allowed both groups of entrepreneurs to expand their operations and to specialize. But the behavior of the two industries differed. If the nailmaking industry was stymied by reduced growth in demand and outside competition for that demand, the woolen textile industry was more fortunate. The Verviers industry did not grow without interruption, but it did grow in the eighteenth century, in the process advancing in ways that were unavailable to the nailmakers.

One important reason the textile industry grew in the eighteenth century is that it found new markets for its goods. In the seventeenth century, local consumers—in Liège, in the Spanish Netherlands, or in the Dutch Republic—bought most of the cloth produced in Verviers. Some found its way to destinations farther away, including Germany, Italy, and the Mediterranean basin; but the reasonable price and reputation for quality of Verviers cloth made it attractive to nearby consumers, and they bought the majority of cloth produced.[19] Moreover, production of cloth in the city of Liège was not negligible, and it competed with Verviers for a place in international markets.[20]

After 1700, the situation changed. The city of Liège ceased to be a major center for cloth production. The same protectionist measures that shook the nailmakers cut off Verviers from its Belgian market. Increasingly, Verviers merchants looked east for consumers and sold the majority of their goods in Germany and farther east. Table 7.2 shows the distribution of legal sales (those for which customs duties were paid) in the one year for which we have reliable data, 1744–1745. By that time nearly 90 percent of all sales from Verviers went to places east of the Rhine. Sales to the Austrian Netherlands are low in this table because by 1744 the Verviers merchants had shifted some of their production over to Hodimont, in Austrian territory, to avoid duties. But Hodimont production for sale in the Austrian Netherlands could not have exceeded 2,000 pieces per year in the 1740s and therefore does not materially affect the conclusions to be drawn from Table 7.2.[21]

As important as the markets the Verviers merchants reached are those they did not. They sold very little in the Dutch Republic, and nothing legally in England or France (although there is some reason to believe there was an illicit trade to France). Those large markets, with their prosperous consumers, were almost exclusively served by their own producers. The English, French, and Dutch industries with which the Verviétoise competed were therefore rather different in character from that of Verviers. The Verviers industry was an export industry, whereas its competitors in the largest western European states had domestic markets protected by customs barriers. The size of the domestic market influenced the balance between home and foreign sales. France had the largest population, and most French industrial products were sold at home; with a smaller home market, English industrial production went to both domestic and foreign outlets;

Table 7.2: Woolen Textile Sales from Verviers, September 1744–August 1745 (pieces of cloth)

Destination	Number	Percentage
Germany (meaning all places east of the Rhine)	19,911	86.6
Principality of Liège	1,740	7.6
Dutch Republic	1,272	5.5
Austrian Netherlands	51	0.2
Principality of Stavelot	30	0.1
Total	23,004	100.0

SOURCE: Pierre Lebrun, *L'industrie de la laine à Verviers pendant le XVIIIe et le début du XIXe siècle* (Liège: Faculté de Philosophie et Lettres, 1948), p. 150 (percentages recalculated), tabulated from AEL, Etats, 119.

finally, most Dutch production went to consumers overseas. The dominant overseas markets were central and eastern Europe, the Mediterranean, and the Americas.

We see the difference when we compare Verviers's production with that of its French competitors—places such as Sedan in northern France and Elbeuf near Rouen. Elbeuf exported only about 10 percent of its production, sending the rest to the domestic market.[22] The manufacturers of Sedan both competed and cooperated with Verviers, as noted in the Chapter 6 discussion of labor relations in the eighteenth century.[23] The high-quality textile industry in Sedan grew in the eighteenth century, roughly paralleling that of Verviers.[24] Its products were also exported, but they had much more access to Paris and other points in France than did those of Verviers.[25] The Verviers industry served a highly competitive export industry, whereas its French competitors served a less competitive domestic market.

THE EVOLUTION OF TEXTILE INDUSTRY ORGANIZATION IN THE EIGHTEENTH CENTURY

As the Verviers textile industry grew in the late seventeenth and eighteenth centuries, its operations evolved. Growth spread the industry geographically through the region between the Meuse and the Rhine; it brought on specialization, as workers and entrepreneurs focused their activities; and it concentrated the industry, as a smaller and smaller number of businessmen controlled more and more of it. These processes led by the end of the eighteenth century to the first factories, which in turn signaled the coming of mechanization in the nineteenth century. In this, Verviers followed essentially the same path traversed by other textile industry regions in the eighteenth century.

Verviers was the center of the textile industry in the seventeenth century, although smaller concentrations of merchants operated in other towns: Limburg, Eupen, and Monschau. Many operations were handled in Verviers itself, including the preliminary tasks such as cleaning the wool and most of the finishing operations. Combing, carding, and spinning were done in the countryside, primarily in the villages that surrounded Verviers to the west, north, and east. The only unusual characteristic of the Verviers industry was that most weaving was done in the town itself or in a few adjoining villages, instead of in the larger hinterland that served it for other processes. This early concentration, with weaving done in town rather than in the countryside, was a precursor of later industrial concentration. The only process that was not done in Verviers in the seventeenth and early eighteenth centuries was dyeing. Prior to the mid-eighteenth century, only yarn was dyed in Verviers; the cloth was woven from already dyed yarn, or the semifinished cloth was sent elsewhere for dyeing.[26] In the early years of the Verviers industry, a large quantity of cloth was sent to Leiden for dyeing. In the eighteenth century dyeing was the specialty of nearby Eupen.[27]

No single pattern can describe the origins of this industrial organization. It seems likely that many of the drapers who were its principal operators in the seventeenth century began as weavers or as very small-scale traders. We might put the younger de Fays in this group, although the family was so wealthy that we should more accurately categorize its business dealings as the investments of someone looking for many outlets in which to spread a substantial fortune.[28] In order to have yarn to weave or cloth to sell, the first industrialists put others to work in cleaning, combing, spinning, and so on. A need for bigger outlets led them to long-distance trade. An early eighteenth-century document describes the beginning of the process in seventeenth-century Ensival, a stage that was probably reached in Verviers by the mid-sixteenth century:

> [The early draper] was at the same time merchant, manufacturer and worker, because the different operations were carried out by members of the family, giving a hand to a neighbor when it was a question of work which could not be done by a single person, for example weaving or raising the nap. Anyone who had a bit of money or a bit of credit bought wool for a piece of cloth which once completed they sold, either in Liège or in some other nearby town. All these would-be manufacturers eventually shared in the establishment of a fulling mill. Manufacturing remained for some time on this footing . . . until a few of the most able each made up a little assortment, perhaps a dozen pieces, and attempted a voyage to Frankfort. There they found a success which encouraged them to return with a bit more merchandise. The appetite for profits pushed them to find

manufacturers who did not have the resources to make a quantity of cloth for their own account. These other drapers they provided with wool so they could manufacture cloth, paying them so much per piece.[29]

This document, however oversimplified, effectively describes the beginning of the differentiation between three different kinds of businessmen in the Verviers region textile industry. At the economic pinnacle was the "merchant-draper," who was involved in both manufacturing and trading. He owned his own raw materials or bought finished cloth from one of the others. In an intermediate position was what we might simply call a "draper"—a small capitalist organizing the manufacture of cloth but not involved in trade. He might own the raw materials his employees worked, or he might simply be working on a contract basis for a wealthier draper and be paid by the piece. At the bottom was the simple weaver, who rarely owned his own raw materials and was far from the guild-centered ideal of the master craftsman. By the early seventeenth century in Verviers, and somewhat later in neighboring towns, he was simply an employee, paid by the piece.

This hierarchy was not a caste system. Individuals moved into it at all levels from outside, and while upward mobility to the highest levels was difficult, anyone in the hierarchy could move up or down, depending on luck and ability. Weavers or their sons could become manufacturers; at the other extreme merchants could lose their capital and find themselves mere manufacturers handling other people's work or, worse yet, fallen to jobs as agents or as workmen themselves. On the individual level the system remained fluid and flexible just as on a structural level the groups of economic actors sorted themselves into distinct categories. This is the system Rudolf Braun has described for the textile industry of the Zurich highlands in Switzerland in the nineteenth century. There a new group of industrial entrepreneurs emerged with mechanization. "From which social milieu are they recruited?" he asks.

> With few exceptions they are tradesmen who already under the old regime belonged to the socially dominant class in the industrial districts of the Zurich area, either directly or indirectly on account of the role they played in the domestic system, where they acted as

middlemen between the domestic producers and their urban employers. To them may be added other rural dealers and craftsmen, especially owners of licensed enterprises such as millers and innkeepers, many of whom were also active in the domestic system in an ancillary capacity.[30]

What we see here is a process of economic specialization and concentration. In the early seventeenth century there were 286 "drapers" and 61 "merchant-drapers" among Verviers's 4,500 inhabitants.[31] In the 1744–1745 accounts of exports from Verviers, there were 204 producers of cloth, of whom only 97 produced more than ten pieces in a year. By the early nineteenth century there were still fewer, slightly more than 100 manufacturers. Examined another way, in 1744–1745 12 manufacturers accounted for half of all production; by the end of the old regime only 6 manufacturers accounted for half of all production. The largest operations were indeed considerable, with the two largest, Biolley and Simonis, selling four thousand pieces of cloth per year by the 1770s, and another ten selling at least one thousand each.[32] The process was under way in almost every large center of textile production. It was certainly so in Sedan, where the number of drapers fell from over 100 in 1716, to 60 in 1731, to 42 in 1765. At the same time total production more than doubled.[33]

The process of concentration produced striking wealth, especially in the eighteenth century. When Pierre Dethier died in 1771, he left his heirs 169,000 florins. J. J. Kaison left 198,000 florins in 1786. And buoyed by the great prosperity of the late eighteenth century, there were a number of fortunes of more than 500,000 francs in the first decade of the nineteenth century.[34] The largest of all was that of J. J. Simonis, who died in 1806 leaving an estate of 4.6 million francs. These, of course, were industrial fortunes, built in the manufacture and trade of woolen textiles. The most spectacular fortune in Verviers was a commercial fortune, that of the banker and wool merchant François Franquinet, who died in 1754 leaving more than 2 million florins.[35] Franquinet and his family dominated the wool trade into Verviers beginning in the 1720s. They were heavily involved in international trade, buying wool in Spain and selling finished cloth in central and eastern Europe. Their large volume of currency transactions made it easy for them to become bankers in the eighteenth-century sense of the word: they handled currency exchanges for others. The scale of Franquinet's wealth shows how successful trade could be in the eighteenth century. The great eighteenth-century fortunes, even in Verviers, were mercantile fortunes. Only in the nineteenth century did industrial fortunes exceed them.

As the top of the hierarchy increased the scale of its operations, new intermediate levels of management were established. In the Verviers region these new management levels were a consequence of the growing differences between the merchant-draper and the mere draper. The draper or small-scale manufacturer was more than a weaver. He and his family may have worked on the cloth, but he probably also employed others to work in his small shop and gave out materials to spinners and weavers who worked in their own homes. This was the cottage industry production of cloth, on a very modest scale. The draper differed from the merchant-draper or pure merchant because he was not involved in international trade and never dealt either with foreign merchants or ultimate consumers. He sold his finished product to one of the local merchant-manufacturers or merchants. From the point of view of the small-scale manufacturer this was not a bad arrangement, but from the merchant's point of view it left something to be desired.

The vital trade-off in traditional industry was investment versus control. By purchasing finished cloth from the small-scale manufacturer, the merchant or merchant-manufacturer was able to obtain cloth to sell in distant markets without investing in raw materials or equipment and without needing to supervise an undisciplined labor force. Yet at the same time he gave up control over the manufacturing process. The workers were at two removes from his management. He might not be able to control adequately the types and the quality of the cloth produced. Moreover, if the merchant's competitors were willing to pay unreasonably high prices for cloth, he might be bound to their pricing scheme; if the small drapers were short of working capital, he might find little cloth to purchase. This is the dilemma of the modernization of industry at the end of the old regime: obtaining more control meant committing more capital, and managing a larger and larger enterprise meant devising new administrative schemes.

FAÇONNAIRES AND EARLY FACTORIES

The continuing expansion of the Verviers industry put great pressure on the cottage industry system. The capital resources of the small manufacturers on whom the industry depended may have restricted expansion. This shortage of capital spurred the expansion in the eighteenth century of a new class of business-men, similar to the small manufacturer but without their own working capital. In the Verviers region they were called *façon-naires*, but we find them in other regions, including Switzerland, France, and England.[36] The *façonnaire* was simultaneously the merchant-manufacturer's agent and an independent business-man. From the merchant he received wool and instructions about the kind of cloth to produce. The *façonnaire* then arranged all the stages of production, either in his own shop or by putting out the work to others, just as if the wool were his own. Once the goods were produced he received a payment sufficient to pay his work-ers and allow a profit. The advantages to the merchant are clear, if limited: to the extent he could depend on the *façonnaire*, he got precisely the cloth he ordered—in terms of type and quality, and at his price—without dealing directly with workers or creating new management systems. He had merely increased his invest-ment in raw materials, a commodity in which he may have been trading already.

On the other side, the workers may have gained from this system too. Unlike some cottage industry systems, the Verviers textile industry was one in which the worker fetched his own materials and later returned the finished product. For villagers living some distance from the towns in which the merchants and drapers lived, this meant a considerable investment of time in carrying their work between home and merchant. The system of *façonnaires* was less centralized, and many of them lived in the villages. The workers gained time to work (no doubt at the cost of lower pay), and the villages gained a new group of middle-class citizens. The simultaneous concentration of the largest mer-chants in Verviers and the rise of the *façonnaires* to meet growing demand spread the industry throughout the countryside and far-ther and farther from the central town.

The account books of one *façonnaire*, Thiry Thiriart of Ensival, survive for part of the 1730s and 1740s.[37] From them we can learn about the conduct of the *façonnaire's* business. Thiriart worked primarily for two merchants, the brothers Jean and Lambert Franquinet of Verviers. The Franquinet family controlled a large part of the business of importing wool from Spain into Verviers and were active in the business of exporting cloth (produced by a number of *façonnaires*) from Verviers.[38] In Thiriart's account we see him receiving orders for a number of pieces of cloth—usually between ten and forty at a time—and recording their size and identifying marks when they are completed. He is paid by the *aune* (a measure of cloth), depending on the kind and quality of cloth and on the market value of his services at the time. Usually he receives between 38 and 47 florins per *aune,* and his total annual revenue amounts to several thousand florins per year.

Thiriart produced too much cloth each year to have done much of the work on it himself. Surely, he employed workers in his shop and farmed out some of the work to people who worked at home. His account book fails to record the payments to these workers, so we do not know how much they were paid or how much profit he made. That he had much of the work performed by employees in his shop is clear from the fact that he records the purchase of various pieces of cloth-making equipment and expendable supplies (materials, such as soap, consumed in the manufacturing process). In the early 1730s he records the purchase of oil (to lubricate wool) at various times. In 1736 he purchased two pairs of shears for 17 écus and a barrel of oil for 65 florins. In 1739 he bought and erected on leased land a tenter frame. The construction of the frame cost him 212 florins; the rent on the land was 10 florins a year.

The emergence of very large scale manufacturers and traders, and their increasing dependence on *façonnaires* to produce cloth, is but one step in the concentration of the Verviers woolen industry as it matured in the eighteenth century. By the late eighteenth century another stage of development was under way. After moving toward decentralized production for a century, the largest manufacturers began to centralize production. Obviously there had always been shops owned by manufacturers. After all, some operations, such as fulling, simply could not be done without centralized investment. But these new operations, which we see in the last third of the eighteenth century, brought the whole range of textile production activities under the eye of the merchant-manufacturer. Here we see the beginning of the move toward real industrial development for its own sake and the emergence of manufacturers who were interested primarily in efficient production and secondarily in marketing, instead of the reverse.

Cottage industry was not very efficient, and it was difficult to manage. Its inefficiency was a direct result of the costs of each transaction: moving materials around the countryside was expensive and time consuming. The manufacturer may have maintained his profitability by making use of *façonnaires*, but he did so at the cost of what he paid workers. As soon as he encountered a shortage of workers, his costs would increase sharply. The distance between workers and owners led to management problems. On one side it resulted in confusion over instructions and the exact product required. It also raised the manufacturer's costs by permitting embezzlement and by leaving him unable to control the amount of time it took to complete a given piece of work. Embezzlement was constantly complained about by employers.[39] Workers regularly returned only some of the raw materials left in their possession; the rest they accumulated and sold. And the owner had few means with which to force workers to complete an assignment on time or not to take on the work of a competitor. Despite these limitations, cottage industry prospered because it had low fixed capital costs, and it prospered under two circumstances: where low labor costs offset its inefficiencies, or where demand was so great that manufacturers tolerated them. Where competition was great, or where other pressure—such as a shortage of labor—was put on the industry, businessmen tried better and more efficient ways to manage it. This is what happened in the Verviers textile industry, beginning in the 1760s, soon after the same kinds of changes began in a number of other European industrial centers, in England and France.

The process almost certainly began when manufacturers tried to take on high-profit and relatively technical operations in the preparation and finishing part of the business. These allowed them to deal more effectively with competition by varying the finished look of their cloth.[40] In Verviers the first stage of this process took place in the 1760s, when dyeing, which had been done at nearby Eupen, was taken over. The leader of this movement appears to have been Jean Biolley, who succeeded in 1765 in producing rich colors in his new dyeshop.[41] A year later he wrote to the city council asking that he be temporarily exempt from service on that body. He wrote that "the prosperity and great success of his newborn factory and dye-works absorb all his time, and prevent his putting it usefully to the public good."[42]

The concentration that started by bringing technical finishing processes under the manufacturer's control eventually led him to oversee closely operations that had been done elsewhere. At least one large textile firm in Verviers, Dethier, was by the 1760s concerned about its costs and profits in the production of cloth. We see this in their records, because by 1760 they had devised a very detailed system of keeping track of the cost of producing each piece of cloth, and the consequent profit or loss.[43] Table 7.3 reproduces part of the register. We see that each piece of cloth has a line devoted to it. On one side of the page the characteristics of production are recorded, including its size at various stages in the production process and the name of the weaver. On the facing page are recorded the costs of producing it: raw materials, basic preparation, weaving, dyeing, and overhead. The total cost is compared with the sale price, and the difference recorded in either the profit or loss column. Dethier must have made money in this period: there are few entries that show losses, and after a few months the record keepers even give up on calculating profit and loss. Only the expense columns are filled in; the sale price, profit, and loss columns are left blank.

Within a few years the Dethier firm had instituted an even more detailed approach to management record keeping. Each bale of wool was entered into a register of work "put into production" (*mise en fabrique*), which occupied a whole page or several pages in a very large register. These registers constitute a remarkable series, running almost continually from 1769 to 1812, that shows the operation of a primitive textile factory.[44] In addition to the costs and some facts of production, these new registers show who spun the yarn, the dates the spinners began and ended, and the amount of time it took to weave the cloth. We do not know how the firm used these registers, but their detailed record keeping about the time spent and the expense of cloth production must have provided a clear way of evaluating the efficiency of the production system used.

These production management records are called "registers of placement in the factory." This might suggest that the Dethier firm's desire to control the production process went beyond record keeping to the creation of a factory environment in which virtually all the work was done under their immediate supervision. If that was the case, it could be argued—as it is in what follows—that the consolidation of control led to the creation of primitive factories in the eighteenth century, and the existence of factories made the eventual mechanization of production all but inevitable. Nor was Dethier the only firm using factories in this period. In 1774, Paul and Wilhelm Scheibler built a spinning mill in the town of Dalhem, on the Meuse River.[45] The Scheiblers were part of a Protestant family from the town of Monschau, which already operated a small factory for their textile business there.[46] Whether we should call these factories or not is among the questions debated by economic historians. Some, such as David Landes, argue that a factory by definition required powered machines; collections of manual workers were employed in "workshops" or "manufactories."[47] What we call these places is not really important, so long as we know what was involved. They were primarily collections of workers under the owner's eyes.

Although there is some evidence that by the 1770s much production in Verviers as elsewhere was done under a single roof, in primitive factories, we can be certain that not all the work described in the Dethier registers was done in a factory, per se, owned by the manufacturer. First, Dethier continued to employ *façonnaires*.[48] But much more important is the fact that while all the other operations were done in the factory, spinning was still largely done in the countryside and weaving was done by domestic workers in Verviers itself.[49] There were still many spinners in Verviers's hinterland in 1800.[50] At the very end of the eighteenth century both spinning and weaving were being brought into the factory—the former much more rapidly than the latter, which because it had traditionally been done in town was subject to much better control than spinning. One final important reason that the factory developed only slowly is that the evolution of management and control was simply too slow. The operation of a large factory was possible but not likely to emerge all at once. Only after the advantages of mechanization were firmly established did the need for factories in

Table 7.3   Record Keeping in the Dethier Firm, 1760*

Wool Batch or Sack Number	Quantity of Wool (lbs)	Quality/ Length	Weaver	Length After Weaving (aunes†)	Weight from Press (lbs)	Length After Pressing‡ 9/4 aune wide	8/4 aune wide	Value of Wool
17785	160		Lesquet	41	26.00		32.25	
				40	26.00		32.25	
				41	25.25		33.50	
				42	24.50		32.00	
			Total Item 17785:	164	102.75		131.00	274.00
17786	40		Lesquet	44	28.00		35.25	68.25
17787	80	11.5/102	Gautier	43	28.00	35.25		
		10.5/100	Duspeaux	42	27.00	33.25		
			Total Item 17787:	85	55.00	68.50		181.50
17788	160		Henrard	42	27.00		33.25	
				43	27.00		32.50	
				41	25.50		32.50	
				44	26.00		32.25	
			Total Item 17788:	170	105.50		130.50	274.00
17789	160	10 /100	L. Mordan	40	27.00	29.50		
		10.5/102	Nautay	40	27.00	30.00		
		11 /100	Mordan	40	27.50	30.00		
		10 /102	Lange	40	27.00	29.50		
			Total Item 17789:	160	108.00	119.00		360.00

SOURCE: AEL, Dethier, 2618 (1760–1762).
*Quantities of money are expressed in Liégeois florins.
†A Liégeois *aune* was 0.656 meters long, or about 26 inches.
‡Cloth was produced in Verviers in a variety of widths, measured in *aunes*. The most common width was 9/4 *aune*, or 1.48 meter. It was also produced in widths of 8/4 *aune* (1.31 meter) and 10/4 *aune* (1.64 meter).

certain industries become clear and the persistence of older methods of production erode.

Whatever our reservations about the speed at which the Verviers textile industry moved toward the factory, there should be no question about its direction. The Dethier firm, like others in the region from Liège to Aachen, had a factory organized by the end of the eighteenth century.[51] The need for efficiency, for

Waste Warp	Waste Woof	Cost of Weaving	Cost of Dyeing	Cost of Preparation	Gen. Expenses	Total Cost	Sales Proceeds	Profits
43.40	0.00	142.60	45.50	84.75	38.40	590.25	652.60	62.17
41.50		39.60	12.10	21.20	9.60	150.75	175.70	25.00
23.25	21.65	23.35	25.85	53.75	19.75	349.00	422.90	73.85
0.00	0.00	153.00	59.20	84.75	38.40	609.35	650.00	40.65
41.80	43.60	44.00	30.40	107.60	89.55	669.95	737.25	67.30

quality control, and for control of theft had led them in this
direction, even before the Industrial Revolution brought mechanization. Pierre Lebrun draws this conclusion: "The industrial
revolution could not, evidently, provoke concentration because
it already existed."[52]

CONCENTRATION AND ITS USES

Manufacturers moved away from cottage industry because they
faced competition or because labor shortages and problems of
labor control spurred them toward technical innovation. These

were the reciprocal spurs to concentration and mechanization. Concentration in Verviers echoed eighteenth-century industrial development elsewhere, because it solved a common set of problems. Management had become more and more difficult, and employers sought to control their work force. The need did not arise all at once in the last third of the eighteenth century. It had been growing for some time, as J. D. Chambers has noted: "In these circumstances, an infusion of fixed capital in the form of labour saving devices and centralised control was an inevitable corollary, and for more than a century before the factory system emerged, attempts were being made to provide both."[53]

In Verviers, as elsewhere, the more technical processes saw the first attempts at concentration, which were probably the result of competition. In textiles the finishing operations received the first attention, hence Biolley's 1765 factory and dye works. Industrialists could modify a standard product such as worsted cloth by changing finishes—through different dyes and colors and through slightly different naps and appearances.[54] This allowed them to enter new markets and to stay ahead of the competition in their older ones. This competitiveness in the evolution of new products out of old ones was part of the emerging art of marketing and advertising that grew up in the eighteenth century. The Wedgwood pottery works, one of the earliest innovators in the concentration of industrial activity, was a leader in this approach.[55] They needed to maintain close control of these processes to get the quality, speed, and flexibility that their market and their competition demanded. Technical innovation led to secrecy, which itself spurred manufacturers to enclose workers to safeguard proprietary techniques—as they had done early in silk production, armaments, and specialized glassmaking.

Spinning was another area in which concentration and mechanization took place in response to a cycle of business conditions: labor shortages, labor control, and competition, in alternation. In the Verviers region, as elsewhere on the European continent, the initial moves toward concentrating spinning in primitive factories was a response to the need for better control of labor. It also may have been the case in England, but the process of mechanization and concentration took place there almost simultaneously. That makes it difficult to separate the two. The English manufacturers built their mechanized factories in order to deal with labor shortages in the face of an increase in cotton production.[56] The flying shuttle, invented in 1733 but not widely adopted until the 1750s and 1760s, doubled the productivity of weavers by allowing them to work more quickly.[57] Every weaver needed the yarn produced by several spinners, so an increase in weaving put tremendous pressure on the spinning business. Manufacturers had a difficult time finding yarn to meet their orders. They applied machines to cotton production first, beginning in 1770; wool was not far behind. Demand for worsted stockings boomed in the last third of the eighteenth century, and the supply of spun worsted fell behind demand. The difficulty of spinning worsted delayed the development of a suitable machine until after 1785.[58] The spread of mechanized spinning in England put competitive pressure on Continental manufacturers. French and Swiss cotton producers were forced to emulate the English cotton manufacturers, and as we will see in the next chapter the Verviers industry adopted mechanized spinning in 1802.[59]

The process of industrial concentration was not new in the eighteenth century. Large establishments had been common since at least the sixteenth century. They developed where state sponsorship was involved, where state interests were strong, where raw materials were valuable, and where technical secrets needed to be preserved.[60] Shipbuilding and armament production, from the time of the Venetian Arsenal, were characterized by large-scale operations, especially when controlled by the state.[61] Silk manufacture was another industry that promoted large-scale enterprise, both because the raw material was valuable and because manufacturers tried to keep the process secret.[62] These enterprises certainly contributed to the development of expertise in dealing with scale, but the role of the state and the role of processes outside the commercial mainstream made them exceptional. They were only approximate precursors of the mechanized factory in the nineteenth-century sense.

Nor was industrial concentration limited to textiles in the eighteenth century. It took place anywhere that there was a demand for fairly large quantities of industrial products. The best examples of industrial concentration outside the older industries such as silk and munitions are English. The Wedgwood pottery works saw advances in scale, concentration, and division of labor in the eighteenth century.[63] Its organization is one of the classic examples of the Industrial Revolution, and one of the best outside textiles. Another excellent example is the London brewing industry.[64] The production process was ideally suited to increases in scale, because the process involved liquids rather than solids (which could be moved about more easily), and was well suited to economies of scale. A single person could fill or empty a large vat as easily as a small one. In every case what we get are more production controlled by fewer businessmen and more production accomplished under one roof or in a single compound.

The process of concentration was accompanied by new social arrangements that emerged in industrial communities. It put more wealth and power in the hands of the owners and less in the hands of the workers. This is partly the process of proletarianization discussed in Chapters 5 and 6, but it may also be more. Stephen Marglin has argued that the industrialist added little or nothing in the way of efficiency to the industrial process.[65] The same functions could have been carried out by a worker acting on his own. All the boss did by setting up the division of labor was expropriate income from the worker. Marglin's critics argue the Smithian position—that in a number of ways the capitalist did more for industrial productivity than simply take money from the worker's pocket and put it in his own.[66] The critics seem to have the advantage for the time being: however exploitative the cottage industrialist, the early factory master, or their successors (and we should not question the manufacturer's desire to exploit his workers), their businesses were more efficient than those of independent masters, and the factories were more efficient than cottage industry. Whatever conclusion we draw, there is no doubt that the concentration of economic power in the hands of a number of early industrialists made them wealthy, and this wealth made it possible for them to invest in factory building and machines. From the merchant manufacturer came many early factory operators, and from the early factory operators came many of the true industrialists of the nineteenth century. The process was one of continuing transitions.

This chapter has been about the operation of early industry in its heyday, and about its slow evolution toward factory organization and mechanization. The late seventeenth and eighteenth centuries were good times for industrial development. Industrial output grew in an era of expanding demand and new trade routes both within and outside developed Europe. The most successful industrialists, although still working with traditional production techniques, devised new means to organize manufacturing and spur sales. In the Liège-Verviers-Aachen region we see two traditional industries reach maturity in differing ways. The nailmakers responded to stagnant markets by forming a cartel that allowed most of the manufacturers to persist in difficult times. The cloth manufacturers, on the other hand, responded to more steady growth by consolidating operations and striving for operational efficiency. In this they were like many of their foreign competitors.

The message here is that in the eighteenth century many industries matured into forms in which concentration and large-scale production could take place. These processes occurred because of conditions in the economy as a whole. They prepared the ground for mechanization by creating a group of industrial leaders with the means and the experience to experiment with other advances in production. This is a model of the path toward the economy of the late nineteenth and early twentieth centuries, a time when the industries of Liège and of Verviers peaked. It is, to a great extent, a demand-side model of industrial development. Where industrial demand was increasing naturally, or could be made to increase by aggressive promotion or the opening of new markets, industrial innovation took place. It was not certain to happen, and it was not linear in development, but the innovation that took place was mostly of a sort that allowed traditional operations to be done more efficiently. Once the process began, it could be sustained, as we saw in Chapter 5. In the Verviers textile industry, as in France and England, operations were consolidated so that larger businesses handled the export trade of cloth. That led to more rationalized production under the control and the eye of the merchant-manufacturer. The concrete results were early factories. The early industrialists reacted to changing circumstances of supply and demand by consolidating operations. Their concentration led, given the conditions of the times, to mechanization. Thus there was a logic to industrial development in the eighteenth century, under which it moved from cottage industry to early factories in response. The next step was mechanization.

NOTES

1. For England this period has been the subject of an important book by Maxine Berg, *The Age of Manufactures, 1700–1820* (London: Fontana, 1985).
2. For a general summary of industry in this region and in this period, see Georges Hansotte, "Pays de fer et de Houille," in *La Wallonie: Le pays et les hommes. Histoire-économies-sociétés*, ed. Hervé Hasquin, 2 vols. (Brussels: La Renaissance du Livre, 1975), 1:269–294.
3. The general descriptions of Liégeois nailmaking are drawn from Georges Hansotte, *La clouterie liégeoise et la question ouvrière au XVIIIe siècle*, Anciens Pays et Assemblées d'Etats, No. 55 (Brussels: Editions de la Librairie Encyclopédique, 1972); and J. M. Remouchamps, "La fabrication des clous forgés à la main," *Enquêtes du Musée de la Vie Wallonne* 3 (1931–1935): 55–125.
4. Hansotte, *La clouterie liégeoise*, 15.
5. H. Angenot, "Un marchand cloutier verviétois au XVIIme siècle," *BSVAH* 13 (1913): 129–169. The manuscripts are located in the Historical Manuscript Collection of the Municipal Archives of the City of Verviers.
6. AV, Man. 77/60.
7. Angenot, "Un marchand cloutier," pp. 136, 145–149.
8. Ibid., p. 150.
9. Ibid., p. 139.
10. For parallels, see Jürgen Schlumbohm, "Seasonal Fluctuations and Social Division of Labour: Rural Linen Production in the Osnabrück and Bielefeld Regions and the Urban Woolen Industry in the Niederlausitz, c.1770–c.1850," in *Manufacture in Town and Country Before the Factory*, ed. Maxine Berg et al. (Cambridge: Cambridge University Press, 1983), pp. 92–123.
11. Angenot, "Un marchand cloutier," p. 138.
12. Ibid., pp. 142–144, 153–161.
13. The documents we have for Lambert de Fays are his "grand journal" for the years 1632–1645 and some of his letter books for the 1640s. AV, Man. 77/48, 49, 51, 62.
14. Hansotte, *La clouterie liégeoise;* and Hansotte, *La métallurgie et le commerce international du fer dans les Pays-Bas autrichiens et la Principauté de Liège pendant la second moitié du XVIIIe siècle* (Brussels: Academie Royale de Belgique, 1980). The description of the evolution of nailmaking around Liège in the eighteenth century that follows in the next few paragraphs is based on these two works.
15. Richard W. Unger, *Dutch Shipbuilding Before 1800* (Assen: van Gorcum, 1978).
16. Ibid., pp. 9–10.
17. Hansotte, *La clouterie liégeoise*.
18. V. Tahon, "L'industrie cloutière au pays de Charleroi," *Documents et*

Rapports de la Société Archéologique de Charleroi 36 (1914–1921): 4–71; and A. Hansay, "Contribution à l'histoire de la politique mercantile au XVIIIe siècle en France et dans le pays de Liège," in *Mélanges Paul Frédéricq* (Brussels: H. Lamertin, 1904), pp. 338–342.

19. Lebrun, *L'industrie de la laine à Verviers pendant le XVIIIe et le début du XIXe siècle* (Liège: Faculté de Philosophie et Lettres, 1948), pp. 150–152.

20. Savary's *Dictionnaire universel de commerce* listed textiles among Liège's products even in the eighteenth century. Etienne Hélin, "Liège d'après quelques manuels à l'usage des negotiants," *Le Vieux Liège* 6 (1961–1965): 216–228.

21. Ibid., pp. 150–151.

22. Pierre Dardel, *Commerce, industrie et navigation à Rouen et au Havre au XVIIIème siècle* (Rouen: Société Libre d'Emulation de la Seine-Maritime, 1966), p. 111.

23. Gérard Gayot, "La longue insolence des tondeurs de draps dans la manufacture de Sedan au XVIIIème siècle," *Revue du Nord* 63 (1981): 105–134.

24. Gérard Gayot, "Dispersion et concentration de la draperie sedanaise au XVIIIème siècle: L'entreprise des Poupart de Neuflize," *Revue du Nord* 61 (1979): 127–148; and Tihomar H. Markovitch, *Les industries lainières de Colbert à la Révolution* (Geneva: Librairie Droz, 1976), pp. 135–169.

25. Compare the total production figures in Markovitch, *Les industries lainières*, with the export figures in Dardel, *Commerce, industrie et navigation*, pp. 114–115.

26. Paul Bertholet, "Les industries d'Aix-la-Chapelle, Eupen, Hodimont, Maestricht, Montjoie, Stavelot-Malmedy, Verviers et de leurs environs, vues par un negotiant Français vers 1755," *BSVAH* 61 (1980): 124, 130–132.

27. Lebrun, *L'industrie de la laine*, p. 206. Renier dates the introduction of competitive dyeing in Verviers to 1765. Jean Simon Renier, *Histoire de l'industrie drapière au pays de Liège* (Liège, 1881), 68.

28. The de Fays became lords of the village of Andrimont by the end of the eighteenth century and spent a fortune building a chateau. See AV, Man. 77.

29. Published in Emile Fairon, *Les industries du pays de Verviers* (Verviers, 1922), p. 17 (reprinted as "Histoire économique du pays de Verviers" in *BSVAH* 43 [1956]: 26). Fairon does not give an archival source for this statement.

30. Rudolf Braun, "The Rise of a Rural Class of Industrial Entrepreneurs," *Journal of World History* 10 (1967): 556–557.

31. Lebrun, *L'industrie de la laine*, p. 348.

32. Ibid., pp. 521–523.

33. Markovitch, *Les industries lainières*, pp. 148–152. See also Gayot, "Dispersion et concentration de la draperie sedanaise."

34. Lebrun, *L'industrie de la laine*, p. 485. After Germinal in the year XIII

(March 1805), one Liégeois florin was roughly equivalent to 1.2 francs.

35. Paul Bertholet, "L'étonnante fortune du marchand-drapier Verviétois François Franquinet (5-9-1671, 21-9-1754)," *BSVAH* 61 (1980): 137–173.

36. On Switzerland, see Braun, "The Rise of a Rural Class of Industrial Entrepreneurs"; on France, William M. Reddy, "Modes de paiement et contrôle du travail dans les filatures de coton en France, 1750–1848," *Revue du Nord* 63 (1981): 138; on England (in the hosiery trade), John Rule, *The Experience of Labour in Eighteenth-Century English Industry* (New York: St. Martin's Press, 1981), p. 141.

37. AV, Man. 55.

38. Bertholet, "L'étonnante fortune."

39. Rule, "Exploitation and Embezzlement," Chapter 5 in *The Experience of Labour*, pp. 124–146; and John Styles, "Embezzlement, Industry and the Law in England, 1500–1800," in *Manufacture in Town and Country Before the Factory*, ed. Maxine Berg et al. (Cambridge: Cambridge University Press, 1983), pp. 173–210.

40. D. C. Coleman, "Textile Growth," in *Textile History and Economic History: Essays in Honour of Miss Julia de Lacy Mann*, ed. N. B. Harte and K. G. Ponting (Manchester: Manchester University Press, 1973), pp. 1–21.

41. Renier, *Histoire de l'industrie drapière*, p. 68.

42. AV, F. 110/17.

43. AEL, Dethier, 2618 (1760–1762) and 2619 (1777).

44. AEL, Dethier, 2451–2484.

45. René Leboutte, "Un exemple d'industrialisation des campagnes: La manufacture de draps Scheibler, Ronstorff, Rahlenbeck à Dalhem (1774–1890)," *Cinquième congrès national d'archéologie industrielle. Le textile. Gand, 26–27 novembre 1977* (Ghent: Rijksuniversiteit Gent, 1979), pp. 111–120; and Leboutte, "De lakenfabriek Scheibler, Ronstorff, Rahlenbeck te Dalem (1774–1890): Een voorbeeld van industrialisatie op het platteland," *Studies over de sociaal-economische geschiedenis van Limburg* 24 (1979): 24–82.

46. Paul Schoenen, *Das Rote Haus in Monschau* (Cologne: Dumont Schauberg, 1968).

47. David S. Landes, "What Do Bosses Really Do?" *Journal of Economic History* 46 (1986): 601–605.

48. In the Dethier archive there is a "Livre de façonniers" that covers the period 1769–1779. AEL, Dethier 2606. There is no evidence that the employment of *façonnaires* ended in 1779, only that a subsequent register was either not kept or has been lost.

49. Lebrun, *L'industrie de la laine*, pp. 276–287.

50. See the censuses taken around this year discussed earlier, in Chapter 6.

51. On early factories in Verviers, see Lebrun, *L'industrie de la laine*, pp. 276–282.
52. Ibid., p. 282.
53. J. D. Chambers, "The Rural Domestic Industries During the Period of Transition to the Factory System, with Special Reference to the Midland Counties of England," *International Conference of Economic History, Aix-en-Provence, 1962* (Paris: Mouton, 1965), 2: 439.
54. Coleman, "Textile Growth."
55. Neil McKendrick, "Josiah Wedgwood and the Commercialization of the Potteries," in Neil McKendrick, John Brewer, and J. H. Plumb, *The Birth of a Consumer Society: The Commercialization of Eighteenth-Century England* (Bloomington: Indiana University Press, 1982), pp. 99–144.
56. Stanley D. Chapman, *The Early Factory Masters: The Transition to the Factory System in the Midlands Textile Industry* (Newton Abbot: David & Charles, 1967), pp. 46–47.
57. Ibid., and David Landes, *The Unbound Prometheus: Technological Change and Industrial Development in Western Europe from 1750 to the Present* (Cambridge: Cambridge University Press, 1972), pp. 84–85.
58. Chapman, *Early Factory Masters*, pp. 101–124.
59. On Switzerland, see Charles P. Kindleberger, "The Historical Background: Adam Smith and the Industrial Revolution," in *The Market and the State: Essays in Honour of Adam Smith*, ed. Thomas Wilson and Andrew S. Skinner (Oxford: Clarendon Press, 1976), pp. 24–25. On France, see Gay L. Gullickson, "Proto-industrialization, Demographic Behavior and the Sexual Division of Labor in Auffay, France, 1750–1850," *Peasant Studies* 9 (1982): 108–109; and Serge Chassagne, "L'enquête dite de Champagny, sur la situation de l'industrie cotonnière française au début de l'Empire (1805–1806)," *Revue d'Histoire Economique et Sociale* (1976): 336–370.
60. Landes, "What Do Bosses Really Do?" p. 603.
61. Frederic C. Lane, *Navires et constructeurs à Venise pendant la Renaissance* (Paris: SEVPEN, 1965).
62. Carlo Poni, "All'origine del sistema di fabbrica: tecnologia e organizzazione produttiva dei mulini da seta nell'Italia settentrionale (secoli XVII–XVIII)," *Rivista Storica Italiana* 88 (1976): 444–497.
63. Neil McKendrick, "Josiah Wedgwood and Factory Discipline," *The Historical Journal* 4 (1961): 30–55.
64. Peter Mathias, "An Industrial Revolution in Brewing, 1700–1830," in *The Transformation of England: Essays in the Economic and Social History of England in the Eighteenth Century* (New York: Columbia University Press, 1979), pp. 209–230; and Mathias, *The Brewing Industry in England* (Cambridge: Cambridge University Press, 1959).
65. Stephen A. Marglin, "What Do Bosses Do, Part I," *Review of Radical Political Economy* 6 (1974): 60–112 (reprinted as "What Do Bosses Do?" in *The Division of Labour: The Labour Process and Class Struggle in*

Modern Capitalism, ed. Andre Gorz [Hassocks: Harvester, 1976], pp. 13–54). A revised version of this paper appears as "Knowledge and Power," in *Firms, Organization and Labour: Approaches to the Economics of Work Organization,* ed. Frank H. Stephen (New York: St. Martin's Press, 1984), pp. 146–164.

66. Landes, "What Do Bosses Really Do?"; and Kindleberger, "The Historical Background," pp. 17–25.

CHAPTER 8

Epilogue: Mechanization and Its Meaning

The revolution in the Verviers textile industry took place at the very end of the eighteenth century.[1] In November 1799 an English machine builder named William Cockerill arrived in Verviers and contracted with J. F. D. Simonis of the Biolley-Simonis firm to build machines for the mechanized transformation of wool. By early 1801, the machines were in place and the region's industry was made over, some fifteen years after the mechanization of the English industry.[2] At the beginning, Cockerill and his family had an exclusive contract with Biolley-Simonis. This was modified in 1803, when his son William and his son-in-law James Hodson set up a separate business. William Cockerill, Jr., and James Hodson built machines for other textile manufacturers in Verviers, and they soon had competitors.[3] Among the many spin-offs of the Cockerill empire was the firm of John Cockerill, established in Liège and then Seraing, which became one of the largest iron, steel, and heavy industrial firms in Europe.

By 1812, when the local official Louis Thomassin wrote his *Mémoire statistique,* the region's industry was thoroughly mechanized.[4] Half of the production of Verviers and Hodimont came from factories in which machines did everything—from clean and mix the wool to teasel and partly shear it. Only weaving was not mechanized. Water was the first power source; it had long been used in the Verviers industry for fulling. Each complete set of machines was called an *assortiment.* In 1812, there were 4 *assortiments* operating in Limburg, 32 in Ensival, 47 in Hodimont, and 89 in Verviers. In the years that followed, machines spread to the villages of the region: A spinning factory opened in Charneux in 1814. Not long thereafter, the steam engine arrived. The first engine of the type constructed by Watt was installed in 1816; by 1830 there were 22 in Verviers, 47 in the *arrondissement* (an ad-

229

ministrative unit smaller than a province or department, consisting of a number of communes).[5]

Verviers was among the first regions on the European continent to take up mechanized textile production.[6] Its industry mechanized rapidly, and for a few years it stayed ahead of its Continental competitors. The primacy of the Verviers industry, sometimes argued heatedly by Pierre Lebrun and others, is not our major concern.[7] It had, after all, lagged behind English industry at the beginning, and it probably stayed somewhat behind. What is more important to ask is why the Verviers industrialists mechanized when they did, and why this is important. This chapter deals briefly with the revolutionary origins of mechanization, but it is really about the evolutionary development of industry in the Meuse-Rhine region, a topic in all the earlier chapters.

We have no direct testimony from Simonis, his partners, or his competitors about why they installed machines in the factory buildings they had been using since the late eighteenth century. The Simonis archive contains no correspondence for this period, and his competitors, David and Dethier, do not appear to discuss machines in their correspondence.[8] Nevertheless, their reasons should not be difficult to fathom. The large producers in the Verviers textile industry had done well during the 1790s.[9] Their emigration in 1794–1795, to avoid French troops, had only briefly disrupted their prosperity.[10] The price of wool and of textiles had increased, and stable profit margins had produced more than satisfactory profits. The integration of the Austrian Netherlands and the principality of Liège into France opened large new markets. There is reason to believe that demand for the well-regarded Verviers cloth exceeded supply.[11] Firms such as that of Simonis could afford to expand production, having made profits averaging over 100,000 florins a year during the 1790s.[12]

The industrialists of Verviers were well aware of the introduction in England of machine production for cotton and wool. Their use of factories in Verviers, Hodimont, and Ensival certainly prepared them for the organizational problems posed by grouping workers under one roof. What they lacked was the technical know-how, which Cockerill provided. This does not mean that the availability of technology fully explains the introduction of machines in Verviers. Cockerill had left England in

1794, with the idea that he would sell his skill as a builder of spinning machines. He traveled to Russia, Sweden, and Germany in an unsuccessful search for customers before Simonis brought him from Hamburg to Verviers.[13] What distinguished Simonis was his willingness to seek out and employ Cockerill, when others were unwilling to do so.

In the context of his business, Simonis did not take a very large risk by ordering the machines. It is true that he ordered twelve full sets of machines, at 12,000 francs each; and he ordered them for his personal account, not for the family business.[14] Only after the visible success of the machines, in 1801, did the firm concur in the decision to order them and pay him a bonus of 20,000 francs for his initiative. This demonstrates the self-confidence of the textile industry in Verviers. The Simonis family was exceptionally wealthy by this time. Jacques Joseph Simonis and his wife Marie Agnes Franquinet left an estate valued at over 4 million francs, not including the business. Each heir (including J. F. D.) received about 460,000 francs, made up of cash, land, and outstanding loans.[15] The firm's secret operating accounts in the early nineteenth century usually reported cash balances over 1 million francs.[16]

Simonis invested a substantial amount in machines, but it was an amount readily repaid out of his share of the firm's cash in hand. Moreover, it was an amount that the firm was able to repay out of profits in less than two years. And he was probably not required to pay the full cost of the machines until most of those profits were in hand, because these machines were usually sold against a bill of exchange due six months or a year after the date of delivery. The 20,000-franc bonus should be seen as a very substantial tip, not as a big prize to the man who took a risky and revolutionary step.

We should not underrate the importance of the revolution that the mechanization of industry brought about. In eastern Belgium and western Germany it transformed economic and social life at a pace that was surely impossible and unthinkable in the seventeenth and eighteenth centuries. Yet we should hesitate before overglorifying the Industrial Revolution, at least in this context. The introduction of machines was a logical step in a process that saw greater capital investment by industrialists, and greater centralization of their operations, in order to manage and control their labor force better. Mechanization was a logical continuation of earlier processes.

Moreover, the victory of mechanization was only slowly achieved, if we look at all the elements of industry in the region from Liège to Aachen. Mechanized textile production did not immediately replace manual textile production. Hand spinning died out by the 1830s, but hand weaving was only slowly overtaken by mechanized weaving. And although the textile industry mechanized rapidly, other industries did not. Just as Raphael Samuel has shown for England, a very large part of industrial production remained artisanal until the end of the nineteenth century.[17] This was true of the nailmaking industry in the Verviers region. Even the more progressive Liégeois armaments industry failed to centralize its production into a large mechanized factory until the 1880s.

When we gauge the Industrial Revolution in Verviers and Liège by its mechanization in the nineteenth century, we are struck on the one hand by its speed and precocity and on the other hand by its slowness. When we evaluate the entire process we find a more gradual evolution. This is especially the case if we study not just the late eighteenth and nineteenth centuries but a much longer period—a period that begins in the seventeenth century and continues until the early twentieth century. The installation of machines by Simonis was part of a continuing process by which the Verviers textile industry was built. Mechanization was just one of many evolutionary and more or less rational business decisions taken by the industrialists of the late eighteenth and nineteenth centuries. These decisions were taken not in some revolutionary spirit that sought change for its own sake, but to increase business and deal with particular problems of competition and management. Moreover, they were often taken by men such as Simonis who were successful practitioners of earlier industrial forms.

The preceding few sentences outline the central message of this book: that industrial growth and change was a logical and evolutionary process, undertaken by businessmen from an older milieu who were in search of solutions to immediate problems.[18] I believe that this was true in the English cotton industry in the eighteenth century, but the amount of change required to convert a tiny industry to a mammoth one has obscured the process.

It can be seen more clearly in the development of older and larger industries such as metallurgy and the production of woolen textiles in the Low Countries in general, and in smaller areas such as Liège-Verviers in particular. In these regions the economic and social developments that accompanied growth and change in industrial production built on a strong base. The changes that occurred were incremental, and they permitted the participants in older forms of economic activity—be it agriculture, trade, or industry—to maintain much of their place and their traditions. This is why we see traditional businessmen such as Biolley building factories in the eighteenth century and Simonis investing in mechanization in the early nineteenth century. It is also why—despite significant changes in the nature of society and the sure creation of an industrial proletariat—social relations in the region examined in Chapter 6 retained so much stability.

The preceding chapters have several common threads. A central narrative theme has been the route by which industrial leadership in worsted textiles arrived in Verviers. The route by which leadership in the iron business reached Liège has been a subsidiary point. Beginning with "the first crisis of urban industry"—the subject of Chapter 2—we have seen the rising importance of worsted cloth, the changing patterns of industrial organization, and the movement of the industry's geographical centers from place to place in western Europe. The rise and fall of the Flemish towns and the English towns, then Hondschoote, Venice, and Leiden, and the eventual rise of places such as Yorkshire and Verviers have animated this discussion. These final victors prevailed in the seventeenth and eighteenth centuries, and it is these regions that first mechanized the production of wool. They prevailed because they produced and successfully sold high-quality cloth at attractive prices, made possible first by an unregulated urban and rural work force, and later by mechanization.

The narrative of economic evolution is matched by one of social evolution. The growth of industrial activity brought with it social changes; but these social changes were—like the economic changes—logical and evolutionary, built on past practice and on continuing customs. There was social disruption in the textile and metal industries in the eighteenth century, but there was also social stability. Even the creation of a wholly new category of exclusively industrial workers did not easily erode the social system that had existed. Farming and traditional trade and crafts remained important sources of employment; and in the nineteenth century they would again prevail, as industry became more and more centralized. Never were they eliminated.

The emphasis placed here on continuity has some important intellectual ties to Franklin Mendels's concept of protoindustrialization, but we should not make a doctrine out of either the general idea of continuity or the more specific idea of protoindustrialization. There is a logic to economic development, even if all economic actors and all economies do not always do what is in their best interests. Much of this book is about failure, and the Verviers textile industry itself eventually failed—for many of the same reasons its predecessors did. The logic of economic development over most of the past thousand years has led to greater manufacturing efficiency and less expensive products, but it has not done so without setbacks. That it was logical and evolutionary does not mean that economic history is inevitable and always progressive. This book has not been about the inevitable glory that was Verviers. Given the current dire situation in which the economy of eastern Belgium finds itself in the 1980s, such a book would be wildly inappropriate. The logic of economic development at issue here says that certain business environments succeed better than others. It tells us that monopolistic producers compete poorly with unregulated ones, in a relatively open market; that access to markets is vitally important, no matter how access is achieved; and that flexible approaches to production and distribution have always done well. The winners have been the unregulated, the flexible, and those who have access to markets. The losers have been the monopolistic, the inflexible, and those closed out of markets.

In all this I do not want to refute the *revolution* in the Industrial Revolution but rather to stress its irrelevance. In part this is because I think very important changes had already preceded mechanization. The other part of the argument is that mechanization was a logical response to problems that arose in late eighteenth- and nineteenth-century industry. These problems were solved in much the same way that earlier problems had been solved; and they slowly shifted the locus of industry, as earlier solutions had slowly shifted the locus of industry. New products, new processes, and new industrial locales emerged, involving new kinds of businessmen and new kinds of workers.

NOTES

1. The history of the Industrial Revolution in Verviers is presented in Pierre Lebrun, *L'industrie de la laine à Verviers pendant le XVIIIe et le début du XIXe siècle* (Liège: Faculté de Philosophie et Lettres, 1948), pp. 232–254. He restates his position in P. Lebrun et al., *Essai sur la révolution industrielle en Belgique, 1770–1847,* 2nd ed. (Brussels: Académie Royale de Belgique, 1981), pp. 161–260. Lebrun supersedes J. S. Renier, *Histoire de l'industrie drapière au pays de Liège et particulièrement dans l'arrondissement de Verviers depuis le moyen-âge jusqu'à nos jours* (Liège, 1881), although Renier includes some details worth knowing.

2. On the introduction of machines in the English woolen and worsted industries, see J. de Lacy Mann, *The Cloth Industry in the West of England from 1640 to 1880* (Oxford: Clarendon Press, 1971), pp. 123–156; D. T. Jenkins, "Early Factory Development in the West Riding of Yorkshire," in *Textile History and Economic History. Essays in Honour of Miss Julia de Lacy Mann,* ed. N. B. Harte and K. G. Ponting (Manchester: Manchester University Press, 1973), pp. 247–280; and Jennifer Tann, "The Employment of Power in the West-of-England Wool Textile Industry, 1790–1840," in ibid., pp. 196–224.

3. Henri Delrée and Etienne Hélin, "Introduction des fameuses mécaniques anglaises à Verviers," *Bulletin de la Société Royale le Vieux Liège* 11 (October–December 1986): 197–206; Delreé and Hélin, "Contre les machines, pour le plein employ? Un réquisatoire de Laurent-François Dethier (1757–1843)," *Bulletin de la Société Royale le Vieux Liège,* forthcoming 1987.

4. L. Thomassin, *Mémoire statistique du département de l'Ourthe* (Liège, 1879).

5. Lebrun et al., *Essaie sur la révolution industrielle,* p. 174.

6. Some mechanized cotton spinning was done in France as early as the 1770s. C. Engrand, "Concurrences et complémentarités des villes et des campagnes: Les manufactures picardes de 1780 à 1815," *Revue du Nord* 61 (1979): 174.

7. Lebrun et al., *Essaie sur la révolutino industrielle,* p. 174.

8. These collections can be found in the Archives de l'Etat à Liège. The David collection contains a copy of the first contract for machines with the Cockerill firm: AEL, David, 4248.

9. Renier, *Histoire de l'industrie drapière,* p. 78.

10. Ibid., pp. 76–77.

11. This is a point made by Lebrun, in *L'industrie de la laine,* p. 238.

12. Ibid., p. 508; and AEL, Simonis, 8.

13. According to Renier, Cockerill was discovered in Hamburg by a M. Mali, who was Simonis's manager charged with buying wool. *Histoire de l'industrie drapière,* p. 79.

14. Lebrun, *L'industrie de la laine,* p. 242. By 1807 the price had fallen to 7,500 francs per set.

15. AEL, Simonis, 7, "Copie de documents relatifs au patrimoine de Jean-François Simonis, 1792–1829," pp. 47–64.
16. AEL, Simonis, 8, "Livre, comptes et bilans secrets commencé l'an 1801, fini l'an 1824 inclus."
17. Raphael Samuel, "Workshop of the World: Steam Power and Hand Technology in Mid-Victorian Britain," *History Workshop Journal* 3 (1977): 6–72.
18. See also François Crouzet, *The First Industrialists: The Problem of Origins* (Cambridge: Cambridge University Press, 1985); and Henri Pirenne in "The Stages in the Social History of Capitalism," *American Historical Review* 19 (1914): 494–515. Pirenne believed that every capitalist age created its own leadership, because the older leadership left to find more comfortable social niches outside commerce. That may have been true in the Middle Ages, but it was certainly not true in the period under discussion in this book.

Bibliographical Essay

The reader interested in the history of European industry between the late Middle Ages and the building of the first factories has a long task ahead of him or her. The quantity of material available is enormous, much more than can be mentioned in this bibliography or in the notes that accompany the text. This essay is selective. What I have tried to do is identify both the most important issues in the book and the most important historiographical themes that surround them, and direct the reader to a variety of starting points that will make those issues and themes accessible.

One objective of this book has been to emphasize the long continuities in Europe's industrial history since the late Middle Ages. There are few works that deal with these long continuities. The most influential in recent years have been the three volumes of Fernand Braudel's *Civilization and Capitalism, 15th–18th Century* (English translation, New York: Harper & Row): *The Structures of Everyday Life* (1981), *The Wheels of Commerce* (1982), and *The Perspective of the World* (1984). These books are flawed and anachronistic, but their ability to make the reader reconsider important questions is without equal. Braudel's view is not only long but wide, and his decision to include the world outside Europe gives the book a twentieth-century flavor that is inappropriate to a discussion of early modern times. There are few besides Braudel who have attempted to bring a long perspective to the movement of economic and social history. Among them, but even more anachronistic than Braudel, is Immanuel Wallerstein, in *The Modern World System*, 2 vols. (New York: Academic Press, 1974–1980). Wallerstein provides a strongly stated point of view about the ways in which economic power shifted location in the sixteenth, seventeenth, and eighteenth centuries. The first volume, especially, has a number of inaccuracies, and the world-wide perspective is as difficult as Braudel's. Both volumes have the further disadvantage of being relatively little interested in the role played by industry.

In the absence of overarching interpretations of the economic or social sides of industrial history, the best starting points are the multivolume surveys of economic and social history published in the last few years. In English, the best continue to be the volumes in the *Cambridge Economic History of Europe* (Cambridge: Cambridge University Press, various dates) that deal with this period. Another good starting point is Carlo Cipolla, ed., *The Fontana Economic History of Europe*, 6 vols. (London: Fontana, 1972–1974). Both these histories provide good information about the various components of economic history, but they have the disadvantage of being disjointed collections of articles on special topics, which sometimes fit together well and sometimes do not. Both series are now dated, but this problem is more severe for the Cambridge history, some volumes of which are now thirty years old, and virtually all of which are at least twenty years old. This is especially marked in discussions of demography and industry, where the fields have evolved considerably since the 1950s.

The French histories are better integrated than the English. The best works are syntheses about French history: the *Histoire économique et sociale de la France,* edited by Braudel and Ernest Labrousse; and the *Histoire de la France urbaine* and *Histoire de la France rurale* edited by Georges Duby. The French alternative to the English series, with a world-wide perspective, are the six volumes edited by Pierre Léon, *Histoire économique et sociale du monde* (Paris: Armand Colin, 1978). All the French works are somewhat less scholarly than their English equivalents, but include excellent artwork and graphics. They nonetheless contain syntheses by the most prominent French historians of important work on topics of interest.

Once we go beyond works of very general focus, we can concentrate on specialized topics. The rise and fall of cities is of great importance to the story told in this book. A good introduction can be found in Paul M. Hohenberg and Lynn Hollen Lees, *The Making of Urban Europe, 1000–1950* (Cambridge, Mass.: Harvard University Press, 1985). This book is strong in several ways. It is interested in the very long-term development of cities, which provides a useful counterpoint to the perspective here. It achieves its interest in the long-term and in urban systems by giving the reader an excellent background in the ways geographers and others have looked at systems of cities. Finally, it explicitly deals with the industrial development of cities and of the countryside by developing a "protoindustrial" model of urban development. Another book that explicitly looks at the relationship of cities to the countryside and the rise of rural industry is Jan de Vries, *European Urbanization, 1500–1800* (Cambridge, Mass.: Harvard University Press, 1984). De Vries starts with the demographic development of European cities by tracking estimates of their population. He goes beyond that to develop models of urban growth and decline, and then to relate that to overall population growth in town and countryside. For the particular problem of urban decline, its causes and consequences, see Myron P. Gutmann, "The Dynamics of Urban Decline in the Late Middle Ages and Early Modern Times: Economic Responses and Social Effects," in *Ninth International Economic History Congress, Bern, 1986: Debates and Controversies* (Zurich: Verlag der Fachvereine, 1986), pp. 23–56. This paper is a report on a meeting about urban decline. It summarizes theoretical positions and very recent research. Sources for the history of individual cities that declined or otherwise underwent difficulties are mentioned below.

Another way to break up the long history of industry is into sections about individual periods and individual industries. The industrial history of the Middle Ages is a major topic, deserving of a new book on its own. The traditional story can be found in the chapters by E. M. Carus-Wilson (on textiles) and John Nef (on mining and metallurgy) in volume 2 of the *Cambridge Economic History.* They are out of date by now, as are the textbooks by Henri Pirenne, *Economic and Social History of Medieval Europe* (New York: Harcourt Brace, 1937), and Robert S. Lopez, *The Birth of Europe* (New York: Evans, 1967). However, in the absence of a better starting point they must be consulted.

Textiles were the most important European industry until the nineteenth century. The techniques are ably described in R. Patterson, "Spinning and Weaving," in *A History of Technology*, ed. Charles Singer et al., 8 vols. (Oxford: Clarendon Press, 1954–1984) 2:190–210. For England, the articles in E. M. Carus-Wilson, *Medieval Merchant Venturers: Collected Studies* (London:

Methuen, 1967), provide the basic information. A. R. Bridbury, *Medieval English Clothmaking: An Economic Survey* (London: Heinemann, 1982), is not a real attempt to survey the field. Rather, it is an extended attack on Carus-Wilson and her followers. It is worth reading, but it is not as definitive as it claims. For Flanders, G. de Poerck gives a good introduction to technology in *La draperie médiévale en Flandres et en Artois*, 3 vols. (Bruges: De Tempel, 1951). On the history in more general terms, see Georges Espinas, *La draperie dans la Flandre français au moyen-âge*, 2 vols. (Paris: Picard, 1923). Although there is no more recent survey of medieval and early modern textiles, the subject was largely brought up to date in a conference, most of the contributions to which were published in Marco Spallanzani, ed., *Produzione commercio e consumo dei panni di lana (nei secoli XII–XVIII)* (Florence: Leo Olschki, 1974). In the years following that publication, the journal *Textile History* has published extensively and provided ongoing bibliographies.

The introduction of the "new draperies" and the transformation of textile industries are central to understanding the "crisis of urban industry" described in the text. Pirenne's article discussed in Chapter 2 is "Une crise industrielle au XVIe siècle. La draperie urbaine et la 'nouvelle draperie' en Flandre," in *Histoire économique de l'occident médiéval* (Brussels: Desclée, De Brouwer, 1951), pp. 621–643. Pirenne's article was originally published in 1905 and therefore reflects relatively early research results. Herman van der Wee has brought the issue of the long-term development of the textile industry in the southern Low Countries up to date in "Structural Changes and Specialization in the Industry of the Southern Netherlands, 1100–1600," *Economic History Review*, 2nd ser., 28 (1975): 203–221. Both Pirenne and van der Wee see the ultimate victory of the light drapery industry centered in the Flemish town of Hondschoote. The Hondschoote industry is the subject of a monograph by Emile Coornaert, *Un centre industriel d'autrefois: La draperie-sayetterie d'Hondschoote (XIVe–XVIIIe siècles)* (Paris: Presses Universitaires de France, 1930). For England, the introduction of the new draperies is ably described by D. C. Coleman in "An Innovation and Its Diffusion: The New Draperies," *Economic History Review*, 2nd ser., 22 (1969): 417–429. He gives a practical description of types of cloth and their relationship to the production process, beyond narrating the introduction of new technical processes.

The metal industry was smaller than textiles, but it was nonetheless among the most important industries in Europe even prior to the nineteenth-century boom. For the Middle Ages, see Rolf Sprandel, *Das Eisengewerbe im Mittelalter* (Stuttgart: Anton Hiersemann, 1968); Sprandel, "La production du fer au Moyen Age," *Annales ESC* 24 (1969): 305–321; and Philippe Braunstein, "Innovations in Mining and Metal Production in Europe in the Late Middle Ages," *Journal of European Economic History* 12 (1983): 573–591. These works bring up to date Nef's overview from the *Cambridge Economic History*, as well as supplementing H. R. Schubert, *History of the British Iron and Steel Industry from c.450 B.C. to A.D. 1775* (London: Routledge & Kegan Paul, 1957). The metal industry in the early modern period has not been extensively studied, but there are good summaries in two volumes (one about iron and one about copper) edited by Herman Kellenbenz: *Schwerpunkte der Eisengewinnung und Eisenverarbeitung in Europa 1500–1650* (Cologne: Böhlau Verlag, 1974) and *Schwerpunkte der Kupferproduction und des Kupferhandels in Europa 1500–1650* (Cologne: Böhlau Verlag, 1977).

Much of this book is about Liégeois industry and its history. There is no good full-length history of Liégeois industry in any period. The reader must therefore turn to individual works. The industry of Liège has had its good and its great historians, who have taken the study of this small region beyond the scale of local history and genealogy. The best of the active economic historians is Georges Hansotte, who ably summarizes the state of current knowledge in "Pays de fer et de houille," in *La Wallonie: Le pays et les hommes. Histoire-économies-sociétés*, ed. Hervé Hasquin (Brussels: La Renaissance du Livre, 1975), 1:269–294. Hansotte's specialty is the metal industry. For a more detailed survey of that industry in the sixteenth and seventeenth centuries, see Hansotte, "La métallurgie wallonne au XVIe et dans la première moitié de XVIIe siècle. Un état de la question," in *Schwerpunkte der Eisengewinnung und Eisenverarbeitung*, pp. 126–146. Hansotte builds on the work of two of his predecessors. Jean Lejeune, *La formation du capitalisme moderne dans la principauté de Liège au XVIe siècle* (Liège: Faculté de Philosophie et Lettres, 1939), is problematic (in part because he does not adequately understand the word "capitalism," which he places in his title) but still very interesting. Of far more durability has been Jean Yernaux, *La métallurgie liégeoise et son expansion au XVIIe siècle* (Liège: George Thone, 1939).

There are three important sources for the history of the Liégeois economy in the eighteenth century. On metallurgy, the new point of reference is Hansotte, *La métallurgie et le commerce international du fer dans les Pays-Bas autrichiens et la Principauté de Liège pendant la second moitié du XVIIIe siècle* (Brussels: Academie Royale de Belgique, 1980). The reader should not ignore the large mass of Hansotte's earlier work on smaller topics. Most important among these is his *La clouterie liégeoise et la question ouvrière au XVIIe siècle* (Brussels: Editions de la Librairie Encyclopédique, 1972), but the monographs about forges and firms (see the bibliographies of these two works and of the chapter in *La Wallonie*) that he has published over a long career are models of the work of a good historian. The Verviers textile industry is the second component of the region's industry. Its most important history is Pierre Lebrun, *L'industrie de la laine à Verviers pendant le XVIIIe et la début du XIXe siècle* (Liège: Faculté de Philosophie et Lettres, 1948). The striking success of Lebrun's work is not that it needs no updating after forty years but that it addresses so many questions that are important today.

The third component of the Liégeois economy was agriculture. Joseph Ruwet was most concerned with that, and the most important work remains his *L'agriculture et les classes rurales au pays de Herve sous l'ancien régime* (Liège: Faculté de Philosophie et Lettres, 1943). Ruwet's work focused on the Herve Country to the east of the city of Liège. The work of Ivan Delatte was more general, especially *Les classes rurales dans la principauté de Liège au XVIIIe siècle* (Liège: Faculté de Philosophie et Lettres, 1945). It has not held up as well as Ruwet's work, and there has been no general work on Walloon or Liégeois agriculture in this period to replace it. There have been more specialized works, however. In *War and Rural Life in the Early Modern Low Countries* (Princeton: Princeton University Press, 1980), I wrote about the impact of war on agriculture and economy in the seventeenth and eighteenth centuries. Paul Servais, in a series of works, has followed Ruwet and illuminated the connection between agriculture and industry in the Herve Country. His book *La rente constituée dans la ban de Herve au XVIIIe siècle* (Brussels: Credit Communal, 1982) explains in admirable detail the role played by credit in an agricultural and cottage industry economy. His more recent essays, "Les structures agraires du Limbourg et des pays d'Outre-Meuse du XVIIe au XIXe siècle," *Annales ESC* 37 (1982): 303–319, and "Industries rurales et structures agraires: Le cas de l'entre-Vesdre-et-Meuse aux XVIIIème et XIXème siècles," *Revue Belge d'Histoire Contemporaine* 13 (1982): 179–206, describe the interaction of agriculture and industry.

The notion of crisis used to explain the seventeenth century both here and elsewhere has not engendered a clear-cut historiography. The concept began as a way to explain seventeenth-century "decadence" in general and then to explain the cycles of early modern economic and demographic history: growth in the sixteenth century followed by decline in the seventeenth and then growth in the eighteenth. The analytic schemes that have been used to explain the seventeenth-century "crisis" can be found in two books of essays and one small text. Trevor Aston, ed., *Crisis in Europe* (Garden City: Doubleday Anchor, 1967), includes the original essays published in *Past & Present* by E. J. Hobsbawm and H. R. Trevor-Roper, plus the replies to them. Only the two principal essays are important. Geoffrey Parker and Lesley M. Smith published a more sophisticated collection of essays, *The General Crisis of the Seventeenth Century* (London: Routledge & Kegan Paul, 1978). A number of these are important, especially the editors' introduction and the essays by Niels Steensgaard, John Elliott, and A. Lloyd Moote. Theodore Rabb, *The Struggle for Stability in Early Modern Europe* (New York: Oxford University Press, 1975), provides a good general summary and an interesting point of view. To the dilemma of whether there was a crisis or not, he sees the answer in solving the terminological problem. Rabb finds his solution in the medical definition of "crisis"—a turning point at which the patient either recovers or dies—and detects such a turning point in the second half of the seventeenth century. Jan de Vries, *The Economy of Europe in an Age of Crisis, 1600–1730* (Cambridge: Cambridge University Press, 1976), remains the best short summary of the economy of the seventeenth century.

Discussion of the crisis relies on a number of case studies, for

Leiden, Venice, and Nördlingen. The classic works on Leiden are the results of a lifetime's work by the Dutch economic historian N. W. Posthumus. He collected and organized the documents, wrote the narrative history, and foresaw the need for high-quality series of quantitative data. The documents are published in *Bronnen tot de geschiedenis van de Leidsche textielnijverheid,* 6 vols. (The Hague: M. Nijhoff, 1910–1922). The history of the textile industry is in *De geschiedenis van de Leidsche lakenindustrie,* 3 vols. (The Hague: M. Nijhoff, 1908–1939). For a newer view, see the article by Robert S. Duplessis and Martha S. Howell, "Reconsidering the Early Modern Urban Economy: The Cases of Leiden and Lille," *Past & Present* 94 (1982): 49–84. They report the history as well as suggesting a reinterpretation of the material presented by Posthumus.

For Venice, the work of Domenico Sella is most important and largely accessible in English. The reader can begin with "The Rise and Fall of the Venetian Woolen Industry," in *Crisis and Change in the Venetian Economy in the Sixteenth and Seventeenth Centuries,* ed. Brian Pullan (London: Methuen, 1968), pp. 106–126. Other important works by this master are "Industrial Production in Seventeenth-Century Italy: A Reappraisal," *Explorations in Entrepreneurial History* 6 (1969): 235–253; and *Commerci e industrie a Venezia nel secolo XVII* (Venice: Instituto per la Collaborazione Culturale, 1961). On Lombardy, another Italian region, see his *Crisis and Continuity: The Economy of Spanish Lombardy in the Seventeenth Century* (Cambridge, Mass.: Harvard University Press, 1979). This work, better than most others, brings together the conflicting story of decline and advance that characterizes the seventeenth century. For Nördlingen, see Christopher R. Friedrichs, "Early Capitalism and Its Enemies: The Wörner Family and the Weavers of Nördlingen," *Business History Review* 50 (1976): 265–287; and Friedrichs, *Urban Society in an Age of War: Nördlingen, 1580–1720* (Princeton: Princeton University Press, 1979).

Many of the questions raised in this and earlier works of interpretation about the early modern economy could be more easily solved with better quantitative analysis. For the sixteenth and seventeenth centuries even national-level data are difficult to acquire. That is not true for the eighteenth century, and the quantitative study of the eighteenth century economy and its relationship to population growth has been a major topic of recent research. For an introduction, see Jan de Vries, "The Decline and Rise of the Dutch Economy, 1675–1900," in *Technique, Spirit and Form in the Making of the Modern Economies: Essays in Honor of William N. Parker, Research in Economic History*, supplement 3 (1984): 149–189; and N. F. R. Crafts, *British Economic Growth During the Industrial Revolution* (Oxford: Clarendon Press, 1985). On the demographic side, E. A. Wrigley, "The Growth of Population in Eighteenth-Century England: A Conundrum Resolved," *Past & Present* 98 (1983): 121–150, presents an overview. There he reports the results of the major work he did with Roger Schofield, *The Population History of England, 1541–1871: A Reconstruction* (Cambridge, Mass.: Harvard University Press, 1981). This book has become the starting point for understanding both the future methodology of historical demography and the quantitative development of the English population. As such, it is probably the most important work in demographic history published in the 1980s.

The other side of industrial growth and its consequences is the protoindustrialization debate. The starting point is Franklin Mendels, "Proto-industrialization: The First Phase of the Industrialization Process," *Journal of Economic History* 32 (1972): 241–261. For a more recent statement, see his "Protoindustrialization: Theory and Reality," in *Eighth International Economic History Congress, Budapest, 1982: "A" Themes* (Budapest: Akademiai Kiado, 1982), pp. 69–107. The other classics of the history of protoindustrialization are Rudolf Braun, *Industrialisierung und Volksleben: Die Veränderungen der Lebensformen in einem ländlischen Industriegebiet vor 1800 (Zürcher Oberland)* (Erlenbach: Eugen Rentsch Verlag, 1960); and David Levine, *Family Formation in an Age of Nascent Capitalism* (New York: Academic Press, 1977). To these must be added a very important monograph by Gay L. Gullickson, *Spinners and Weavers of Auffay* (Cambridge: Cambridge University Press, 1986). Gullickson shows in convincing detail how much variety there was in early industrial development, and in its social consequences. This she does by describing a case of early industrial development that was different from the classic cases, and different from the case described in this book.

There have been some other, more specialized, works that

have developed or contradicted important parts of the protoindustrialization hypothesis or an expanded variant of it. Two works give more specific information about the role of the growth of the proletariat in population increase: Rudolf Braun, in "Early Industrialization and Demographic Change in the Canton of Zürich," in *Historical Studies of Changing Fertility*, ed. Charles Tilly (Princeton: Princeton University Press, 1978), pp. 289–334, develops the demographic side of the descriptive social history he reports elsewhere. Charles Tilly, "Demographic Origins of the European Proletariat," in *Proletarianization and the Family*, ed. David Levine (Orlando: Academic Press, 1984), pp. 1–86, gives an overview and framework to the role of the growing proletariat in the growth of the European population. It is important to note that Tilly is not confined by the protoindustrialization hypothesis, because he builds his proletariat from agricultural as well as industrial workers. In addition, there are several collections of essays worth noting. The *Revue du Nord* has published two special numbers, one in volume 61 (1979) and one in volume 63 (1981). Pierre Deyon and Mendels published a collection of essays contributed to the 1982 International Economic History Congress as *La proto-industrialisation: Théorie et réalité. Rapports* (Lille: University of Lille, 1982). Also interesting is Peter Kriedte et al., *Industrialization Before Industrialization* (Cambridge: Cambridge University Press, 1981).

There have been a number of critiques of both the economic and the social component of the protoindustrialization concept. Each has its own point of view, so perhaps a list is appropriate. The most important are: D. C. Coleman, "Proto-Industrialization: A Concept Too Many?" *Economic History Review*, 2nd ser., 36 (1983): 435–448; Myron P. Gutmann and René Leboutte, "Rethinking Proto-Industrialization and the Family," *Journal of Interdisciplinary History* 14 (1984): 607–621; Paul G. Spagnoli, "Industrialization, Proletarianization and Marriage: A Reconsideration," *Journal of Family History* 8 (1983): 230–247; and Rab Houston and K. D. M. Snell, "Proto-industrialization? Cottage Industry, Social Change, and Industrial Revolution," *The Historical Review* 27 (1984): 473–492.

The transformation from cottage industry to factory is another major topic for discussion. The most important work is still being done on British industry, an imbalance that remains to be redressed. The background can be found in the literature of the Industrial Revolution, as written over the past twenty-five years. The best starting point for the technological development is still David S. Landes, *The Unbound Prometheus: Technological Change and Industrial Development in Western Europe from 1750 to the Present* (Cambridge: Cambridge University Press, 1972). For a good summary of overall economic conditions, see the essays in Roderick Floud and Donald McCloskey, eds., *The Economic History of Britain Since 1700*, 2 vols. (Cambridge: Cambridge University Press, 1981); and Joel Mokyr, ed., *The Economics of the Industrial Revolution* (Totowa, N.J.: Rowman & Allenheld, 1985).

On the eighteenth century and the transformation itself, there is an excellent book on England: Maxine Berg, *The Age of Manufactures, 1700–1820* (London: Fontana, 1985). More specialized but also fascinating is Pat Hudson, *The Genesis of Industrial Capital: A Study of the West Riding Wool Textile Industry c. 1750–1850* (Cambridge: Cambridge University Press, 1986). Finally, there are a number of interesting articles in Maxine Berg, Pat Hudson, and Michael Sonenscher, eds., *Manufacture in Town and Country Before the Factory* (Cambridge: Cambridge University Press, 1983).

INDEX

Aachen, 63–64, 66–67, 186. *See also* Liège-Aachen region
Age of Manufactures, The (Berg), 5
Amsterdam, 55, 75
Antwerp, 40, 42–43, 55
Armament production, 221
Arrondissement, 229–230
Arte de Calimala, 29–30
Assortiment, 229
Auffay, 157–158, 180

Baptisms, registers of, 133, 135
Beggar weddings, 129
Belgium, 119. *See also* specific cities in
Berg, Maxine, 5
Biolley-Simonis, 229–231
Biolley, Jean, 211, 216
Birth rates, 52, 125, 147. *See also* Fertility
Blaschke, Karlheinz, 148
Bottesford, 157
Brabant, 32–34, 55
Bräker, Ulrich, 176
Braun, Rudolf
  and entrepreneurs in cotton industry, 210–211
  and hybrid society, 157
  and improvements caused by cotton industry, 128–129
  and labor force in cotton industry, 157
  and proletarianization, 145, 148
Brewing industry, 222
Bridbury, A. R., 35
Bruges, 32, 40

Capitalism
  of Liège, 58–61
  and textile industry, 43–44
Carding wool, 23–24
Carus-Wilson, E. M., 34–36
Chambers, J. D., 220
Champagne, 32
Champs, Arnuld des, 60
Charleroi, 206
Charleville, 206
Cleaning wool, 22–23
Cloque, 184
Clothiers, 37
Coal industry, 56–58
Cockerill, William, 229–231
Cockerill, William, Jr., 229
Colaert, Jacob, 43
Cole, W. A., 118, 120–121
Coleman, Olive, 35–36
Combing wool, 23–24
Comines, 180
Competition
  in cottage industry, 215
  in Flemish textile industry, 38–40, 42–43
  in Leiden textile industry, 101
  and Venice, 109–110
Concentration
  and Industrial Revolution, 219
  origin of, 216
  and technological innovations, 220
  uses of, 219–222
  in Verviers, 220
Confraternity of Shearmen of Verviers, Ensival, Hodimont, and Francomont, 186

Migration. *See also* Mobility
and Leiden textile industry,
87–88
to Liège-Aachen region, 51
to Verviers, 137–142, 147
Mining, 17, 58
Mobility, 175–179. *See also*
Migration
Monopolies, 15–16
Mortality
and economic growth, 126,
130
in Liège-Aachen region, 52–54
in Verviers, 137–141
Muese-Rhine region, 86, 208

Nailmaking industry
de Fays in, 199–203
labor in, 204–205
in Liège, 195–199, 203–206
organization of, 195–199
as prefactory industry,
203–206
strikes in, labor, 204–205
in Verviers, 195–199
National states, 55–56. *See also*
Government
Nef, John, 5
Netherlands, 119. *See also* specific
cities in
New draperies, 38–40, 42–43
Noone, 186
Nördlingen, 10, 101–104

Occupational structure, 174–175

Papermaking industry, 8,
106–108
Paris, 55
Pirenne, Henri, 16, 31, 44
Political change. *See* Political
growth
Political growth. *See also*
Government
and Leiden textile industry,
95–96
in Liège-Aachen region, 55–56

in seventeenth century, 92–93
and urban industry, 110–111
Politics. *See* Government;
Political growth
Poor, 172–175
Population growth
and consumer industries, 108
and cottage industry, 127–128
cycles of, 6–9
and demand, 108
and economic growth, 9–12
in eighteenth century,
115–116, 132
in England, 126
and fertility, 130–131
in France, 125–126
and industrial growth, 132
and Leiden textile industry,
87–88
in Liège-Aachen region,
51–54, 75–77, 79–80
local, 132–133, 135–142
and marriage patterns, 126
and proletarianization,
125–132
in seventeenth century, 51,
93–94
in sixteenth century, 50–51
in Verviers, 133, 135–147
Population History of England, The
(Wrigley and Schofield), 136
Prefactory industries
in monopolistic environment,
15–16
nailmaking, 203–206
textiles, 206–208
Preindustrial, 6
Pricing, 94
Processing industries, 59. *See also*
specific types of
Production, 18–20, 94, 197
Profits, 121
Proletarianization
and Braun's work, 145, 148
and population growth,
125–132
Proletariat, 127

ABOUT THE AUTHOR

MYRON P. GUTMANN was born in Chicago and attended Columbia College and Princeton University. He is Associate Professor of History at the University of Texas at Austin, where he is a member of the Population Research Center. His previous book is *War and Rural Life in the Early Modern Low Countries*.

A NOTE ON THE TYPE

This book was set in a *digitized version* of Baskerville, originally a recutting of a typeface designed by John Baskerville (1706–1775). Baskerville, a writing master in Birmingham, England, began experimenting about 1750 with type design and punchcutting. His first book, set throughout in his new types, was a Virgil in royal quarto published in 1757, and this was followed by other famous editions from his press. Baskerville's types were a forerunner of what we know today as the "modern" group of typefaces.